"What happens when a biblical scholar, a virtue ethicist, an ecofeminist, and a theologian of science sit together to talk ecology? You get a lively discussion that proves to be nothing short of transformative. This volume is no mere introduction to 'ecotheology.' It is a model for conversation that reaches toward a multivalent ecological ethic drawing from the rich resources of Scripture, science, theology, Christology, ethics, and experience. This dialogical exploration offers the wisdom that is needed for people of faith to address the greatest crisis facing planetary life in human history."

— William P. Brown
Columbia Theological Seminary

"Regarding ecotheology as a marginal subdiscipline of Christian doctrine appears fatal for the deep understanding of faith. Four respected voices in North American theology enrich this long-standing field with discussions about climate justice, love, virtue ethics, earthkeeping (rather than stewardship), and eschatology and hope. The editors' and authors' profound and eloquent chapters and comments make obvious how the environmental agenda challenges and transforms long-established doctrines in theology. Their work enables faith communities and theologians to draw on their own spiritual sources and contribute new practical wisdom and wonder to the environmental movement."

— Sigurd Bergmann
founder of the European Forum for the Study of Religion and the Environment

"*Ecotheology: A Christian Conversation* is genuinely a conversation, a theological-moral dialogue set amidst creation in crisis for the purpose of framing, generating, and guiding Christian faith-based action. It succeeds splendidly! Each of the authors of the four essays evokes probing responses from the other three authors. The result is deepened theological substance and critical, constructive response. Were I teaching any course on Christianity and our planetary emergency, this would be my lead text."

— Larry Rasmussen
Union Theological Seminary, New York City

"*Ecotheology* is an exceptional contribution to religious thinking on human responsibilities in, with, for, and to creation. In this book, creation is viewed not as a single event-moment from millennia ago, but as an ongoing process within and upon which humans reflect on their world together with other members of the community of creation. This is an important work: it should stimulate Christians'—and others'—reflections on and concrete community commitments to address Earth's and Earth's creatures' endangerment and extinction at the hands of *homo sapiens*."

— John Hart
Boston University School of Theology
editor of *The Wiley Blackwell Companion to Religion and Ecology*

"In concise and accessible style, this book lets us listen in as four leading ecotheologians set forth their distinctive visions for Christianity and ecology—and then respond to each other in robust and charitable dialogue. It is illuminating to see where the authors disagree and challenge each other, but most encouraging are the remarkable convergences and shared commitments that emerge in the conversations opened up here. This will serve as a very useful introduction for students and be of interest to everyone in the field."

— Jonathan A. Moo
Whitworth University

"Too many students remain unconvinced that Christian theology has anything serious to say about a deeper ecological awareness. This book corrects that bad impression by introducing students to ecotheology with theological sophistication and ecological insight. This company of excellent scholars has given us a textbook that advances the crucial task of showing why the environment matters for theology and for a helpful Christian witness."

— Willie James Jennings
Yale Divinity School

"The editors of this book can be congratulated for drawing together some classic but still vital ethically relevant strands in ecotheology, focusing on the key ideas worked out by four renowned scholars in biblical studies, ecological ethics, and systematic theology. This book will be perfect for students and researchers who are newcomers to ecotheology, introducing not just core discussions, but also providing exemplars on how to think theologically in the context of a changing climate. It also helps the reader by opening up a discussion among authors, with each using the analytical tools of their speciality."

— Celia Deane-Drummond
University of Oxford

"Jorgenson and Padgett have accomplished something breath-taking here—a conversation of some of the brightest minds about caring for creation as Christians in this world. Drawing from the deep well of brilliance from some of the most notable ecotheological luminaries, this exquisite volume makes huge strides forward in assisting Christians formulate a biblical, theological, practical, and sustainable expression of discipleship that takes Earth-care seriously in the twenty-first century. A tour de force, indeed. Highly recommended."

— A. J. Swoboda
Bushnell University, Oregon

"Join a scientist, two ethicists, and a biblical scholar as they draw us into a wonderful conversation on God's love for the earth, the ecological crisis, and the community of creation. Creation itself joins the conversation, as a 'resilient creation once spoken into being still speaks.' This book asks: will we Christians listen to creation's voice?"

— Barbara Rossing
Lutheran School of Theology at Chicago

"A fine exercise in ecumenical dialogue with insightful biblical exegesis. This is a work of advocacy, in places passionate and prophetic, and an exploration of ecological virtues of both personal character and social transformation. Its eschatology is focused on the redemption of all things and built on hope in God's faithfulness. This is a book rooted in narratives, designed to stimulate the growing importance of ecotheological conversations in our churches and, more importantly, to provoke urgent action in 'earthkeeping' and sustained responsible care for God's earth."

— David Atkinson
author of *Renewing the Face of the Earth: A Theological and Pastoral Response to Climate Change*

"*Ecotheology* is a rare example of critical and meaningful dialogue among scholars. Its vision, that the whole creation and each creature has a meaningful place in the purposes of God, offers a powerful and potent reimagination of the Christian tradition. This is the type of work desperately needed to restore hope in the face of ecological violence and to motivate the church to concretely and decisively embrace a love of earth."

— Matthew Eaton
King's College, Pennsylvania

ECOTHEOLOGY

A CHRISTIAN CONVERSATION

EDITED BY

KIARA A. JORGENSON

ALAN G. PADGETT

WILLIAM B. EERDMANS PUBLISHING COMPANY
GRAND RAPIDS, MICHIGAN

Wm. B. Eerdmans Publishing Co.
4035 Park East Court SE, Grand Rapids, Michigan 49546
www.eerdmans.com

Published 2020
Printed in the United States of America

26 25 24 23 22 21 20 1 2 3 4 5 6 7

ISBN 978-0-8028-7441-2

Library of Congress Cataloging-in-Publication Data

Names: Jorgenson, Kiara A., 1979– editor. | Padgett, Alan G., 1955– editor.
Title: Ecotheology : a Christian conversation / edited by Kiara A. Jorgenson, Alan G. Padgett.
Description: Grand Rapids, Michigan : William B. Eerdmans Publishing Company, 2020. | Includes bibliographical references and index. | Summary: "Theocentric scholarly dialogues on creation care"—Provided by publisher.
Identifiers: LCCN 2020012146 | ISBN 9780802874412 (paperback)
Subjects: LCSH: Ecotheology.
Classification: LCC BT695.5 .E326 2020 | DDC 261.8/8—dc23
LC record available at https://lccn.loc.gov/2020012146

To our students and the growing generation of ecotheologians

Contents

Foreword

In the beginning, God told humans to "be fruitful and multiply; fill the earth and subdue it" (Gen. 1:28 NKJV). That instruction was given to a very small number of people on a planet that was able to provide in abundance for the needs of all living things, but today it has become obsolete—and not only obsolete, one may argue, but unrecognizably warped from God's original intention.

As human population closes in on eight billion, overconsumption, exploitation, and destruction abound. A 2019 intergovernmental report found that 75 percent of terrestrial environments and 66 percent of marine environments have been "severely altered" by human activity.[1] On land, humans have reduced the productivity of soils by 23 percent, and we dump nearly four hundred million tons of toxic waste into the oceans every year.2 Researchers have even found microplastics in the oceans' deepest trenches.[2] We share our planet with eight million known animal and plant species, and new ones are constantly being discovered. But a million of those species, scientists estimate, are threatened with extinction, many within the next few decades.[3]

Overlaying everything is climate change, the ultimate threat multiplier. The Industrial Revolution brought us many benefits: doubling Western life spans, improving our quality of life, and providing the electricity, transportation, and other goods and services we take for granted today. However, it was powered by fossil fuels. These fuels, when burned, produce greenhouse gases that build up in the atmosphere, holding in heat that would otherwise escape to space.

1. Intergovernmental Science-Policy Platform on Biodiversity and Ecosystem Services (IPBES), "Global Assessment Report on Biodiversity and Ecosystem Services," 2019, https://ipbes.net/global-assessment.

2. X. Peng et al., "Microplastics Contaminate the Deepest Part of the World's Ocean," Geochemical Perspectives Letters 9 (2018), doi: 10.7185/geochemlet.1829 https://www.geochemicalperspectivesletters.org/article1829/.

3. Peng et al., "Microplastics Contaminate."

Carbon dioxide levels today are higher and temperatures are rising faster than at any other time in human history. We are the sole cause of this change.

What have we gained from this? Many in the developed world *do* benefit from an improved quality of life as we consume the equivalent of several planets' worth of resources every year.[4] But this imbalance means that others go without. In the case of climate change, our continued dependence on fossil fuels and our wastefulness primarily benefit the wealthiest countries and companies in the world.[5] Since the 1960s, climate change has increased the economic gap between the richest and poorest countries by as much as 25 percent.[6] Only ninety coal, oil, and gas corporations, many of which are counted among the richest companies in the world, are responsible for two-thirds of greenhouse gas emissions since the dawn of the Industrial Era.[7]

What do we stand to lose? We have already witnessed how fossil fuel extraction pollutes pristine ecosystems and increases the risk of birth defects, diseases, and cancers for nearby communities. The air pollution from burning fossil fuels is responsible for the deaths of millions of people every year, and it's estimated that one out of every six deaths worldwide is the result of air, water, or soil pollution.[8] The highest proportion of these occur in some of the world's poorest countries, such as Bangladesh and Somalia.

Nearly 50 percent of tropical rainforests have disappeared, and with them over 50 percent of our biodiversity. In addition to the devastating direct im-

4. The calculation of how many planets, in terms of land and resources, would be required to support human population if everyone lived the same way that you do is eye-opening. If you'd like to see what your calculation is, you can use an Ecological Footprint Calculator like this one: https://www.footprintcalculator.org/.

5. Lawrence Livermore National Laboratory estimates that, in 2019, 67.5 percent of the energy generated in the United States was wasted (see https://flowcharts.llnl.gov/commodities/energy). A 2019 report by the American Council for an Energy-Efficient Economy estimates that US carbon emissions could be reduced 50 percent through efficiency measures alone (see https://www.aceee.org/research-report/u1907).

6. N. Diffenbaugh and M. Burke, "Global Warming Has Increased Global Economic Inequality," Proceedings of the National Academy of Sciences 116, no. 20 (2019): 9808–9813, https://doi.org/10.1073/pnas.1816020116.

7. D. Starr, "Just Ninety Companies Are to Blame for Most Climate Change, This 'Carbon Accountant' Says," Science, 2019, https://www.sciencemag.org/news/2016/08/just-90-companies-are-blame-most-climate-change-carbon-accountant-says.

8. Philip J. Landrigan et al., "The Lancet Commission on Pollution and Health," The Lancet 391, no. 10119 (2017), https://www.thelancet.com/commissions/pollution-and-health.

pacts on animals and plants, use of fossil fuel also affects the quality of our air and water, as the purifying filtration capacity provided by natural ecosystems is diminished. Healthy ecosystems also protect coastlines from storm surge, ensure genetic diversity in our food supply, and buffer us from the risk of diseases like coronavirus being transmitted from animal to human populations.[9]

We've also seen the harmful effects of our unsustainable land use on the soil's ability to produce food. The world loses thirty million acres of productive land every year with, as UN Secretary-General António Guterres warns, "far-reaching consequences including falling crop yields, massive food loss, rising tensions over natural resources, forced migration and weakened resilience to climate change."[10] Since the 1980s, crop losses from climate change impacts alone have averaged $5 billion per year, much of this in the world's poorest countries.[11]

What is at risk is, ultimately, the life-giving ability of our planet. And those who have the least to lose are already losing the most, as these changes heighten the injustices and inequalities in our social and economic systems, pushing the marginalized and disadvantaged further into poverty.

Before we can address climate change though, we must understand why it's happening and what that means for us and every other living thing that shares our home. The direct causes of climate change are our greenhouse gas emissions: 75 percent from fossil fuel use, 14 percent from largely industrialized animal agriculture, and the remaining 11 percent from deforestation and unsustainable land use. The indirect causes, however, are not so simple to tease out. They include our attitudes, assumptions, flawed beliefs, and the many uncomfortable truths we've chosen to ignore.

At the heart of our short-sightedness is the myth of an infinite earth, one still waiting to be filled and subdued. Until just a few centuries ago the earth was, for all intents and purposes, infinite. Its land and oceans provided for our needs and

9. World Wildlife Federation, "The Loss of Nature and Rise of Pandemics," posted March 31, 2020, https://wwf.panda.org/wwf_news/?361716/The-loss-of-nature-and-rise-of-pandemics.

10. António Guterres, "Message to the Seventh Kubuqi International Desert Forum," Kubuqi Desert, China, July 27, 2019, https://www.un.org/press/en/2019/sgsm19680.doc.htm.

11. David B. Lobell and Christopher B. Field, "Global Scale Climate–Crop Yield Relationships and the Impacts of Recent Warming," *Environmental Research Letters* 2, no. 1 (March 16, 2007), https://iopscience.iop.org/article/10.1088/1748-9326/2/1/014002/meta.

took up the waste we produced. A few urban centers such as Rome and London were already struggling with sewage and air pollution, and some vulnerable populations like whales were already collapsing because of growing demands for whale oil. But overall, if humans needed more, there was usually somewhere to get it.

Today, however, we know our planet truly is finite. We also know that the earth's life support system is complex and nuanced, involving a series of *planetary boundaries* that we must not exceed in order for earth to continue to be "hospitable to human life."[12] The nine planetary boundaries begin with the depletion of the stratospheric ozone that protects us from the sun's life-threatening ultraviolet radiation; they include chemical pollution, deforestation, and the flow of nitrogen and phosphorus from fertilizers into the biosphere and ocean; and they end with one that has already been surpassed, climate change.[13]

Climate change is not more important than biodiversity loss, pollution, or deforestation. Rather, the reason we care about it is because it multiplies all of these other threats. From planetary boundaries that affect all living things to our entirely human challenges of poverty, hunger, disease, lack of access to basic health care and employment opportunities—climate change makes all of these worse. That's why fixing climate change is so important: because we cannot solve any of these other problems if we don't address it. And if we delay significant action until climate change stresses our already stressed economic, geopolitical, and resource systems past their breaking points, it will be too late. Our capacity to fix it will be gone.

We often envision iconic species such as the polar bear or coral reefs as the "canary in the coal mine." But, as the scientists of Polar Bears International told me, what they've learned from decades of studying these incredible bears is that the next item on the endangered list is *us*. Not the survival of the human species but rather human civilization as we know it. And this means that if we don't fix climate change soon, soon we won't have a chance to. Instead, it will fix *us*.

We have already exceeded the boundaries of what will sustain life in all its diversity on this planet. We scientists, however, can't solve this problem alone. We diagnose, we quantify, we even forecast the results of different decisions we as a society can make, such as, what are the consequences of continuing to depend on fossil fuels as our primary energy source compared to a future

12. J. Rockström et al., "Planetary Boundaries: Exploring the Safe Operating Space for Humanity," *Ecology and Society* 14, no. 2 (2009): 32.

13. W. Steffen et al., "Planetary Boundaries: Guiding Human Development on a Changing Planet," *Science* 347, no. 736 (2015), DOI: 10.1126/science.1259855.

in which we transition to clean sources of energy? But we can't prescribe or implement the solutions. They must come from our collective choices as humans: informed by the science, yes; but as every contributor to this volume argues, the change begins with each of us.

So where *do* we begin? What needs to change in our attitudes and assumptions? As Christians, we follow a rich and diverse set of traditions and beliefs. There is no one single approach to ecotheology but rather a range of perspectives that overlap to some degree and to which any individual may ascribe partial or entire weight. And as you read this volume, you'll see that we don't have to agree about everything, and that is its strength. By reading ideas that challenge us and by giving them due consideration, we deepen our understanding of not only what we believe but why we believe it. Overall, however, the essays in this book complement each other because, as Christians, we all agree on the role of God as creator of all. We also agree that Christians are called to have compassion for the poorest and most vulnerable who today are disproportionately impacted by environmental degradation, pollution, and climate change.

What is the first tangible step to change? *Talk about it*; have a conversation where you connect the dots between who you are, what you believe, the things you value, and how these are being affected by our exploitation of our planet. Share hopeful stories of people like Yeb Saño, a Christian from the Philippines who walked more than nine hundred miles to the Paris Climate Conference in 2015 as a pilgrimage for climate action. Or Young Evangelicals for Climate Action, who've united over thirty thousand young people across the United States to advocate for clean energy and climate action. Tell people about faith-based organizations like A Rocha, which are transforming urban wastelands into wildlife habitat and green spaces; countries like Bhutan that are already carbon-negative and prize happiness over economic productivity; or the dozens of cities and companies like Apple and Lego, which are already powered by clean energy.

Talking may seem inconsequential, even trivial. But while most North Americans agree on the reality of climate change and the solutions to fix it, they still see it as a problem removed from their own lives. When people are asked, "Do you think this will affect you?" and "Do you discuss global warming, even occasionally?" the answer is a resounding *no*.[14] Because if you don't

14. https://climatecommunication.yale.edu/visualizations-data/ycom-us/.

talk about something, why would you care about it? And if you don't care, why would you act, or encourage others to, or advocate for the system-wide change we ultimately need? Friends and family, people who share our values, are the best people to have these conversations with,[15] and these conversations initiate a positive feedback loop. The more you talk about it, the more you learn and know.[16] The more you know, the more concerned you are. And the more concerned you are, the more you talk about it – and are willing to do something about it!

Ultimately, though, the purpose of these conversations is to share both our concern and our hope with each other: because without hope, we will become a self-fulfilling prophecy of despair. And as Christians, we have a secret weapon; we know that fear is not from God. Instead, he gives us a spirit of power, to act; a spirit of love, to care for others; and a sound mind, to make good decisions based on the truth his creation is telling us (2 Tim. 1:7).

This hope is not achieved through our own effort. It is not the result of positive thinking or positive circumstances or attempting to believe or speak it into existence. Our hope, as the apostle Paul reminds us, lies not in this world (Rom. 15:3). Rather, it comes from knowing, as Cynthia Moe-Lobeda calls it, "the end of the story": that "God's life-saving, justice-seeking love is stronger than all else."[17] And until we reach that end, we are called to walk in the good works which God prepared beforehand (Eph. 2:10), buoyed by what John Haught terms our most fundamental ecological virtue: hope.

Katharine Hayhoe

15. A. Malka, J. Krosnick, and G. Langer, "The Association of Knowledge with Concern about Global Warming: Trusted Information Sources Shape Public Thinking," *Risk Analysis* 29, no. 5 (2009), DOI: 10.1111/j.1539-6924.2009.01220.x; A. Leiserowitz et al., "How Americans Communicate about Global Warming in April 2013" (New Haven, CT: Yale Project on Climate Change Communication and George Mason University Center for Climate Change Communication, 2013), https://environment.yale.edu/climate-communication-OFF/files/Communication-April-2013.pdf.

16. M. Goldberg et al., "Discussing Global Warming Leads to Greater Acceptance of Climate Science," *Proceedings of the National Academy of Sciences* 116, no. 30 (2019): 14804–5, https://doi.org/10.1073/pnas.1906589116.

17. See page 82 in this volume.

Acknowledgments

No book comes together by the efforts of its authors alone, and this conversation in print is no different. We are grateful to James Ernest and David Bratt, our fine editors at Eerdmans, for their enthusiastic acceptance of this project. Our debt and heartfelt thanks to our wonderful co-authors is natural yet real nonetheless, and as they are also friends, we feel this even more deeply than most editors.

I (Alan) would like to thank my family, first of all, for their support and encouragement on this project, over many years. Especially important has been my most excellent and much beloved wife, Dr. Sally Bruyneel. I have learned a great deal about love for the earth, both in theory and practice, from her. The on-going support of my seminary community in this time of global pandemic crisis has been essential to the work that I have been able to devote to this project. Thank you.

I (Kiara) wish to express gratitude to family and friends who have offered support in this early-career work. My young daughters Olia and Ingrid bring humility and wonder to each encounter with our magnificent Earth. They are my teachers. May the dialogue within this volume be worthy of the world their generation deserves to inherit. I thank too my loving spouse Andrew who cares so deeply about processes, be they those of our fragile ecosystems or my very own. And a word of thanks to my marvelous colleagues at St. Olaf College who continue to teach me a great deal about the value of a purposeful conversation.

Finally, we give thanks for our students. They have asked challenging questions and pressed us to make plain the relationship between Christian faith and environmental care and justice. It was their concerns that prompted our initial vision for this book, and it is to them that we lovingly dedicate the volume. *Ecclesia semper reformanda est.*

Introduction

For the Love of the World: A Dialogue on Ecotheology

Alan G. Padgett and Kiara A. Jorgenson

Our planet suffers greatly, and change from within our human communities needs to happen now. From growing problems of threatened biodiversity; to global pollution of water, air, and land; to extreme weather stimulated by rapid climate change, the problems we face as an interconnected living world are challenging, even daunting. We are in nothing less than a crisis. This ecological crisis calls for concerted and significant action by people everywhere, and particularly by people living in high-consuming contexts such as the United States. We need to engage now in practices that bring healing to the earth and limit the damage that modern life and civilization bring. Our planetary future depends upon it.

Like other types of liberative theology, ecotheology is first and foremost concerned with guiding and stimulating right action. We need to continue and deepen our personal, communal, and international action to bring justice and healing to a planet in peril. But action alone—without integrated thought, understanding, wisdom, or critical thinking—can lead us astray. We can make things worse if we are not careful and engage in thoughtless acts. Theological understanding has a vital role to play in this practical wisdom.

What is more, many people today still need to grasp the importance of our present environmental crisis. Inside and outside the church, persuasive work still needs to be done. Theological, philosophical, and scientific work should champion and bring into being liberation and reparation for Earth's living systems. As an interdisciplinary field within the environmental humanities, ecotheology speaks to relevance of beliefs, thoughts, and axioms as well as the critical role of praxis. This is why in ecotheological works natural science and social science frequently partner with variant forms of eco-criticism in the work of reinterpreting Scripture; revising and teaching new modes of worship, prayer, and preaching; reimagining the boundaries of Christian doctrine; re-forming the mission of the church; and the like.

This volume seeks to further this emergent and urgent outlook in theology. By asking four major voices in the field to set forth their understanding for a broad audience of thoughtful readers, we hope to stimulate and guide further crucial work in ecotheology. But like all proposals from individual theologians, these essays are neither final nor definitive. We believe that the conversation among these theologians, from different perspectives and approaches, not only will be interesting and informative but will also stimulate our own theological imagination.

In the early 1950s, before ecotheology was a recognized term or academic field, Lutheran minister and scholar Joseph Sittler encouraged the church to take up what he considered the most insistent and delicate task awaiting Christian theology—an articulated theology *for* the earth. He warned, "If the Church will not have a theology for nature, then irresponsible but sensitive [people] will act as midwives for nature's un-silence-able meaningfulness and enunciate a theology for nature. For earth . . . unquenchably sings out her violated wholeness, and in groaning and travailing awaits with [humankind] the restoration of all things."[1] The wicked and complex problem of climate change grows worse, the ramifications publicly evident in higher global temperatures, depleted water systems, food insecurity, climate migration, vanishing ecosystems, turbulent weather, rising oceans, and the like. Add to this ongoing ecological concerns such as widespread water and air pollution, deforestation, and the destruction of animal habitats, and the picture becomes bleak. Yet, a resilient creation once spoken into being still speaks. But have we Christians listened? Even where we have taken due notice, what have our responses been?

As anyone even vaguely familiar with the realm of religion and ecology is aware, Christian theologies and related biblical Scriptures since 1950 have been critiqued as explicitly anthropocentric, inherently aligned with modernist materialisms and economic systems that promote harmful industry, and

1. Joseph Sittler, "A Theology for Earth," *Christian Scholar* 37 (1954): 367–74, at 370.

ultimately inadequate when addressing the complexities of climate change. But as Christianity's most influential eco-critic, Lynn White Jr., once stated, the religious nature of our environmental problems requires religious answers, or at least responses. "More science and technology are not going to get us out of the present ecological crisis until we find a new religion or rethink our old one. . . . Since the roots of our trouble are so largely religious, the remedy must also be essentially religious, whether we call it that or not. We must rethink and refuel our nature and destiny."[2] Because White was a practicing Christian, this last point may have seemed natural to him.

Since the 1970s, Christian theologians and practitioners, biblical scholars, and ethicists have followed his advice and reimagined Christian environmental heritage and legacy. The majority of the seven-thousand-plus titles on Christianity and ecology published in the past fifteen years have taken up White's challenge with abandon, seeking to redefine critical Christian doctrines in light of ecological realities and scientific discovery. Other Christians working on these themes come to the table by invitation, a welcome from the scientific community, which recognizes now more than ever the necessity of the humanities in the shape-shifting of values. Still other Christian scholars see discussion on creation care as mission-critical, given that so many younger people indicate concern over environmental justice issues. These variant reasons for engaging in the debate have often led to disparate views on Christian ecotheology, which have in turn led to much defending of views rather than coalescing of differing traditions' various strengths. Deliberating in theoretical and abstract realms, Christianity's short tenure in the department of ecological ethics has largely focused on the deconstruction and reconstruction of doctrines, interpretations, and beliefs, frequently leaving aside more practical perspectives.

In the creation of this work, we maintain that for Christian theology, practice, and witness to prove environmentally fruitful rather than harmful, all these differing perspectives are necessary. Rather than highlighting one over another or seeking to synthesize views into a comprehensive approach, we celebrate the space shared among seemingly alternative or competing views and advocate for bringing to bear the many resources Christianity has to offer.

2. Lynn White Jr., "The Historical Roots of Our Ecologic Crisis," *Science* 155, no. 3767 (March 10, 1967): 1207.

Ecotheology: A Typology

In working with people of good will everywhere to oppose the destruction of the earth and work for healing and justice, it is important for Christians of all kinds to be aware of the various secular or humanistic theories of ecological ethics. The world simply needs all kinds of people, everywhere, to begin making a difference to a planet at an ecological crisis point. We have to work together, and work globally, with people of all religions and none at all. Yet the focus of this work is different.

Equally important for those of us who are Christian is the ongoing work within Christianity itself, globally, to educate and promote a Christian ecotheology among Christians everywhere. The flowering of ecotheology has brought, and will no doubt continue to bring, a diversity of theologies into the open. This is important for the crucial work of localization and contextualization, for despite overwhelming evidence of global pollution and ecological devastation, alongside solid biblical and theological reasoning toward ecological justice, far too many Christians today deny the importance of such work or place it well below other duties and activities in priority. As Jim Antal writes near the beginning of his helpful book *Climate Church, Climate World*: "Since 2008 [when he tried to organize four hundred churches for action] discussion of climate change has been drenched in disputation, denial and despair." Yet there are signs of hope: "Also since 2008, many, many churches have embraced their calling as followers of Christ and communities of faith to be bold and courageous in proclaiming truth in the public square."[3] Our hope is that this book will help Christians to better understand this truth about God and creation, so as to better proclaim it and lead change to enact it in a hurting world.

Any quick and basic outline of various kinds of theology, or much else that is complex, is bound to be a simplification: ours is no different. For each model or type, we will talk about its character and connect it with a typical and plausible moral ground for its perspective. We do not assume that these are the only ways of putting together ecotheology and metaethics, but only that they are natural enough and not uncommon in the literature. The realities of specific authors and theories are always more complex and interesting. Part of

3. James Antal, *Climate Church, Climate World* (Lanham, MD: Rowman & Littlefield, 2018), 10.

the purpose of this book is to stimulate further, careful reading in the rich and growing literature of ecotheology. We start this brief survey of various types of ecotheology with the model of stewardship.[4]

Starting with Stewardship

Stewardship is a fairly straightforward model with a long history in Christian thought.[5] The basic notion here is that stewards take care of property belonging to someone else. The biblical analogy of being a shepherd of the sheep is often brought forward, as shepherds in biblical times usually worked for somebody who owned the flocks they watched. Biblical scholars have argued recently that stewardship is a more appropriate way of understanding the classic phrase from Genesis that humans are created to have "dominion" over the animals of the earth than the typical Enlightenment interpretation of becoming "rulers of nature."[6] Theologically the idea of stewardship fits well with the place of human beings in a world that is created by God and fundamentally owned by God. Since the whole world is the Lord's, we cannot have absolute control over creatures, nor should we treat creation as existing only for our own needs.

While not a specific Christian theological approach, stewardship is commonly used in pluralistic and secular contexts. This generation then becomes stewards of the earth for future humans. For rhetorical effect, these future generations can be identified as "our children and grandchildren." In such a case stewardship has a purely humanistic focus rather than a theocentric one. Still, this model can be useful when talking about motives for moral behavior toward the natural world with groups that embrace a variety of worldviews and religious perspectives.

4. For a more developed and different typology, see Willis Jenkins, *Ecologies of Grace* (Oxford: Oxford University Press, 2008).

5. Douglas John Hall, *The Steward: A Biblical Symbol Come of Age* (Grand Rapids: Eerdmans, 1990).

6. Walter Brueggemann, *Genesis*, Interpretation: A Bible Commentary for Teaching and Preaching (Atlanta: John Knox, 1982), 32; Eleonora Montuschi, "Order of Man, Order of Nature: Francis Bacon's Idea of a 'Dominion' over Nature, " in *Order: God's, Man's, and Nature's* (unpublished collection of discussion papers from the London School of Economics, 2010), https://iris.unive.it/retrieve/handle/10278/24867/23441/MontuschiBacon.pdf; see also her anthology, *Nature and Scientific Method: Essays on Francis Bacon's Imagery of Scientific Inquiry* (Milan: Albo Versorio, 2015).

In terms of Christian ethics, advocates of this model in ecotheology would naturally be drawn to a divine command theory. The Bible becomes a primary source of moral teaching, as we seek to understand God's will for the care of creation. The positive implications of this focus on the biblical witness is a reexamination of the Bible. Biblical scholars of all kinds have worked to rediscover lost voices in the biblical text often overlooked by our traditions. In some cases, even English translations have not properly expressed the earth-friendly character of the original text. For example, Genesis 2:15 famously states that the newly created human being is placed in the forest of Eden "to dress it and to keep it" (KJV).[7] A green hermeneutic of Scripture embraced by biblical scholars has discovered that the words are more oriented toward service to the earth than was previously thought. Richard Bauckham's contribution to this volume is a fine example of such work. The phrase could be translated as "to take care of it and to look after it" (CEV)—a far more earth-friendly reading. More conservative and Bible-oriented Christian groups have tended to embrace the stewardship model along with a divine-command ethic and a green biblical hermeneutic as the source for the ethics of earth care.[8] Our task in this model is to follow our calling as Christians to obey God's will in caring for the earth, since we've been commanded by God to be good stewards.

Ecotheology as Ecojustice

A significant change came to Christian theology with the rise of liberative and revolutionary movements in the 1960s. These included the green revolution, black power, the civil rights movement, and the second wave of feminism. Especially significant for ecotheology was the work of feminist thinkers who expounded and uncovered in the "logic" of patriarchy an analogous oppression of the natural world and of the bodies of women.[9] The resulting movement of

7. Unless otherwise indicated (as here, for example), biblical quotations in this book come from the New Revised Standard Version.

8. See, e.g., Francis Schaeffer, *Pollution and the Death of Man* (Wheaton, IL: Tyndale House, 1970).

9. See, e.g., Françoise d'Eaubonne, *La Féminisme ou la Mort* [Feminism or death] (Paris: Horay, 1974). She coined the term "ecofeminism" in this work. See also part 1 of Hallie I. Austen, *The Heart of the Goddess: Art, Myth, and Meditations of the World's Sacred Feminine*, 2nd ed. (Rheinbeck, NY: Monkfish, 2018).

thought in ecofeminism was the first liberative movement to combine a holistic understanding of human oppression and ecological pollution. Christian feminist theology developed this insight for Christian thought.[10] Latin American liberation theology came to similar perspectives about this same time, especially in the thought of Leonardo Boff.[11] Black, womanist, indigenous, and other critical theorists and theologians further developed these intersectional insights regarding race, poverty, and ecological destruction.[12] Collectively they contend that context is important, and particularity is essential, even when we are thinking about global problems. Cynthia Moe-Lobeda's contribution in this volume is a good example of this kind of holistic ecological analysis, which includes human oppression and liberation in a more comprehensive vision of shalom. In various ways and with many voices, ecotheology has developed a cry for justice: for humans, to be sure, but also for the earth itself.

The ground for this moral imperative is often put in terms of rights: human rights for humans, yes, but also the right to live and to flourish for the whole community of creation. The resulting notion is that of ecojustice, where the earth itself receives justice because the rights of all living things are granted and protected. The question of whether the moral grounding of "rights" can be extended to all living things has been controversial. But as Simone Weil once pointed out, "rights" can be parsed ethically in terms of obligations.[13] The right to freedom of speech can thus be understood as an obligation upon the government and other citizens not to censor or stifle free speech and its propagation. In terms of ecojustice, the right to live and flourish enjoyed by all living things could be understood as both an obligation on people to cease damaging living things and systems, and an obligation to heal and care for those places we are so actively destroying as a species. What is beyond dispute

10. E.g., Rosemary R. Ruether, *Gaia and God* (San Francisco: Harper, 1992). See further Karen J. Warren, ed., *Ecofeminism: Women, Nature, Culture* (Bloomington: Indiana University Press, 1997); Karen Baker-Fletcher, ed., *Sisters of Dust, Sisters of Spirit: Womanist Wordings on God and Creation* (Minneapolis: Fortress, 1998); and Ivone Gebara, *Longing for Running Water: Ecofeminism and Liberation* (Minneapolis: Fortress, 1999).

11. Leonardo Boff, *Ecology and Liberation* (Maryknoll, NY: Orbis, 1995).

12. See, e.g., Jace Weaver, ed., *Defending Mother Earth: Native American Perspectives on Environmental Justice* (Maryknoll, NY: Orbis, 1996).

13. Simone Weil, *The Need for Roots* (London: Routledge, 2002; French original 1949), 2–3.

is the greater insight that the intersection of ecological destruction with human systems of oppression—racism, poverty, sexism, and the like—opens up a new emphasis on justice that has significantly changed our understanding of and quest for full liberation.

Character in the Community of Creation

While ecojustice focuses on duties and obligations and divine command on behaviors, virtue theory focuses on moral character and practical wisdom. Justice can sometimes be a rather abstract idea; virtue theory seeks a practical wisdom that guides us toward the good in our daily life. The development and use of such virtues as humility, self-control, wisdom, compassion, justice, courage, and hope are vital to a human community that can bring healing to our wounded planet. Proponents of this view argue that ecojustice's central interest in practical wisdom requires greater attention given to the moral character of each person in the community as a whole.

Understood as the collective unity of individual moral agents, moral community extends from humans to living systems all around us. In this volume Richard Bauckham represents an important voice in this discussion, and his scholarship has contributed to general conversation on this topic. When we recognize that we're part of a larger community of creation, we can more easily overcome the power hierarchy humans have typically embraced with respect to our fellow creatures. With respect to our moral character, embracing the idea of the community of creation in God provides virtues with an extension for compassion, justice, love, self-control, and the other virtues beyond the confines of anthropocentric points of view. The neighbor becomes not merely the human neighbor but the broader neighbors of the world around us, all of us creatures of the one God. Steven Bouma-Prediger's argument to move beyond stewardship into moral character, a contribution to our present conversation, is a clear and persuasive version of ecological virtue theory.

Deep Incarnation and a Sacramental Universe

So far our typology has examined the moral grounds for concrete, practical acts to bring healing and shalom to a hurting planet. One strand of ecotheology draws upon what one might call a divine "incarnational principle." It takes the enfleshment of God as an analogy for God's being in the all of creation. On such a view, the full incarnation of the second person of the triune God as Jesus is not a bolt from the blue but is in keeping with a kind of analogical being-with and participation-in that the Creator has always been about. The Lutheran theologian Niels Henrik Gregersen has called this "deep incarnation," while others speak of a "sacramental" approach to nature.[14] Working to heal the earth and uphold the rights of our fellow creatures, in this light, becomes a spiritual practice. We are working with God and participate in God's ongoing act of creation and renewal. Christian theology has tended to focus on such participation only in the dimension of human history. This sacramental view of nature pushes us to understand that God is equally present and at work bringing new things and overcoming evil in the realm of creation itself.

The moral motive and ground of such care for creation thus become fused with the impulse of reverence toward the Creator. While creation must not be identified with the Creator in keeping with the fundamental truths of the Ten Commandments, to recognize that God participates in and flows through the creative world grants a sacredness to the world with powerful practical and moral implications for how we treat our home planet. The essay by John Haught fits into this approach but adds an important dimension: the dimension of the promise of God. Hope is needed in our intergenerational struggle. Many of us think of eschatology as a problem, and far too many Christians use it as a basis for rejecting the radical changes we all need to embrace in the light of our present ecological crisis. Haught argues to the contrary, that a truly Christian eschatology is vital to a full-orbed ecotheology.

So, where does this book land in the current discussion in ecotheology? As the brief typology just surveyed implies, a defining feature of this work is its dialogical structure. Rather than making a case for a particular approach to ecotheology or surveying variant theoretical approaches, our contributors seek to tease out similarities and differences in an ecumenical and introductory fashion so that Christians and other interested people might appreciate the need for a consistent and coherent approach to planetary living.

The compendium is also unique in its interdenominational representation. Herein the reader will find Reformed-evangelical, Anglican, Lutheran,

14. Niels Henrik Gregersen, "*Cur Deus Caro*: Jesus and the Cosmos Story," *Theology and Science* 11 (2013): 370–93.

and Catholic voices. The diversity of theological viewpoints gives texture to the reading and application of relevant biblical texts, as one might expect, as well as insight into how certain theological concepts and doctrines relate to others. In this sense the book reaches far beyond an introductory environmental reader.

Finally, the book's intended American audience, and therefore seemingly narrow scope of contributors, proves unusual. Indeed, at first glance the astute reader might ask, "Why not include voices from the global majority?" And while in the context of wider ecumenical dialogue the centering of global voices is paramount—for in most cases it is the global majority poor who are most impacted by environmental degradation—we hold a presumptive and practical belief to attend "to our own." All four contributors who share in the titles of scholar, activist, and citizen hold two things in common. First, they all hail from highly consumptive contexts in the modern world and aim to name and address these realities head-on. Second, all four have decidedly positioned themselves within globally diverse communities of faith with an aim to learn and share insights within their own privileged contexts. Here they do the very important work of informing the global elite, yes, but they also provoke readers to consider their own participation in institutions and systems at the local level that uncreate human and biological communities.

The dialogical nature of this work requires careful attention to terms and language. All four perspectives fall loosely under a broad Christian approach. Rather than "nature," all four contributing scholars often use the theological term "creation" because on some level they champion the Christian belief in an intentional and sovereign Creator who crafted the world in love and continues to engage within it. The term "creation" is decidedly theocentric in scope and situates conversations about ecological ethics within a larger doctrinal framework, where other doctrines such as soteriology, Christology, pneumatology, and eschatology easily relate.

The related concept of work toward a healthier creation might be easily associated with long-standing approaches to Christian stewardship, a model of environmental engagement under heavy scrutiny in recent years. Critics of stewardship models rightfully note how the concept borders on management, reinforcing harmful anthropocentric emphases. As will be teased out in this volume, contemporary conversations underscore the interconnectedness of all life and thereby seek to render ecological action more a matter of right relationship than right management. Richard Bauckham and Steven Bouma-Prediger illustrate this well in their careful analysis of specific texts on land-human relationship.

In contrast, some contemporary theological communities understand work to overcome the destruction of the earth to be a matter of justice, where the concern proves largely social, structural, and political. And while all four contributors prove sympathetic to the justice-oriented approach, indeed championing it in their own ways, the dialogue among them pushes the conversation further, to include personal and spiritual transformation. This is perhaps most evident in the dialogue shared between Moe-Lobeda, who utilizes social-political methodologies in her theological engagement, and Bouma-Prediger, who most exemplifies an ecological virtue-ethics approach focusing on moral character.

Our Christian Conversation

At this point a brief introduction to the argument found in each main chapter is called for. Richard Bauckham's chapter focuses on the reinterpretation of the biblical witness. Describing and rejecting the Baconian project of "dominion" as domination, he begins by rereading the classic text Genesis 1:26–28. After exploring and rejecting this early modernist perspective, he moves to the notion of responsible stewardship found in more recent, earth-friendly scholarship. While stewardship has some positive contributions to make, Bauckham argues that it does not embrace the fullness of what the Genesis story is telling us. He moves toward a "community of creation" view of human being as the image of God, by reexamining Genesis 1 and 2 and other texts in the broader witness of all Scripture. The result places humans in a more leveled and mutual relationship with our fellow creatures, a view of humanity more in keeping with current ecological understanding.

Questions of a community's constitution and how members of communities might see, think, and act are central to Cynthia Moe-Lobeda's chapter on incarnate love. In response to the embodied and social devastation of climate violence, she argues for more radicalized forms of sacramental love, wherein promises of God's unceasing love for all creation can be actualized, structural sin is addressed head-on, and love becomes a public justice-seeking, earth-relishing, life-saving force of resistance and rebuilding. Moe-Lobeda is primarily concerned with the uprooting of moral inertia among climate-privileged sectors of the church. She briefly addresses the roots of Christian complicity, complacency, and privatized morality as she sees them and concludes her chapter with many practical guideposts for revitalized moral-spiritual agency.

Like Bauckham, Steven Bouma-Prediger begins with the notion of stewardship and gives reasons to "retire" this word along with the associated term "dominion," to describe a biblical understanding of human relationship with creation as a whole. Instead he makes a case for understanding Scripture to teach that humans are *earthkeepers*. He fills out this biblical and theological understanding by turning to the doctrine of our vocations in Christ and to a virtue ethic for earthkeepers. Arguing that what we do flows from who we are, he turns to the moral character of the earthkeeper. He sketches the nature of virtue as such and sets forth a coherent environmental virtue ethic. Long-cherished Christian virtues such as humility, self-control, love, hope, and perseverance, along with newer virtues such as attentiveness and imagination, are given a broader scope that includes the community of creation as a whole.

In his contribution to this dialogue, John Haught joins Moe-Lobeda's efforts by setting forth a sacramental view of creation in the context of radical ecological degradation. He rejects an alternative viewpoint named "archaeology," by which he means a kind of reductive physicalism for understanding the natural history of the cosmos. But he likewise sets forth and sets aside a more traditional sacramental view, "analogy," because it thinks of the cosmos as already saturated with the eternal present of God's being. Instead, Haught proposes an alternative sacramental view of creation, which places becoming and divine promise at the center of its cosmology. This move recognizes the unfinished character of creation and provides a fully eco-friendly place for Christian hope and eschatology. Haught thus places our own spiritual life, passion, and action toward wholeness in creation within the larger adventure of cosmic becoming. We live now in and with a cosmos moving toward a future, fuller communion with the Creator, gaining hope from the divine promise to renew all things. This move places the moral grounds for ecojustice in the sacredness of nature as participation in the presence and grace of God.

We hope the above *hors d'oeuvres* have stimulated your appetite for the riches of this volume and the texture of each viewpoint as the authors themselves lay it before us. The structure of the book indicates its intention, to lift up the value of intra-Christian conversation and the need for a multivalent ecological ethic. Each chapter begins with an extended essay from one author, which is followed by three brief responses. The responses are not intended to be full peer reviews but instead offer brief thoughts for further reflection and development. Unlike some other dialogical works, space isn't given for rebuttal, as the overall book isn't apologetic in nature but rather generative. Our editorial goal is to illuminate similarities and differences in perspectives and to provide new avenues for Christian imagination. Our aim is thus to assist individuals and communities to develop their own ecotheology and to explore the spiritual and theological dimensions of cultivating a greater love of the world.

1 ~ Being Human in the Community of Creation

A Biblical Perspective

Richard Bauckham

We human beings are trashing God's creation. To some extent we have been doing so throughout history, but in the modern period the damage we do has increased exponentially. This is the brutal fact that must set the context for any responsible Christian thinking about the relationship between humans and other creatures.

Take, for example, the oceans. They and the immense number and diversity of living creatures that inhabit them constitute a very large proportion of God's creation on this planet, as the psalmist realized (Ps. 104:25), even though he cannot have known just how vast are the oceans or just how extraordinary the species that live in them—still innumerable even to modern science. Scientists have barely begun to explore the dark depths of the oceans, which turn out to be unexpectedly teeming with strange life-forms.

For most of history, humans have felt powerless in the face of the sea and have not thought we could possibly do any damage to it. Until recently that was largely the case. People may have overfished local areas, but the problem was always local and temporary, and, since fish are naturally very fertile, stocks always recovered. Any debris we dumped in the sea was literally a drop in the ocean. But in the last half century much has changed. The huge increase in demand for fish by a growing human population, crucially combined with industrial methods of fishing that destroy far more life than the fish they take, have reduced much of the ocean floor to underwater deserts. Our pollution of the oceans has become deadly to marine life, creating ever-increasing "dead zones"—oxygen-depleted regions of sea close to land, where the largest populations of marine creatures would naturally occur but now struggle to survive.

Then there is plastic. We used to think of it as one of the most useful and benign of human inventions. Unfortunately, much of it ends up in the oceans, where it floats along the currents and endangers marine creatures and sea birds. Millions die every year from entanglement with plastic rubbish and ingestion of plastic bags. Plastic never degrades; it merely disintegrates into tiny particles that get into the marine food chain with poisonous effect. It is hard to see how this plastic pollution can ever be effectively reversed, even if it is halted. Finally, in the oceans, human emissions of greenhouse gases are causing both warming and acidification, dramatically changing the functioning of marine ecosystems. Coral reefs, which are unique communities of life, have become well-known casualties.

At creation God "blessed" the creatures of the sea, endowing them with fecundity, and told them to "be fruitful and multiply and fill the waters in the seas" (Gen. 1:22). They have done so spectacularly well—until now. By desertifying the oceans and rendering them inimical to life, modern humans are directly opposing and frustrating the creative intention of God for the sea and its creatures. Whatever the meaning of our God-given "dominion over the fish of the sea" (Gen. 1:26), an issue to which we shall return, this cannot be it.

I have sketched this specific area of ecological destruction, as an example, as it is the one of which most of us have been most oblivious until very recently. From our land-based and human-centered perspective, we have not noticed. But the more we do notice what is going on in a world of which no part is now immune from the effects of human activity, the more extensive our disastrous impact on other creatures turns out to be. To follow where the argument of this essay will take us, we should note the phrase "other creatures," which I have deliberately used rather than a term such as "the environment" or "the natural world." Other creatures are not just something else besides us, a nonhuman world from which we are separate, but our fellow creatures. We and they are all creatures of God—however diverse—and we belong with them in this world that God has made for his own delight and for the interdependent flourishing of us all.

Dominion as a Project of Domination

We human beings are trashing God's creation. How and why has this come about? There is no simple or single answer. A very general theological answer might be: human sin and human fallibility, two factors that are closely intertwined in much of human history. But we also need to think about how humans in particular cultures understand their relationship to the rest of the natural world, because undoubtedly some ways of thinking of that relationship influence human behavior in ways that are more or less damaging to other creatures. The most relevant culture in any discussion of the roots of the modern ecological disorder is the modern West, which has also influenced much of the rest of the world in the modern period. In the early modern period, the Bible and the Christian tradition were so important that even relatively new intellectual developments, such as the origins of modern science, occurred within a Christian framework of thought, though later, especially in the wake of the Enlightenment, the intellectual traditions of the West developed in a more secular direction.

In this context, what we could call the Baconian interpretation of Genesis 1:26–28 has a special importance. I use this term to refer to an understanding of the human dominion over other creatures whose genealogy goes back to Francis Bacon in early seventeenth-century England.[1] If historical theology were not defined as narrowly as it usually is, Francis Bacon would have a significant place in it. Bacon created the vision that inspired the great scientific-technological project that has in large part made the modern world. The extent to which Bacon foresaw where this project would take us—including humans redesigning animals, for which bioengineering now has the means—is astonishing, though, like most utopians, he foresaw only the benefits and none of the downsides.

In creating the ideology of scientific-technological progress that is so characteristic of the modern world, Bacon gave it an exegetical-theological basis in a reading of Genesis 1:26–28. He was the first person to interpret the dominion

1. Among Bacon's many works, see especially the *Instauratio Magna* [The great instauration] (London, 1620). See further Richard Bauckham, *Living with Other Creatures: Green Exegesis and Theology* (Waco, TX: Baylor University Press, 2011), 47–55.

given by God to humans at creation as a mandate for the progressive exploitation of the resources of creation for the improvement of human life. Previously it had often been seen as justification for the use of creation for human benefit, but only in the sense of authorizing the ordinary ways in which people already made use of the nonhuman creation: farming, hunting, fishing, mining, and building. It was not seen as a project humans were commanded to pursue.[2] But Bacon, in the context of the new sense of human power over the natural world that came with the Renaissance, understood subduing the earth and ruling over creatures to be a goal for which science and technology were the means. In fact, he understood science and technology as the means by which humans could recover the power over creation that they had before the Fall. Whereas the role of religion in human life was to remedy the effects of the Fall in the spiritual and moral sphere, the task of science and technology was to restore the human dominion over the earth. He envisaged it as the labor of dedicated scientists over many generations, as indeed it became.

Bacon's vision was a lofty humanitarian ideal: scientists were to work for the good of humanity. But his view of the value of the natural world was purely utilitarian: the natural world was made by God as a resource from which humans could fashion things of much more benefit to human life. It was given in order to be remade by human ingenuity. Notions such as human responsibility for creation, care for creation, and conservation of the natural world would have sounded very strange to Bacon. His language about the dominion is aggressive. The human task is to conquer nature and force her under torture to work for human benefit. In fact, the language of conquering nature runs right through the Western tradition of science and technology. Only in the twentieth century was it filtered out of common scientific discourse. In the course of the modern period, Bacon's vision was secularized. Many scientists and engineers were, of course, devout people, as many still are. But it was not difficult to drop God from the Baconian project. That nature is *God's creation* made no real difference to the pursuit of the project. Essentially nature became raw material for the *human* creative enterprise.

There is much more to modern science than the role Bacon gave it. A quite different impulse in the ecoscientific enterprise—to understand, to appreciate, and therefore to conserve—is also deeply rooted in the modern scientific

2. Bauckham, *Living with Other Creatures*, 25.

tradition and has fortunately come into its own, alongside the utilitarian attitude to nature, in the recent past. At the same time, the Baconian vision of exploiting and transforming nature for human benefit has become more and more problematic. During at least the last half century, in addition to delivering undoubted benefits, the Baconian project has also been immensely destructive in ways that were either unheeded or unanticipated in its heyday. If we care about the trashing of God's creation, the Baconian project needs radical reassessment, as it has received in the green movement, among both Christians and others. For Christians, it must mean going back to the Bible and asking whether Bacon's reading of Genesis 1:26–28 is justified or adequate.

Stewardship Is Not Enough

Moved by the ecological consciousness of our time, many Christians have abandoned the Baconian interpretation of the human dominion over other creatures. Probably most of these would say that Genesis 1:28 is not a mandate for exploitation but an appointment to stewardship.[3] In other words, the human role in relation to other creatures is one of care and service, exercised on behalf of God and with accountability to God. Creation has value not just for our use but also for itself and for God, and Christians are to care for creation as something that has inherent value.

The notion of stewardship—along with kindred terms such as "guardianship" or "earthkeeping" or (the one I prefer) "responsible care"—has, I believe, proved very valuable in enabling Christians to reimagine the human relationship to the rest of creation and to begin to undertake the responsibilities that entails in our age of ecological catastrophe. However, I also think that this model has serious limitations. The notion of stewardship actually goes back to the seventeenth-century English lawyer Matthew Hale, who understood it in legal terms: humans are God's estate managers charged with looking after and improving his property. While this certainly included a notion of the inherent value of the natural world, it also stressed the need for wild nature to be

3. For a fuller discussion of the inadequacy of the stewardship model, see Richard Bauckham, *Bible and Ecology: Rediscovering the Community of Creation* (London: Darton, Longman & Todd, 2010), 1–12; Norman Wirzba, *The Paradise of God: Renewing Religion in an Ecological Age* (New York: Oxford University Press, 2003), 128–32.

restrained, corrected, and improved. Left to itself, the natural world is chaotic and violent. It needs humans to impose order on it and to develop its otherwise wasted potential.[4] With such a pedigree, it is possible for "stewardship" to encourage nothing more than a somewhat softer version of the project of mastering and improving nature through technology. This is probably not what most Christians who use the term understand by "stewardship," but it illustrates the ambiguity of the term. We now know, of course, that nature is intricately ordered in ways that encompass change, but we are more prone to disrupt its order than to improve it. Modern ecological science teaches us great respect for the order of the natural world, but the notion of stewardship itself need not include that. A related problem is that, as is widely agreed, we now urgently need to preserve wilderness, to let wild nature be itself without human interference, insofar as that is still possible. The notion of "stewardship" too easily implies that nature in some way needs us if it is to realize its full potential.

However, the main reason I think we need to go beyond the notion of stewardship is this: much modern Christian thinking about the human relationship to the rest of creation is deeply in error, in that it has been understood as a purely vertical relationship, a hierarchy in which humans are placed over the rest of creation in a position of power and authority. The "stewardship" interpretation has this in common with the Baconian reading. But humans are also related horizontally to other creatures; we, like they, are creatures of God. To lift us out of creation and so out of our God-given embeddedness in creation has been the great ecological error of modernity. We urgently need to recover a biblical view of our solidarity with the rest of God's creatures on this planet, which is our common home. We need to locate ourselves once again where we belong—within creation.[5]

Creation as a Community

For this purpose I advocate the idea of the "community of creation" as a model for conceiving this world of diverse creatures to which we belong. Since the word "community" usually refers to a human community, some readers may

4. Bauckham, *Living with Other Creatures*, 59–60.

5. See John Mustol, *Dusty Earthlings: Living as Eco-Physical Beings in God's Eco-Physical World* (Eugene, OR: Cascade, 2012), 30–53.

find this extension of the word strange and may misunderstand it. But the word has long been used in ecological science to refer to the diverse living inhabitants of a particular ecosystem together with the inanimate components of their environment. It evokes the way that such creatures are interdependent and interrelated in many complex ways.[6] In taking the word in a theological sense, I am extending it to refer to the whole global ecosphere, and by referring to the community of *creation,* I am making its relationship to God its Creator an integral part of the concept. To see ourselves within the community of creation is to become aware of our own creaturehood and of all we share with the other creatures of God on this planet. We are not independent of the rest of creation but participants in the interconnectedness of life and the many components of inanimate nature. To see the natural world around us, below us, and above us as a community to which we belong is to reenter creation, the community from which in many ways modern humans have become estranged. It is to recognize the relationships of which, in modern urban and industrial civilization, we have become oblivious but which have never ceased to sustain our life and our flourishing. It is to live in conscious mutuality with other creatures.

Human communities are more or less diverse, and people have a variety of different roles and relationships within them. The community of creation is immensely more diverse, and so the interrelationships of its members are correspondingly much more varied. So the notion of a community of creation does not exclude a distinctive place and role for humans within it. But the point is that such a place and role are *within* creation, assumed and exercised in relation to *fellow creatures.* Common creaturehood is fundamental to everything else. Certainly we must beware of anthropomorphizing the rest of creation, projecting onto it the kinds of relationships that characterize human community. We must recognize the genuine otherness of other creatures. Many of them have almost inconceivably different ways of living or existing. Indeed, to reenter creation is to be liberated from the confines of a purely human-made world, which is what their environment feels like to many modern people. God's creatures are extraordinarily different and relate in innumerably different ways. God made us to be part of that amazing profusion and complexity.

6. See, e.g., Peter F. Sale, *Our Dying Planet: An Ecologist's View of the Crisis We Face* (Berkeley: University of California Press, 2011), 171–98.

The Bible does not use the term "community of creation," but I find it a useful way of encapsulating much that the Bible does say.[7] To appreciate that, we must break out of the traditional tendency to focus on Genesis 1:26–28 in isolation from its context in the rest of Scripture. A good place to begin is the great psalm of creation—Psalm 104—which is in many ways a liturgical equivalent to Genesis 1, celebrating God's creation within a framework of praising him for it.[8] It moves from a poetic evocation of God's original acts of creation to a panoramic view of the parts and members of the created world. A representative sample of living creatures is depicted, each with its place in the world given it by its Creator, each given by God the means of sustenance for its form of life. This is a wonderfully diverse creation (cf. v. 24), and within this diversity humans appear simply as one of the many kinds of living creatures for whom God provides (vv. 14–15, 23). As well as living creatures, the psalmist attends to the springs, the rivers and the rain, the mountains, and the earth itself (v. 13), as well as the sun and the moon.

What gives wholeness to this reading of the world is not human mastery or the value humans set on it but the value of all created things for God. This is a theocentric, not an anthropocentric, or even a biocentric, view of the world. God's own rejoicing in his works (v. 31) funds the psalmist's rejoicing (v. 34), as he praises God, not merely for human life and creation's benefits for humans but for God's glory seen in the whole creation. The psalmist is taken out of himself, lifted out of the limited human preoccupations that dominate most of our lives, by his contemplation of the rest of God's plenitude of creatures.

The Community of Creation in Genesis 1

Genesis 1 paints a similar picture of a world of many diverse creatures, all valued by God. Most of the many categories of creatures depicted in the psalm also feature in the work of the six days of creation, though here we find a more schematic account, with a carefully delineated structure that conveys a sense of the order that the Creator has given to creation. Also, note that the scheme of six days not only comprises a chronological sequence but is also ordered spatially. God first creates, on the first three days, the physical universe, and

7. See also Bauckham, *Bible and Ecology*, 87–92.

8. For a fuller account, see Bauckham, *Bible and Ecology*, 64–72.

then, on the following three days, its inhabitants. On the first day God creates day and night, on the second the sea, on the third the dry land. The inhabitants of each sphere follow in the same order: on the fourth day the heavenly bodies, on the fifth day the sea creatures, and on the sixth day the land creatures—all the land creatures: animals, reptiles, insects, and humans. Humans do not get a day to themselves. They are, from the perspective of this scheme of creation, land creatures, though the rest of this account of their creation distinguishes them as special among the land creatures. But we should not rush ahead to this human exceptionality without noticing how the rest of the account prepares us to understand it correctly.

There are several formulaic refrains that recur throughout the account. One repeated phrase is "of every kind" or "according to their kind" (the translations vary). We hear of fruit trees of every kind, seed-bearing plants of every kind, sea creatures of every kind, birds of every kind, wild animals of every kind, domestic animals of every kind, creeping things of every kind. The phrase occurs ten times in all, scattered across the accounts of the third, the fifth, and the sixth days. To say that this passage recognizes biodiversity is an understatement. It *celebrates* biodiversity. It paints a picture of a world teeming with many different forms of life. In another recurring formula, God "blesses" the creatures he made on the fifth and sixth days. This term means that the Creator gives them fertility, enabling them to "be fruitful and multiply." Thus both diversity and abundance belong to the Creator's will for creation. We may recall that these characteristics of the nonhuman creation were very much more evident before humans came to fill the earth in the rampaging way that we have done.

Probably the most important refrain that runs through the whole account is: "God saw that it was good." At the end of his work of creation on every day of the six, God looks at his work, is satisfied with it, admires it, and pronounces it good. At the end of the sixth day, the formula varies: surveying the work of all six days, God "saw that it was very good." The whole is greater than the parts. It all belongs together, and the finished whole is more than good. If we are tempted to think that it is simply the creation of humans, the last act on God's agenda, that makes creation "very good," we should note carefully that what God approves in this way is "everything that he had made." Humans are essential to the completed whole, but so is every other component of this complex creation. There is no indication that any part is more essential than any other. In fact, the sequence of the six days makes it clear that they are necessarily interrelated. None of the creatures of the fifth and six days could live without those of the first four days: this is why they are created in that sequence. A similar sequence of dependence partly explains the creation of humans only at the end of the sixth day. Even without considering their unique role, it is evident that their living and flourishing are entirely dependent on the creatures of the previous days, and, among the land animals, at least on the domestic animals that are specially designated as such ("cattle of every kind"), even though their presumably vegetarian diet (cf. v. 29) means they are not so obviously dependent on other living creatures. We soon find, however, that their special task, the dominion, puts them, uniquely, in relationship to all other living creatures, even those of the sea. While all the creatures form an interconnected community, humans turn out to be the most connected of all. In God's intention this was for the good of all creatures; in practice it has brought untold damage to the rest of creation.

That refrain, "God saw that it was good," approving each day's work, makes it unmistakable that God sees all his creatures as intrinsically valuable. Even what I have called the environments (the work of the first three days) do not have to wait for inhabitants before God pronounces them good. The creatures do not have merely instrumental value (value for other creatures, though the members of an interdependent community do have value for each other), and they are certainly not created merely for human use. They are good in themselves in God's sight. I have called this intrinsic value, a category that secular people as well as religious believers can understand. But because God is the source of all good and it is God who has made the creatures good, the best way of expressing the value of the creatures is that they have value for God. They matter to God, and in the end that is why they must matter to us.

There is no progression in value as the narrative of the six days unfolds. This is made particularly clear by the account's spatial construction, according to environments, and a sequence whose logic is dependence, not value. It would make no sense to suppose, for example, that insects are more valuable than birds, fish more valuable than the heavenly bodies. So this account does not accord with that modern (not really scientific) view of evolution as an ascending scale that culminates in humans. The uniqueness of humans in Genesis 1 is not a position at the top of some ascending scale of value.

Perhaps the most important way the refrain "God saw that it was good" prepares us for a proper understanding of our special role within creation is that it invites our agreement. From our own appreciation of the creatures (such as we see in Ps. 104), we can echo God's approval and delight at every stage of the creative process. Building on our existing appreciation of the creatures, it invites us to share God's evaluation of them. It invites us, surely, to *love* this world that God has so wonderfully made. So, prepared by a properly attentive reading of the whole account preceding the creation of humans, a reading that pauses to envisage and appreciate the creatures that God at every stage calls good, we already know, when we reach God's command to humans to have dominion over other creatures, that what God is entrusting to our care is something of priceless value. It is the world that we have begun to delight in as God does. It is the creatures we are learning to love as God their Creator does. Only if we have learned to appreciate the creatures in this way can we begin to be qualified for the vocation of responsible care for them that the text calls dominion. An attentive reading of the whole chapter must rule out the Baconian interpretation of the dominion as a task of exploiting and remaking the creation for the sake of human benefit.

The word "good" is a big word, as general in Hebrew as it is in English. We should not restrict it to limited aspects of creation. But there are features of the account that indicate some of the aspects that God values in his creation. We have already noticed diversity and abundance. A third feature is order. The carefully structured form of the narrative points to an order intrinsic to the world as God has made it. In part, God creates by fixing boundaries: between light and darkness, day and night, waters above and waters below, sea and dry land. These distinctions are expressed in categories that belong to the cosmology of the ancient Near East (see also Ps. 104:6–9), in which, for example, the sky was seen as a dome that supports the cosmic waters of heaven above. But they represent order of a kind that the modern mind can also perceive in the created world, whether by ordinary observation or by science. The account also categorizes the creatures, though necessarily in a very general way ("creeping things" includes both reptiles and insects). The references not merely to each day but to "the evening and the morning" of each day indicate the regularity that God has written into creation, which includes also the years and the seasons (Gen. 1:14) and makes the life of the living creatures possible. Less obviously, linguistic patterns (ten occurrences of the phrase "of every kind," seven each of the two verbs "create" and "make") give symbolic expression to the ordered perfection of the creation. The linguistic patterns combine symmetry with variation, a subtle indication of the way the world is dynamically ordered, in constantly varying but far from chaotic structures. All this suggests that creation has order that the human role within creation must observe and respect, not disrupt. It does not favor the old notion of stewardship as bringing order to the chaos of wild nature.

When the Creator blesses human creatures, at the end of the sixth day of creation, God says: "Be fruitful and multiply, and fill the earth and subdue it; and have dominion over the fish of the sea and over the birds of the air and over every living thing that moves upon the earth" (Gen. 1:28). All too often missed is an important distinction here between the two parts of this statement, the first concerning the earth and the second concerning the living creatures.[9] The first part parallels the blessing of fecundity that God has already given to other creatures. To the sea creatures he said, "Be fruitful and multiply and fill the waters in the seas" (1:22). Like the sea creatures, humans are to flourish in the environment God has given them. The one addition made to the blessing to humans is that they are to "subdue" the earth (Hebrew *'eretz*). This is clearly closely connected with filling the earth. It refers to farming the soil, since it is farming that has enabled humans to live all over the land surface of the planet. Farming made it possible for the land to support a much bigger population of humans than it could otherwise have done. The word "to subdue" (Hebrew *kabash*), when used with humans as its object, means something like "to take by force" or "to make subject" (e.g., 2 Sam. 8:11), but when the object is "land" (*'eretz*), the meaning is more like "to occupy" or "to take possession" (Num. 32:22, 29; Josh. 18:1; 1 Chron. 22:18). If its object in Genesis 1:28 were all the creatures of the planet, it could easily support a Baconian view of the God-given task of humanity: to subdue and exploit the world for human benefit. In fact, its reference is much more limited. All creatures have the right to live from their environment: this is part of the interconnectedness of the created world. For humans, that right includes occupying and farming the land. We should not confuse this with the human dominion, which is the subject of the second part of Genesis 1:28.

9. Ps. 8:6 is sometimes understood to mean that the human dominion is over all creation, but the "all" there is defined by the list of living creatures that follows. Both there and in Gen. 1:26–28 it is presupposed that "rule" can only be over sentient beings.

When God announces the intention of creating humans, who are, uniquely among the living creatures, to be created in God's own image and likeness and are to have dominion over other living creatures (1:26), there is no reference to filling and subduing the earth. Creation in the divine image is connected with dominion, not the subduing of the earth. The latter appears only when God blesses humans and begins by commanding them (like the fish and the birds) to multiply and to fill.

Surprisingly, whereas on the fifth day God told the sea creatures to "multiply and fill the waters in the seas" and the birds to "multiply on the earth" (1:22), there is no equivalent blessing of the land animals on the sixth day (cf. 1:24–25). The account must take it for granted; it is not credible that God should not have blessed these creatures with fecundity. But the omission might make us wonder where they are left by the command to humans to "multiply, and fill the earth" (1:28). Only sea creatures live in the sea, but many different kinds of creatures besides humans live on the dry land. So are humans, expected by God to fill the earth, in competition for living space with all the other creatures of the earth? The answer is given in the usually neglected words that God says to humans after blessing them and giving them dominion: "See, I have given you every plant yielding seed that is upon the face of all the earth, . . . and to every bird of the air, and to everything that creeps on the earth, everything that has the breath of life, I have given every green plant for food" (1:29–30). Why does God here tell *humans* about his provision of food from the earth for other living creatures? Surely it is because humans need to know this. They need to know that the produce of the earth is not intended to feed them alone, but also all the other living species of the earth. Clearly they are not to fill and subdue the earth to the extent of leaving no room and no sustenance for the other creatures who share the land with them and also have a God-given right to live from the soil. So the human right to make use of the earth for life and flourishing is far from unlimited. It must respect the rights of other creatures. In an age of mass extinction and depletion of species, caused by humans, we need to attend to those words of God.

We find a similar concern for restraint in subduing the earth expressed in Israel's land legislation. In the Sabbatical Year, fields, vineyards, and orchards were to lie fallow, "so that the poor of your people may eat; and what they leave the wild animals may eat" (Exod. 23:11; similarly Lev. 25:7). Even within the cultivated part of the land, wild animals are expected to be able to live.

Human Dominion within the Community of Creation

God's command to humans to "have dominion" (Hebrew *radah*)over other living creatures must be understood within the context of the whole account of creation in Genesis 1. It is not the goal of the whole creative process but a key element within the complex whole of God's creation. We have already seen that it presupposes the value of all the creatures for God, which the human dominion must cherish, and the order of the created world, which the human dominion must respect. It is a role of caring responsibility for other creatures, a role within the community of the creatures, a special role but not one that lifts humanity out of the complex web of interrelationships that constitutes that community. Humans are deeply dependent on other creatures for their life and flourishing, more so than any other creature; they, in turn, exercise a duty of care for other creatures, a role that no other creature is equipped to undertake.

The dominion is a form of rule or authority (cf. Ps. 8:6, where the Hebrew verb is *mashal*), and so it is helpful to compare it with the way both ideal human rule (over humans) and God's rule is depicted in the Bible. The Old Testament is notoriously ambivalent about human kingship in Israel, since kingship so easily entailed domination and oppression. Ideally, Israel should be subject only to the just and compassionate rule of God (1 Sam. 8:4–22). Only one passage in the law of Moses envisages a king in Israel: Deuteronomy 17:14–20 allows Israel to have a king of sorts, but it interprets this kingship in a way that subverts common notions of royal rule. The king must be a brother. He is a brother set over other brothers and sisters, but still a brother, and forbidden any of the ways in which rulers exalt themselves and entrench their power over their subjects. His rule becomes tyranny the moment he forgets that the horizontal relationship of sisterhood/brotherhood is primary, kingship secondary. We could apply the principle to human rule over other creatures. It will be tyranny unless it is seen in the context of our more fundamental relationship of community and kinship with other creatures. The dominion entrusts us with authority to care for our fellow creatures.

This analogy should warn us against making too much of the idea that our dominion over other creatures is a participation in God's rule over creation. God is transcendent over creation, as we are not. In the context of the ancient Near East, kings often regarded themselves as gods, exalted above their subjects on a different plane of reality. The Old Testament brings them down to earth. The danger in many modern readings of the human dominion over other creatures has been similar—and similarly idolatrous. Humans have forgotten their created solidarity with the earth and its creatures and assumed the role of gods exercising the godlike power of technology but without correspondingly godlike wisdom and without responsibility for the other creatures of the earth.

Nevertheless, the Old Testament does expect human rule, in the example of kings in Israel, to reflect the qualities of God's rule, especially justice and compassion. So it will be appropriate to consider at this point the Bible's depiction of God's rule over all his creatures. Readers of the New Testament, especially the Gospels, are familiar with the theme of the "kingdom of God" (for which a better term would be "reign") but probably think of it as God's reign over humans. But limiting the kingdom of God to the human sphere is possible only if we neglect the Old Testament background to Jesus's use of this term, which lies especially in the book of Daniel and in the Psalms, many of which celebrate God's universal reign over all his creatures.[10] Psalm 145 in particular is as relevant to our present concerns as is Psalm 104 but is much less well known in this connection.

It focuses intensively on the universality of God's caring and compassionate rule—all humanity and all God's creatures. The word "all" occurs seventeen times.[11] The four central couplets of the psalm (vv. 10–13a) celebrate God's eternal and universal kingdom, making this theme central to the meaning of the psalm. The whole psalm praises God for the way he exercises his governance of creation—with goodness, righteousness, and compassion.

Of special interest for our present concerns are verses 8–9:

> The LORD is gracious and merciful,
> slow to anger and abounding in steadfast love.
> The LORD is good to all,
> and his compassion is over all that he has made.

10. See also Bauckham, *Living with Other Creatures*, 70–75.

11. In the Hebrew it occurs in verses 2 and 16, where it is not in the NRSV, and is absent from verses 10 and 19, where the NRSV has it.

The first of these two verses quotes the Old Testament's definitive description of the character of God, which is frequently echoed in the Old Testament:

> The LORD, the LORD,
> a God merciful and gracious,
> slow to anger,
> and abounding in steadfast love and faithfulness. (Exod. 34:6)

In its context in Exodus, one might suppose that God shows these characteristics primarily in his dealings with his covenant people Israel. There is certainly no indication that they extend beyond God's relationships with humans. But Psalm 145 draws the conclusion that, if this is what God is like, then he must be like that in relation to all his creatures.

That "all that he has made" really does mean all creatures is quite clear from the way the psalm continues after the central section that celebrates God's kingdom (vv. 10–13a). With the word "faithful," verse 13b picks up again the character description of God ("faithfulness" was the one quality in Exod. 34:6 that was omitted in verse 8) and then, in verses 14–15, echoes Psalm 104:27–28, describing God's provision of food for all his creatures. So Psalm 145 connects the account of God's care for all his creatures in Psalm 104 with the character of God as classically described in the revelation to Moses on Mount Sinai in Exodus 34. We should take very seriously the message of this psalm: that God's characteristic love—goodness and compassion (v. 9), justice and kindness (v. 17)—extends to all that he has made. If this is the reality of God's universal rule, then the human dominion over other living creatures will reflect God's rule by showing these same qualities.

Created in the Image of God

The exceptionality of humans among other living creatures is indicated especially by the divine speech in Genesis 1:26, which declares God's intention of creating humanity "in our image, according to our likeness" and of giving humans "dominion" over other living creatures.[12] There is nothing like this in the accounts of the creation of other creatures. Then 1:26–27 recounts the ful-

12. I take the first-person plural in God's speech to be an authoritative "we," strength-

fillment of that intention, with some elaboration ("male and female") and with the addition of the blessing that parallels God's words to the sea creatures and the birds (1:22). As a result, the account of the work of the sixth day extends to a considerably greater length than that of the other days, treating both the land animals in general and humanity as a distinct creation. Since the account is written for humans, this focus on humans is not surprising, but it is more than a matter of focus: humans are exceptional in two very remarkable ways. They are created "in the image of God,"[13] and they are given "dominion" over other living creatures.

These two features are evidently related in some way, and recent interpretation has tended to understand them in very close relationship, such that the more easily intelligible of the two (the dominion) is thought to define the meaning of the other. There are two possible translations of the part of verse 26 that connects the two. According to one translation, there is a loose and undefined connection: "Let us make humans in our image . . . and let them have dominion." According to the other translation, there is a connection of purpose: "Let us make humans in our image . . . so that they may have dominion." In the latter case certainly and in the former case plausibly, creation in the divine image is what qualifies humans to exercise dominion. But in neither case does the dominion necessarily exhaust the significance of creation in the divine image. That it does not is strongly suggested by the summary of verses 27–28 in Genesis 5:1b–2: "When God created humankind, he made them in the likeness of God. Male and female he created them, and he blessed them." Here there is no reference to the dominion at all. No doubt this is because these verses form the opening of the genealogy of Adam's descendants, for which the relevant aspect of human origins is God's blessing of the first humans with fruitfulness. But (as we shall soon see in more detail) the transmission of the divine likeness to the descendants of Adam is also important (cf. 5:3). The absence of reference to the dominion in this passage should warn us against connecting creation in the image of God too closely to it. The dominion fol-

ening the authority of the speaker, like the authorial "we" in Greek and English and the royal "we" in English. Other scholars think of the "divine council" of heavenly beings.

13. Our creation in "the image of God" is a controversial topic, which I did not treat in any detail in either of my two books on ecotheology. Therefore, in this section, I have engaged more with the views of other scholars (with many of whom I disagree) and supported my argument with more footnotes than in the other sections of this essay.

lows from creation in the image, but creation in the image is not necessarily a functional office that authorizes humans to rule, as recent interpretations have tended to suggest.

Such interpretations owe much to alleged parallels from the ancient Near Eastern context of Genesis 1, specifically from Egypt and Mesopotamia. One proposal is that the idea of the image of God in Genesis is modeled on the practice of kings who set up statues of themselves in territories they ruled but in which they were not personally present. Such statues were symbols of the authority of the absent kings. On this analogy, Genesis would mean that humans are images of God that represent his rule in his absence.[14] A different proposal refers to the use of the term "image" to describe Egyptian pharaohs and Assyrian kings as images of a god. This too is said to be a functional notion: as the image of a god, the king is authorized to exercise rule on behalf of the god. But, more than this, especially for the Egyptian pharaohs, the king is understood to be a kind of earthly manifestation of the god. A third proposal posits that Genesis alludes to the cult statues of gods that were set up in their temples to represent them and to make them present. This proposal is easily combined with the second, since the king as the image of a god (especially in Egypt) was a kind of living cultic image, representing and making the god present.[15]

Richard Middleton, who adopts and develops the second and third proposals, sums up the implications for reading Genesis: "The biblical *imago Dei* refers to the status or office of the human race as God's authorized stewards, charged with the royal-priestly vocation of representing God's rule on earth by their exercise of cultural power."[16] Middleton's impressive book develops the notion that Genesis engages in a critique of the royal ideology of the ancient Near East (he prefers a Mesopotamian over an Egyptian background) in which kings were exalted over their subjects by virtue of their authorization to rule like and on behalf of the gods. By contrast, Genesis, by attributing the *imago*

14. This view was popularized by Gerhard von Rad, *Genesis,* trans. John H. Marks, Old Testament Library (London: SCM, 1961), 57–58.

15. There is a good account of these proposals in Richard Middleton, *The Liberating Image: The* Imago Dei *in Genesis 1* (Grand Rapids: Brazos, 2005), 104–29; see also Edward M. Curtis, "Image of God (OT)," in *Anchor Bible Dictionary,* 3:389–91.

16. Middleton, *The Liberating Image,* 235; cf. the fuller summary on 88. The reference to "cultural power" derives from Middleton's expansive understanding of the human dominion in Genesis.

Dei and dominion over the earth (Middleton does not recognize the restriction to living creatures) to all humans, democratizes the royal ideology, giving to all humans the dignity that non-Israelite cultures confined to kings. This thesis may be somewhat overstated because authority to rule *other humans* is not democratized. The question of how human society is to be ruled is not addressed by Genesis 1.

In my view, one serious flaw in all three proposals is that they proceed to establish the meaning of creation "in our image, according to our likeness" (1:26) without reference to Genesis 5:3, where the same phrase recurs (in the stylistic variation, "in his likeness, according to his image"). Since these are the only two occurrences of the expression in the whole of the Hebrew Bible, it is surely astonishing that most attempts to understand the meaning of the phrase on its first occurrence are pursued without reference to the second. Moreover, it is obvious—and generally agreed—that the use of the phrase in 5:3 relates to the abbreviated form of it ("in the likeness") in 5:1, where it reprises the account of the creation of humanity in God's image in 1:27–28. According to 5:3, Adam fathered a son "in his likeness, according to his image, and named him Seth." This is clearly parallel to 5:1–2, where God "created humankind (*adam*) . . . in the likeness of God . . . and named them Adam." But the phrase in 5:3 cannot bear any of the meanings that the three proposals suggest for its meaning in 1:26–27. Seth is not a representative of his absent father, representing his father's rule. Seth is not exercising delegated rule on his father's behalf. He is not being considered, metaphorically, as a cultic statue of his father. He is not a form of his father's own presence. The passage, we should note carefully, does not *say* that Seth inherited from his father Adam's likeness to God, though this may well be *implied* as a consequence of what it does say. It uses the phrase "in his likeness, according to his image," not to refer to Seth's likeness to God, but to refer to Seth's likeness to his father. The obvious meaning is that he resembles Adam in the way that a son resembles his father. The phrase describes the first link in the genealogical chain that leads from Adam to all other humans. It means that human reproduction passes on to the next generation what it is to be distinctively human.

So, if this very distinctive phrase is used consistently, in 1:26 it must mean that humans resemble God in the way that children resemble their parent.[17]

17. Thus Luke 3:38 ("Seth, son of Adam, son of God") is a good interpretation of Gen. 5:1–3.

The difference is that, whereas Seth's resemblance to Adam is the result of biological derivation, humanity's resemblance to God is the result of God's creation of humanity in his own image and likeness.[18] To reach this exegetical conclusion, we do not need parallels in the Near Eastern context. However, it does not render irrelevant the parallels commonly adduced with royal ideology. Rather, it enables us to see their relevance in a different way. The pharaohs were considered the image of Amon-Re because the god begat them by physical generation. For example, he addresses Amenhotep III: "You are my beloved son, who came forth from my members, my image, whom I have put on earth."[19] This relationship between being of divine origin and being the image of a god is also found in Mesopotamian sources, though more rarely[20] and perhaps understood in a more metaphorical sense.[21] Middleton argues that this aspect of royal ideology cannot have influenced Genesis, because it "is conceptually alien to the worldview of the Old Testament . . . , which studiously avoids metaphors of biological relationship between God and humanity."[22] This is true to a very large extent,[23] but the appropriate conclusion would be that the author of these parts of Genesis has adapted the myths of the ancient Near East in this way, just as, according to a scholarly consensus, he has in other ways too. He distinguishes the way humans originated from God sharply from the way human children derive from their parents: they are created by God, not fathered biologically. The transcendence of God over all his creation, including humans, is thereby protected, and the solidarity of humans with the rest of creation (they too are creatures) is ensured. But the author retains terminology ("image" and "likeness") that suggests the resemblance of children to parents. Creation "in the image and likeness" of God points, not merely to an office or task, but to something intrinsic to human nature that bears a resemblance to God. Genesis 5:3 (in relationship with 5:1) means that

18. After reaching this conclusion myself, I was pleased to see it also argued by C. L. Crouch, "Genesis 1:26–7 as a Statement of Divine Parentage," *Journal of Theological Studies* 61 (2010): 1–15.

19. Quoted in Middleton, *The Liberating Image*, 109.

20. Middleton, *The Liberating Image*, 111–12.

21. Middleton, *The Liberating Image*, 126.

22. Middleton, *The Liberating Image*, 104.

23. But see Deut. 32:18; Ps. 90:2.

this resemblance to God is passed down the generations of humanity by the biological production of children who resemble their parents.

A brief examination of the Hebrew words that are here translated "image" (*tselem*) and "likeness" (*demut*) will confirm this conclusion. In particular, these words do not suggest a cult statue of a god. Referring to the human resemblance to God, the two words are used together only in 1:26 (and otherwise only in 5:3). Thereafter, each word is used alone in an abbreviated version of the phrase ("image" in 1:27; 9:6; "likeness" in 5:1). *Tselem* is a rare word. Outside Genesis 1–9 (where it is used four times of the human resemblance to God,[24] once of the child's resemblance to a parent[25]), it occurs in the Hebrew Bible only twelve times. In only five instances does it refer to images of gods.[26] In other cases it mostly refers to sculpted or engraved representations,[27] but there are two seemingly anomalous instances where it refers to something insubstantial (shadow or phantom).[28] Perhaps the basic meaning is a visual representation of something. In the two anomalous instances, the word could then refer to a *mere* visual representation. *Demut* is a rather more common word (twenty-five times in the Hebrew Bible), derived from the verb *damah*, "to be like" (twenty-eight times in the Hebrew Bible). It means "likeness," often referring to appearance, but not necessarily (Ps. 58:5; Isa. 13:4), occasionally to a physical object (a copy).[29] It is never used of the image of a god.[30] It would seem that the two words have been chosen specifically to exclude any thought of statues of gods. While *tselem* might be taken in that sense, the combination with *demut* excludes it.

Also, in Genesis 1:26, 27; 5:1, 3; and 9:6, the two words are used in adverbial phrases. In 1:26, God says, "Let us make humankind in (*be-*) our image, according to (*ki-*) our likeness." (The two prepositions seem to be used inter-

24. Gen. 1:26, 27; 9:6.

25. Gen. 5:3.

26. Num. 33:52; 2 Kings 11:18 par.; 2 Chron. 23:17; Ezek. 7:20; Amos 5:26.

27. 1 Sam. 6:5, 11; Ezek. 16:17; 23:14.

28. Pss. 39:6(7); 39:20.

29. 2 Kings 16:10; 2 Chron. 4:3; Ezek. 23:15.

30. There are several other words used for cultic images in the Hebrew Bible, some much more frequently. See James Barr, "The Image of God in the Book of Genesis—a Study of Terminology," *Bulletin of the John Rylands University Library of Manchester* 51 (1968): 11–26, here 15–24.

changeably; cf. 5:3.) It is sometimes claimed that the Hebrew means "to be our image and our likeness,"[31] but this is unlikely.[32] It is not said that humans *are* the image and likeness of God, but that they resemble God. Two occurrences of the second adverbial phrase elsewhere in the Hebrew Bible are instructive. Psalm 58:4(5) says that the wicked "have venom like (*kidemut*) the venom of a serpent." Here *kidemut*, literally "in the likeness of," clearly means no more than "like." The same is true in Daniel 10:16, where, in a literal translation, an angelic figure is described as "in the likeness (*kidemut*) of the sons of man" (NRSV: "one in human form"). The meaning is that he resembled a human being. We would not think of saying that he *is* the likeness of human beings. It is true that *tselem* seems to have a more concrete meaning than *demut*, always referring to a visible object. The combination of the two terms in Genesis 1:26 could give the sense: "like God in appearance" or "looking like God." This meaning could be supported by referring to visions of God in anthropomorphic form.[33] But it is hard to see how this would qualify humans to have dominion over other living creatures. More plausibly, this suggestion of a visible resemblance is part of the analogy with the parent-child relationship. The most obvious way in which children resemble parents is in physical appearance. But the fact that humans are *created* "in the image" of the transcendent God, not biologically derived from him, makes visible resemblance only analogical. It need not imply that God has visible form in the way humans do, nor that the resemblance of humans to God is limited to their visible appearance. Since, in the Hebrew Bible, human nature is a psychosomatic whole, we should expect the human resemblance to God to be found in that wholeness.

So it seems that creation "in the image and likeness" of God does not mean what it has often been taken to mean in recent interpretation. It does not confer an office or task on humans. It does not make humans God's authorized representatives on Earth, charged with implementing his rule on his behalf. It does not mean that humans are in some sense the authentic version of what cultic statues of the gods were mistakenly envisaged to be. It simply means that

31. David J. A. Clines, "Humanity as the Image of God," in Clines, *On the Way to the Postmodern: Old Testament Essays, 1967–1998*, vol. 2, Journal for the Study of the Old Testament Supplement Series 293 (Sheffield: Sheffield Academic Press, 1998), 447–97, here 470–75.

32. Barr, "The Image of God," 17.

33. Ezek. 1:26–27; Dan. 7:9.

humans, in some important but unspecified ways, resemble God. Dominion over other living creatures seems to be a role for which this resemblance equips them, but there is no reason to think that it exhausts the significance of the resemblance to God.

It is notable that every occurrence of the phrase "in the image/likeness" of God is accompanied by the word "made" or "created." Resemblance to God does not remove humans from the created world or rank them with God rather than with other creatures. It is qualified by the absolute distinction between the transcendent God and creation. Moreover, it does not rule out any resemblance to God in other creatures, who surely reflect their Creator in a vast variety of different ways. In what way, then, does creation "in the image/likeness" of God differentiate humans from other creatures? I think we should recognize that Genesis leaves it a relatively open concept, not narrowly defined in its context.[34] Recent interpretation that links it too closely with the human dominion has been driven by a conviction that, in the historical meaning of the text, creation "in the image/likeness" of God must have a very specific meaning that can be elucidated by an original context in the royal ideology of the ancient Near East. However, in preferring to see the text as, in this respect, relatively open to interpretation, I do not mean that we should be content with any of the ways in which the theological tradition has located its meaning.[35]

These have usually focused on aspects of human nature that were supposed to distinguish humans from other animals, such as rationality, self-consciousness, moral awareness, and obligation, or capacity for knowing and relating to God. One problem with such proposals is that they think of a binary distinction between humans and other living creatures, which characterizes all the latter in negative terms as nonrational, lacking self-consciousness and so on. It appears to value humans for what distinguishes them from other creatures and devalue other creatures on account of their perceived deficiencies

34. In the view of Barr, "The Image of God," 13: "There is no reason to believe that this writer had had in his mind any definite idea about the content or the location of the image of God."

35. There is an extensive historical survey in Stanley J. Grenz, *The Social God and the Relational Self: A Trinitarian Theology of the* Imago Dei (Louisville: Westminster John Knox, 2001), 141–82; and a brief catalogue in W. Sibley Towner, "Clones of God: Genesis 1:26–28 and the Image of God in the Hebrew Bible," *Interpretation* 59 (2005): 341–56, here 343.

when compared with humans. Genesis 1 itself should remind us of the positive value of all other creatures, of the immense diversity among them, and of our kinship with them. What we share with other creatures (which can now be reckoned in proportions of DNA) is not some sort of merely animal part of our nature, to which our distinctively human characteristics are superior but integral to what we are. It includes particular affinities with a range of different sorts of creatures (by no means only the great apes), while many other creatures have their own excellences that we cannot emulate. We belong within the complexly interrelated diversity of God's extraordinarily different creatures.

Another problem with theological accounts that locate the human difference in specific qualities such as rationality or morality is that science is now constantly discovering in other animals capacities and behavior that display those qualities. David Clough gives these examples: "We now have reason to believe that sheep are capable of recognizing hundreds of faces; crows are able to fashion tools in order to solve problems; chimpanzees exhibit empathy, morality and politics, and can outdo human subjects in numerically based memory tests; dolphins are capable of processing grammar; parrots can differentiate between objects in relation to abstract concepts such as color and shape; and sperm whales have developed culturally specific modes of life and communication."[36] It is becoming clear that we cannot draw any hard lines of difference in kind between humans and other animals.[37] It would even be hazardous to claim that humans are the only animals capable of conscious relationship with God. Might not some animals be aware of God in ways appropriate to their life?[38]

The point is not to minimize human uniqueness but to situate it properly in relation to our fundamental kinship with other creatures. If there is no difference of kind, there are vast differences of degree, and it may be that human uniqueness results from the aggregation of such differences of degree. If sci-

36. David L. Clough, *On Animals*, vol. 1, *Systematic Theology* (London: T&T Clark [Continuum], 2012), 30.

37. For an attempt to distingush human commonalities with and differences from other animals, see Mustol, *Dusty Earthlings*, 57–83.

38. The Bible quite often speaks as though animals are in conscious and intentional relationship with God (e.g., Ps. 104:21, 27; Job 38:41; Joel 1:20). It is not easy to know how to understand such passages, but they should caution us against dogmatically claiming that animals cannot know God.

ence continues to develop in this area, we may in the future be able to define human uniqueness more adequately, and this is a good reason for continuing to leave the content of creation "in the image/likeness" of God relatively open. Positively, it is more important to focus on those ways in which Scripture indicates that humans do or can resemble God than to draw lines between humans and other creatures. Most obviously, humans can and should imitate the kind of love that God shows to his creatures (Deut. 10:18–19; Matt. 5:44–48; Luke 6:35–36; 1 John 4:7–12). In the New Testament, such imitation of God is linked to the relationships of humans as children to God as their Father (cf. also Matt. 5:9). I have argued that it is the resemblance of a child to a parent that Genesis evokes when it says that humans were created "in the image/likeness" of God.

In contrast to the functional interpretation of this language as referring to an office or task of representing God, I have argued that it refers to some intrinsic resemblance of humans to God. But, since this resemblance is depicted as that of a child to a father, it also entails the kind of relationship a child has with a parent. Thus a relational understanding of the *imago Dei*, championed by some modern interpreters,[39] can be reached indirectly via the notion of intrinsic resemblance understood as filial resemblance. By creating "in his own image and likeness," God creates "counterparts"[40] with the capacity for loving, obedient, intimate, and understanding relationship with him, creatures who through this relationship can grow into mature resemblance to God, as children do to their parents.

We are now able to address the question: How does creation "in the image and likeness" of God equip humans for the task of "dominion" over or caring responsibility for other living creatures? We could think of some distinctive characteristics of our species that can be observed. For example, we can extend our mental horizons to envisage the world as a whole, as Genesis 1 itself does, and increasingly we understand that world and the complex interrelationships of its diverse creatures. We are also capable of altruistic care for creatures other than our own species, which occurs only rarely and transiently in other animals. These—and others—are aspects of human exceptionality that come to

39. See Middleton, *The Liberating Image*, 22–24; Grenz, *The Social God*, 173–77.

40. The term is used by Claus Westermann, *Genesis 1–11: A Commentary*, trans. John J. Scullion (London: SPCK, 1984), 157–58.

light when we consider the special role of care for other living creatures that God's command in Genesis gives us. Because they enable us to love and care for other creatures, they belong to our creaturely way of resembling God in his love for all creatures. We can quite properly consider them aspects of what it means to be created "in God's image and likeness," something the text of Genesis itself leaves open to interpretation.

We should also see the task of care for other living creatures in the light of the relationship with God that is implied by the analogy of parent and child. This relationship not only enables us to know that this is a responsibility given us by God and that we are responsible to him in our exercise of it, as sons and daughters employed in their parent's business might be. It also enables us to share God's own appreciation of and love for all his creatures, so that our motivation becomes a combination of love for our divine Father himself and love for all that he loves.

While Genesis leaves the meaning of creation "in God's image and likeness" relatively open, it guards it from misinterpretation in one important way. According to Genesis 3:5, the primal human transgression was motivated by the desire to be "like God." Modern interpreters have not usually related this to Genesis 1:26, because source criticism assigns the first and second creation accounts to different authors and usually dates Genesis 2–3 earlier than Genesis 1. But whatever the history of the text, its canonical form, which was certainly the result of intentional editing, juxtaposes the two.[41] Genesis 3:5 suggests that when humans aspire to divine status, as a project of self aggrandizement, they are subverting, not fulfilling, their creation "in the image and likeness" of God. The key to the difference lies in creaturely limits. Creation in the image of God is a matter of resemblance to God in ways appropriate to creaturely being. The aspiration of Adam and Eve to be "like God" was a desire to escape the limits of being creatures among other creatures in God's world and become like God in his transcendent difference from creatures.[42] One version of this

41. This is given due weight by J. Gordon McConville, *Being Human in God's World: An Old Testament Theology of Humanity* (Grand Rapids: Baker Academic, 2016), 31–45; cf. also Nathan MacDonald, "A Text in Search of Context: The Imago Dei in the First Chapters of Genesis," in *Leshon Limmudim: Essays on the Language and Literature of the Hebrew Bible in Honour of A. A. Macintosh*, ed. David A. Baer and Robert P. Gordon, Library of Hebrew Bible/Old Testament Studies 593 (London: Bloomsbury, 2013), 3–16.

42. In the primeval history (Gen. 1–11), this human aspiration to divinity reaches its climax in the story of the tower of Babel (11:1–10).

desire is the modern interpretation, stemming from Renaissance humanism,[43] of creation in God's image as giving humans the status of "gods" over the creation, acknowledging no limits to their power to be what they choose to be or their power to remake the rest of creation as though they were its creators. To resist this mistake, it is vital to insist that creation in God's image makes human exceptionality a form of creaturely difference in the context of many other kinds of differences between creatures in the community of creation.

Putting Us in Our Place

Throughout the history of Christian thought, there has been a tendency to inflate the role of humans in relation to the rest of creation. The modern interpretation of creation in the image of God as an appointment to represent God in his rule has lent itself to this tendency. So, for example, Douglas J. Green writes: "If the opening chapters of Genesis present the Lord as the king over his creation, they also show that he intends to exercise his royal dominion *indirectly*, through the rule of one of his creatures. More specifically, God's plan is to rule creation through a vice regal representative, a creature who stands in his place and rules over the rest of creation on his behalf. The creature who occupies this position of mediatorial kingship is, of course, humanity."[44] If this were God's intention, given in Genesis 1 and Psalm 8, is it not remarkable that in the whole of the rest of the Hebrew Bible there is no allusion to it? In fact, it speaks continually of God's direct action in the natural world, whether in its regularities, its fluctuations, or its specific events,[45] as does also Jesus.[46] An instructive example is Psalm 147, which mingles references to God's actions in the human sphere and God's actions in the natural world without distinction.

43. See Bauckham, *Living with Other Creatures*, 43–47.

44. Douglas J. Green, "When the Gardener Returns: An Ecological Perspective on Adam's Dominion," in *Keeping God's Earth: The Global Environment in Biblical Perspective*, ed. Noah J. Toly and Daniel I. Block (Downers Grove, IL: IVP Academic, 2010), 267–75, here 269.

45. E.g., Lev. 26:14–22; Job 37:2–18; Pss. 65:9–13; 104:10–30; 105:28–36; 107:25–29; Amos 4:7–13; Mal. 3:10–11. In the so-called Noachian covenant (Gen. 9:8–17), the nonhuman creatures of the earth are direct partners of God, alongside humans, not involved indirectly through human representatives.

46. Matt. 5:45; 6:26, 30.

If we look for explicit reference to God's *rule* over the natural world, we can return to Psalm 145, which we have already discussed. This is a psalm explicitly about God's kingdom, which celebrates God's loving and generous treatment of all his creatures, humans and animals, with no suggestion of human mediation in the case of the nonhuman creatures. There is never any indication that the Creator's direct rule of creation is less than satisfactory, owing to the incapacity of the humans to act as God's vicegerents after the Fall.[47] It is this direct rule of God over all creation that the exalted Jesus exercises from the heavenly throne of God (e.g., Eph. 1:20–22), not the dominion of Adam and Eve, who certainly did not sit on the cosmic throne of God or rule over all humanity, as God the Father and Jesus Christ do.

The caring responsibility for other living creatures that humans were given in creation has been abused and neglected on a gigantic scale, but it was never meant to substitute for God's own direct relationship with all creatures. This notion of humans as God's vicegerents with plenary powers is a modern Western one, beginning with the Renaissance humanists who began to speak of humanity as a sovereign and creative god over the world,[48] and has often been assimilated to the Baconian project of recovering humanity's original power through science and technology. It exercises a seductive influence through modern theological talk of humans as "cocreatures" with God, but its catastrophic effects on God's nonhuman creatures in the modern period require us to treat it with considerable suspicion. The human dominion of Genesis 1 needs to be brought down to earth, where it belongs— within the community of creation. It is a role of collaboration with God, not taking his place, and it is a role of collaboration also with the other creatures, who have their own relationships with their Creator, different from ours but appropriate in each case to them.

Another way of developing the idea of humans as representing God is adopted by Richard Middleton, who sees humans as "living cult statues" of God who, like the cultic images of Near Eastern religion, make God present: "Humans are powerful living images of the one true God, called to manifest God's presence by their active cultural development of the earth. . . . By our

47. This seems to be Green's view: "When the first humans sinned, the king was dethroned" (Green, "When the Gardener Returns," 273).

48. Bauckham, *Living with Other Creatures*, 43–47.

faithful representation of God, who is enthroned in the heavens, we extend the presence of the divine king of creation even to the earth, to prepare the earth for God's full—eschatological—presence."[49] This suggests that God is absent from his creation until humans "extend" his presence in it by their occupation and cultural development of it. So, presumably, what this means for wild nature is that God is not present there until humans appropriate it—a novel theological mandate for the humanizing of the whole world and all its creatures (entailing, of course, the extinction of many of them). God's absence from the world until humans make him present is surely a thoroughly unbiblical notion that has infiltrated Middleton's theology from the pagan religions of the biblical period by means of the claim that humans are "living cult images" of the true God. God is present in creation wherever and to whichever of his creatures he graciously chooses to be present (cf. Ps. 139:7–12). The claim that the human vocation is to "extend the presence" of God from heaven "even to earth" is perhaps the most preposterous, even blasphemous, interpretation of creation in the image of God. If humans are God's cultic statue, his actual presence on the earth, it would seem to follow that other creatures should worship them, whereas, as we shall see, the Bible depicts them worshiping the Creator along with their human fellow creatures.

As an antidote to inflation of the human dominion, we should entertain the possibility that God has purposes for his other creatures with which we have nothing to do and to which we are not privy. This was the burden of God's answer to Job (especially chaps. 38–39),[50] and it could also be learned from reflection on the immensity, variety, and (from the human perspective) sheer strangeness of creation as science increasingly shows it to us.

If the idea of divine vicegerency is a way of interposing humans between God and creation, another such way is the idea of humans as priests of creation, at least when this is understood to mean that they mediate between other creatures and God, voicing for creation the praise that it cannot voice for itself.[51] This is not at all how the Psalms and other biblical passages portray the worship offered to God by all creatures.[52] The most extended version of

49. J. Richard Middleton, *A New Heaven and a New Earth: Redeeming Biblical Eschatology* (Grand Rapids: Baker Academic, 2014), 49.

50. See Bauckham, *Bible and Ecology*, chap. 2.

51. See Bauckham, *Bible and Ecology*, 83–86.

52. The idea that all creatures worship God is found in 1 Chron. 16:31–33; Pss. 65:12–

this theme is Psalm 148,[53] which depicts a great cosmic choir, with more than thirty categories of creatures included, beginning with all the angels in heaven and ending with all people on the earth. The psalm calls on all these to praise their Creator (with the implication that ideally they should, even if presently they do not). This is a cosmic choir in which all parts are sung together and complement each other. We could call it a community of praise. It is assumed that all the choristers can, in their own ways, voice their praise. They do not need humans to voice it for them. Nor are humans the conductor or choirmaster. That they come at the end may be significant in this way: it gives us the sense that there is already a cosmic choir of God's creatures, throughout the universe, praising God, and that we are called to join in. The other creatures set the example and help us to worship our common Creator.

Among creatures on the earth (we cannot speak of the angels), it is distinctively human to put the praise of God into words, but evidently other creatures have their own ways of worshiping. (This theme is far too common in the Bible to be dismissed as poetic fancy.) We could say that they bring glory to the Creator simply by being the creatures he made them to be, living for God's glory as he intended. This may not adequately explain all the references to the praise of the creatures in the Bible, but it may help us understand the possibility that other creatures give glory to God.[54] Most important, in our present context, is that in worship we join with our fellow creatures to praise our common Creator. In worship, what counts is not some kind of human authority over other creatures or superiority to other creatures, but our common creaturehood. Indeed, were we to contextualize our worship within the worship of the whole community of God's creatures more commonly and consciously than most Christians do, it could help us recover a stronger sense of our own creaturehood and of our place within the community of creation.

We should not imagine ourselves priests positioned mediatorially between God and other creatures, but we can think of reciprocity or mutuality in our

---

13; 69:34; 89:12; 96:11–12; 97:7–8; 103:22; 145:10; 148; 150:6; Isa. 35:1–2; 43:20; 55:12; Phil. 2:10; Rev. 5:13.

53. For a fuller study of this psalm, see Bauckham, *Bible and Ecology*, 76–82.

54. A helpful discussion is Hilary Marlow, "The Hills Are Alive! The Personification of Nature in the Psalter," in Baer and Gordon, *Leshon Limmudim*, 189–203. The broader issue is how we may think of the subjectivity (distinguished from consciousness) of all creatures, animate and inanimate.

common praise of God. The ways that other creatures reflect the glory of God and offer it back to him can help us to worship, and we can take up the praise of other creatures into our own, giving it voice in language (as in Ps. 148 itself) or depiction in visual art in a liturgical context (as in the figural motifs in the decoration of Solomon's temple, where cultic images of God were absent but depictions of his creatures evoked, perhaps, creation perfected in paradise). Such participation with the other creatures in worship should, like all worship, overflow into the rest of our lives and affect the way we relate to other creatures. Community and reciprocity in worship can foster community and reciprocity in the rest of life.

God's Future for the Community of Creation

When Christians have denigrated or neglected the rest of creation, the reason has often been a failure to discern the place of the other creatures in God's overall purpose for his world. It has seemed as though the real story happens between God and humans, with the rest of creation relegated to an ancillary role, for which there will be no need when God's purpose for humanity reaches its goal in eternity. Of course, the extremely anthropocentric view that the rest of creation was created solely for human use lends itself easily to the view that its existence is of only temporary value, and this anthropocentric view has been very prominent in Christian history. On the other hand, it is not true that the idea of an eschatological future for the whole creation was absent for most of Christian history. It can be found in such major theologians as Augustine of Hippo,[55] and further research on this topic will probably show that it has been more common than those who have championed it in recent times have realized.[56]

The most important point is to recognize that the overall story the Bible

55. Augustine thought that the redeemed will live in heaven but saw this heaven as the upper part of a renewed heaven and earth (*De civitate Dei* 21.4, 11, 24, 29). This aspect of Augustine is oddly missed by the account in Middleton, *A New Heaven*, 291–93.

56. Middleton's historical review (*A New Heaven*, 283–96) is certainly incomplete (for example, it omits the Syrian fathers and the English reformer John Bradford) and, in my view, attaches too much importance to whether the new heaven and earth are conceived as "temporal" or "atemporal" (a secondary issue). On the other hand, it is right to point out that a new world without animals or plants is hardly a future for the whole creation.

tells, from creation to new creation, takes place within a triangular relationship that has God, humans, and the rest of creation at the three corners of the triangle. (Admittedly, this picture fails to represent the enormous diversity of creatures for which "the rest of creation" stands, but at least it provides a clear alternative to the hierarchical picture: God—humans—rest of creation.)[57] The relationships of God to the nonhuman creation and of humans to the nonhuman creation are operative throughout the story, even if the focus is very often on the God-human relationship. The whole story is a double one of God's purpose to perfect a creation that was originally good but not perfect and of God's purpose to redeem a creation that was originally good but has been ravaged by evil. There is one New Testament passage that summarizes the whole story with a strong emphasis on its cosmic inclusivity: Colossians 1:15–20.

This quasi-poetic passage consists of two carefully structured stanzas, one about creation, the other about new creation. Both stanzas echo Genesis 1:1 ("in the beginning God created heaven and earth"), with "created heaven and earth" echoed in verse 16 and "in the beginning" echoed in verse 18, making Jesus Christ both the source of the original creation and the beginning of the new creation.[58] Most important in our present context is that the text makes very clear that this is the story of *everything* in relation to Jesus Christ. There is a verbal pattern like those in Genesis 1: the catchphrase "all things" occurs seven times. Seven is the symbolic number of completeness, and so the phrase "all things" refers to the whole of creation not only in itself but also by its seven occurrences. The phrase itself is commonly used in Jewish literature and in the New Testament as a shorthand reference to the whole of God's creation. We should mentally fill it out with all the categories of creatures listed in Genesis 1, Psalm 104, and Psalm 148, as well as the angelic beings to which the passage itself draws special attention (v. 16). Moreover, there is a kind of *inclusio* between "all things in heaven and on earth" (v. 16), indicating the scope of creation through Christ, and "all things, whether on earth or in heaven" (v. 20), indi-

57. This hierarchical pattern is depicted in a pyramidal diagram in Middleton, *A New Heaven*, 46.

58. But I do not think verse 15a alludes to Gen. 1:26–27. More likely the phrase "the image of the invisible God" alludes to the Jewish idea of the divine Wisdom as "the image of God" (Wis. 6:26; Philo, *Legum Allegoriae* 1.43; cf. Heb. 1:3): see James D. G. Dunn, *The Epistles to the Colossians and to Philemon*, New International Greek Testament Commentary (Grand Rapids: Eerdmans, 1996), 87–90.

cating the scope of reconciliation through Christ. The scope of reconciliation is as wide as the scope of creation.

Thus the main theme and emphasis of this passage run directly contrary to the common idea that, while all things were created by God, salvation concerns only humans. The goal of God's salvific purpose is to rescue his whole creation from the damage done by evil and, through Christ's work of reconciliation, to create a community of reconciled creatures, reconciled to each other because they are also reconciled to God. We could think here of Isaiah's vision of peace between humans and animals, and peace between the domestic animals that belong to the human sphere and the wild creatures that prey upon them (Isa. 11:6–9). How "the blood of Christ" can effect reconciliation in the nonhuman sphere is even more mysterious than its effect in the relationships of God and humans, but there is no doubt that this passage says that it does.[59] The solidarity of humans with other creatures will not be sundered but perfected in the new creation.

59. In a fuller treatment of this topic, study of Rom. 8:18–25 would be especially important. See Richard Bauckham, "The Story of the Earth according to Paul," in Bauckham, *The Bible in the Contemporary World* (London: SPCK, 2016), 95–101.

Responses

From Cynthia Moe-Lobeda

Richard Bauckham succinctly and lucidly summarizes the argument that Francis Bacon's interpretation of Genesis 1:26–28 as a divine mandate to exploit the other-than-human parts of creation for human improvement has been a root of the ecological crisis, and maintains that this argument was in need of radical reassessment in light of the biblical text itself. This interpretation of Genesis 1, Bauckham notes, has been critiqued by many in the Christian ecological movement and has been replaced by various forms of theology to undergird caring for creation rather than dominion over it. He summarizes also the problems with stewardship theologies, one of which is the placing of humans above the rest of creation—lifting us out of the natural world—and thereby negating "our God-given embeddedness in creation." To the contrary, Bauckham demonstrates through rich biblical exegesis that humans are a *part of*, not *apart from*, God's beloved community of creation, creatures called to live in "mutuality" with the others, though having a distinctive role. "Common creaturehood," he writes, "is fundamental to everything else." Moreover, he argues, all of creation has intrinsic worth based on God's declaration that "it is good."

Of particular value is not this argument that, as Bauckham notes, has been made by many others but rather his detailed insightful exegetical work to ground the argument not only in the Genesis texts but also in related texts in the Psalms and the New Testament, and his exegetical refutation of previous arguments for (1) dominion as exploitation, (2) stewardship as "participation in God's rule over creation," (3) *imago Dei* as authorizing humans to serve as God's representative on Earth, (4) human distinctiveness authorizing humans to speak for other creatures or mediate God for them, and (5) other biblical claims that sever human beings' fundamental kinship with other creatures. Noteworthy too is the author's detailed and exegetically rich rendition of Genesis 1 as a testimony to the intrinsic value of the created world and a testimony to the goodness of creation's diversity, abundance, and interdependence.

This work done, Bauckham responds to his primary question: How does being created in the "image and likeness" of God equip humans for our particular role within the community of creation? Responding to this question requires him to reinterpret both "dominion" over and the call to "subdue" the earth in order to clarify that both refer essentially to loving care for creation that models God's goodness and compassion. Only when we have begun to echo God's delight in and love for creation are we qualified for our special vocation of responsible care signified in Genesis by the word "dominion." Our creation in the likeness and image of God does not mean that we are God's representatives charged with implementing God's rule or God's dominion. Nor does it mean that we are priests on behalf of creation mediating between the other creatures and God. Rather, as Bauckham demonstrates, our being created in God's image and likeness means that we resemble God in a way that a child resembles the parent and in a way that enables us to delight in, love, and care for creation as God does.

Important are his exegetically based arguments that, while we are to "subdue" the earth, our dominion is over other living creatures (Gen. 1:26), *not* over the earth, and that our creation in the image of God does *not* include subduing the earth. Other nuances strengthen these arguments.

I appreciate Bauckham's rereading of dominion, subduing, and human distinctiveness. Human distinctiveness, he argues, lies not in qualities such as rationality, toolmaking, self-consciousness, being redeemed by God, or being called to serve God. These qualities, he acknowledges, may not be unique to humans. (For example, God may also have unique purposes for other creatures, and the biblical narrative reveals God's intent to redeem the entirety of creation "from the damage done by evil and, through Christ's work of reconciliation, to create a community of reconciled creatures.") Rather, our distinctiveness lies in differences of degree, the aggregation of which renders unique human capacities.

With one exception, I find myself in agreement with and appreciative of this exegetical work. The exception is his closing image of "a triangular relationship that has God, humans, and the rest of creation at the three corners of the triangle." Bauckham acknowledges that this image fails to represent the diversity of "the rest of creation," but this is not my problem with the image. The problem is that it seems to contradict one basic argument of his essay—that human beings, while unique, are not set apart from the rest of the community of life. "We cannot draw any hard lines of difference in kind between humans and other animals." There are not differences in kind but in degree. We share "common creaturehood," he so avidly argues. The triangle image, to the contrary, sets us qualitatively apart, as far from the other creatures as we are from God.

This one quarrel with Bauckham aside, I am free to raise questions that arise from his assertions and from my previous musing along similar lines.

Intrinsic Worth

The assertion that the entire community of creation has intrinsic worth because God delights in it and finds it to be good (an assertion with which I agree) raises perplexing questions ripe for subsequent pursuit. Does the intrinsic worth and love-worthiness of the community of creation mean the intrinsic worth of all its parts? That is, for example, are we to value and love the polio virus? If not, then on what grounds are we to applaud the intrinsic worth of some parts of creation and not of others (such as the novel coronavirus)? In addition, what are the keys to distinguishing degrees of worth? Certainly, the worth of all creation cannot signify the equal value of all its parts. While we may be called to value and delight in the ant, surely it is not of equal worth to the human being. If the building were on fire and I could rescue an ant in one end of the building or a human in the other, I would choose the human.

The Role of the Rest of Creation

Bauckham writes, "We should entertain the possibility that God has purposes for his other creatures with which we have nothing to do and to which we are not privy." It is a provocative and pregnant suggestion. Here I explore it further. Rabbi Ellen Bernstein points out that God calls upon the earth, not on humans, to enter into the creating task. On day six, God said, "Let the earth bring forth the living creature after its kind." Moreover, in creating Adam,

God appeals to an "us" to do the creating. To whom does "us" refer? The only beings thus far existing are nonhuman ones. Is God calling on them to enter into creating the human? In Deuteronomy God calls upon the mountains to witness. In Psalm 148, all of creation is called upon to praise God. Humans are, as Bauckham notes, to "join in. The other creatures set the example and help us to worship our common Creator." My point is this: Given that other-than-human parts of creation are called to participate with God in creating (and humans are not) and other-than-human parts of creation set an example to "help us to worship" (arguably the purpose of human existence), perhaps God has yet other purposes for the other creatures, purposes that we, in our profoundly limited capacity for knowing both the purposes and the reality of God's relationships with God's creation, are not yet aware. Perhaps God intends not only to redeem all of creation but also to use creation for God's redemptive purposes, just as God used/uses the other-than-human parts of creation for God's creating purposes. Is it possible that the rest of creation has a redemptive role to play?

In a similar vein, might there be a particular teaching role given by God to the other-than-human creatures, perhaps teaching about how to live in alignment with God's intentions for creation? Humans are the only creatures that have gone so madly rogue as to be threatening Earth's capacity to sustain life, so rogue as to be wiping out countless species that God created for God's delight and purpose. Thus we are the one species that is preventing multitudes of other species from doing their God-given task of "being fruitful and multiplying." In light of this human "derangement,"[60] perhaps God intends to use other creatures to teach this wayward humankind.

The Extent of Human Ecological Sin

"We human beings are," Bauckham declares, "trashing God's creation." That "trashing" includes causing extinctions of species in the millions. I am haunted by three implications of Bauckham's insistence that God may have purposes for the other-than-human parts of creation, purposes "to which we are not privy." The first comes with holding this in light of the mass extinctions that

60. The term was coined by Amitav Ghosh in *The Great Derangement: Climate Change and the Unthinkable* (Chicago: University of Chicago Press, 2017).

we are causing. If God's purposes for other creatures include their role in God's redemptive work, what can be said of the species that is knowingly wiping from the face of the earth the tools of God's purposes, and while perhaps not fully aware of what we are doing, having the capacity to be substantively aware and to do otherwise.

Second, the Hebrew *tov*, commonly translated as good, in fact means not only good but a good that is life furthering, The primal act of the God proclaimed in Judaism and then in Christianity is to create not merely a magnificent world but a magnificently *life-furthering* world that mirrors and embodies the life-creating Holy One who brought it into being. Through climate change, we are endangering not the earth but the earth's *life-furthering* capacities, the climate in which life can thrive. The scandalous point is this: We are *undoing* that very *tov*, life-generating capacity. We as a species are "uncreating."

Finally, as Bauckham demonstrates, Genesis 1 claims that human beings are created "in the image of God." Yet, if global warming continues unchecked, we may be, in the words of Catholic moral theologian Daniel Maguire, "an endangered species." How do we make sense of a human trajectory now aimed at destroying the creatures crafted "in the image of God"?

I appreciate Richard Bauckham for his astute exegetical and theological work, and for eliciting these and other vital questions for people of faith seeking to live in accord with the God revealed in Jesus.

From Steven Bouma-Prediger

A hearty thank you to Richard for his thoughtful and stimulating essay. There is much with which I agree, but I also have some questions.

I agree that we humans are trashing God's creation, often without realizing it. Richard briefly mentions the destruction of ocean ecosystems, the increasing presence of poisonous plastic, and the warming of the oceans due to climate change. These are, alas, only three of the ecological degradations that we face.[61] It is hard to ignore the conclusion that we humans are

61. For documentation of ten major degradations, see Steven Bouma-Prediger, *For the Beauty of the Earth*, 2nd ed. (Grand Rapids: Baker Academic, 2010), chap. 2.

having, as Richard puts it, "a disastrous impact on other creatures." We must eradicate our ignorance by becoming more ecologically literate, and we must overcome our indifference by learning to care for our home planet.[62] Our current path of persistent denial is a prescription for even greater disaster for all creatures.

Richard rightly points out that language matters. His deliberate reference to "other creatures"—rather than "the environment" or "the natural world"—reminds us that we are all, human and nonhuman, fellow creatures of God. Indeed, one of the main themes of his chapter is that we humans are interconnected with and embedded in "the community of creation." This cannot be stressed enough. For better or for worse, language shapes how we think about the world and act within it. We are, as Richard emphasizes, rooted in this world and linked to all other living and nonliving things, but our language too often does not reflect this. For example, as Wendell Berry insists, any reference to "the environment" tacitly means "a world separate from ourselves, outside us," while "the real state of things, of course, is far more complex and intimate and interesting than that," since "the world that environs us, that is around us, is also within us." Indeed, "we are made of it; we eat, drink, and breathe it; it is bone of our bone and flesh of our flesh."[63] There is no split between us and the nonhuman world "out there," as if we humans are somehow not part and parcel of this world.[64]

Richard is correct to locate one of the main reasons for our despoliation of the earth in the history of modernity.[65] While acknowledging that there is no single or simple answer, he correctly points to "the Baconian interpreta-

62. For more on eradicating ecological illiteracy, see David Orr, *Ecological Literacy: Education and the Transition to a Postmodern World* (Albany: SUNY, 1992) and *Earth in Mind: On Education, Environment, and the Human Prospect* (Washington, DC: Island, 2004). For more on overcoming indifference, see James Hansen, *Storms of My Grandchildren* (New York: Bloomsbury, 2009), and Mary Pipher, *The Green Boat: Reviving Ourselves in Our Capsized Culture* (New York: Riverhead, 2013).

63. Wendell Berry, *Sex, Economy, Freedom, and Community* (New York: Pantheon, 1993), 34.

64. The body/soul dualism that infiltrates much Christian speech is another example of a common thought pattern that devalues the physical world and assumes that matter does not really matter.

65. For similar historical analyses, see Donald Worster, *The Wealth of Nature: Environmental History and the Ecological Imagination* (New York: Oxford University Press,

tion of Genesis 1:26–28" and its role in legitimating "the ideology of scientific-technological progress" as one of the major factors underlying the common view of creation as merely a pool of resources to be exploited for human purposes. This view of "dominion as a project of domination" must be debunked, and Richard's insightful interpretation of Genesis 1 goes a long way in doing just that.

However, along with the Baconian interpretation of Genesis, another primary explanation for why we are in our eco-mess is materialism.[66] Many people today worship the god More Stuff, what Jesus called Mammon.[67] As a bumper sticker I once saw brazenly put it: "Whoever dies with the most toys wins."[68] Or, as another bumper sticker succinctly stated, capturing much of the contemporary North American worldview: "You are what you drive." Materialism in this sense is defined as "worshipping the god GNP [gross national product]."[69] I do not deny the idolatrous cultural weight of scientism and technicism (to be clearly distinguished from science and technology), but I think these two isms are today almost always accompanied by a third: materialism.[70]

I agree with Richard that we must move beyond stewardship. As I argue in my chapter in this book, while stewardship is a shift in the right direction, taking us beyond dominion as domination, it does not go far enough.[71] As Richard clearly states, stewardship can too easily devolve into some version of the mastery of nature; it cannot easily address the need to preserve wilderness; and it assumes humans are only really in relation to God and not to other

---

1993), and Norman Wirzba, *The Paradise of God: Renewing Religion in an Ecological Age* (New York: Oxford University Press, 2003).

66. Bouma-Prediger, *For the Beauty of the Earth*, chap. 3.

67. See Matt. 6:24 and Luke 16:13.

68. My response to this bumper sticker is that I have never seen a hearse with a luggage rack. Or pulling a U-Haul.

69. Worster, *The Wealth of Nature*, 210.

70. For more on the gods of our age, see Brian Walsh and Richard Middleton, *The Transforming Vision* (Downers Grove, IL: InterVarsity Press, 1984), chaps. 6–9, and Steve Wilkins and Mark Sanford, *Hidden Worldviews: Eight Cultural Stories That Shape Our Lives* (Downers Grove, IL: InterVarsity Press, 2009).

71. See also my essay "From Stewardship to Earthkeeping: Why We Should Move beyond Stewardship," in *Beyond Stewardship: New Approaches to Creation Care*, ed. David P. Warners and Matthew Kuperus Heun (Grand Rapids: Calvin College Press, 2019).

creatures. Another problem is that many assume that stewardship means giving "tithes, treasure, and time" to the church and has nothing to do with caring for creation. I strongly agree with Richard when he argues, echoing Wendell Berry,[72] that "we urgently need to recover a biblical view of our solidarity with the rest of God's creatures on this planet." The concept of stewardship will not get us there.

I think Richard's main claim that we should speak of "creation as a community" has much merit. It emphasizes ecological and, indeed, global interdependence. It implies that there is a Creator and underscores our status as (finite and fallen) creatures. It includes a distinctive role for humans but insists that humans are creatures woven into creation. Richard means with his term "creation as community" much of what I intend by my term "earthkeeping."[73]

Richard's biblical case for "creation as a community" is strong. Psalm 104, what I call the symphony of creation psalm, is a kind of liturgical match for Genesis 1. This wonderful song, filled with all manner of other-than-human creatures (fragrant firs and towering cedars of Lebanon, reclusive rock badgers and migrating storks, rambunctious young lions and the mysterious-aged Leviathan), offers a vision of reality that challenges any anthropocentric worldview. As Richard observes, this is a theocentric (not anthropocentric or biocentric or ecocentric) vision of the world. God the Creator and Provider is at the center of things, much as God is in the litany of creaturely praise found in Psalm 148.

Richard offers an insightful analysis of Genesis 1, much of which is available in more detail in his previous work.[74] The very structure of Genesis 1:1–2:4 suggests a beautiful orderliness, with different inhabitants (days 4–6) occupying their various habitats (days 1–3). We humans do not get our own day, and the order (humans created on day 6) does not imply, as many assume, that humans are somehow more special—the crown of creation. The narrative emphasizes the many kinds of creatures brought forth and celebrates biodiversity.

72. Berry, *Sex, Economy, Freedom, and Community*, 94–95.

73. My argument for "earthkeeping" as a serviceable term is briefly set forth in my chapter in this book. For a more extensive argument, see my essay in *Beyond Stewardship* and also the introductory chapter of my book *Earthkeeping and Character: Exploring a Christian Ecological Virtue Ethic* (Grand Rapids: Baker Academic, 2020).

74. For example, Richard Bauckham, *The Bible and Ecology: Rediscovering the Community of Creation* (Waco, TX: Baylor University Press, 2010), and *Living with Other Creatures: Green Exegesis and Theology* (Waco, TX: Baylor University Press, 2011).

God blesses more than humans, and everything (not just humans) is declared "very good." As Richard affirms, all creatures have intrinsic value—they are "good in themselves in God's sight." We humans find our uniqueness not in a "position at the top of some ascending scale of value" but rather in caring for a "world that we have begun to delight in as God does." Such is our "vocation of responsible care," but this vocation is possible only if we learn to appreciate our nonhuman neighbors as God does. All these are important learnings from this pivotal, though often misunderstood, text.

Richard is especially insightful in his analysis of Genesis 1:28 when he points out that "subdue" (*kavash*) means farming the earth while "dominion" (*radah*) has to do with ruling living creatures. In other words, this text does not sanction humans subduing or taking possession of all living creatures, and dominion does not mean domination—of other creatures or the land. In contrast, we humans are reminded (1:29–30) that the needs and rights of other creatures must be respected. Ruling or having dominion, properly understood, is a kind of care. The ideal, as described in Psalm 72, for example, is to rule the way God rules—with justice and compassion. Insights abound in Richard's careful exegesis.

This brings us to Richard's understanding of humans created in the image of God. As he notes, this is a controversial topic, as it has been for many years.[75] I agree that this text portrays humans as exceptional in two ways: humans are created in God's image and they are given dominion over other living creatures. The controverted questions are: What does each of these things mean, and what is the relationship between these two features of human uniqueness?

Richard calls into question the claim that the *imago Dei* refers to a functional office that authorizes humans to rule as a representative of God—a view put forward most powerfully (of late) by Richard Middleton.[76] Richard Bauckham's argument is that Middleton's case does not take seriously enough the reference to the image of God in Genesis 5:3, which omits any reference to dominion. Thus Richard concludes that being made in the image and likeness of God in Genesis 1:26 "must mean that humans resemble God in the way that

75. G. C. Berkouwer, *Man: The Image of God* (Grand Rapids: Eerdmans, 1962). See also Stanley Grenz, *The Social God and the Relational Self* (Louisville: Westminster John Knox, 2001).

76. J. Richard Middleton, *The Liberating Image: The* Imago Dei *in Genesis 1* (Grand Rapids: Brazos, 2005).

children resemble their parent." The analogy breaks down when it comes to the reason for the resemblance: divine creation in the one case and biological procreation in the other. Hence, "creation 'in the image and likeness' of God points, not merely to an office or task, but to something intrinsic to human nature that bears a resemblance to God." According to Richard, a study of the words "image" (*tselem*) and "likeness" (*demut*) confirms his interpretation: image and likeness of God mean "like God in appearance" or "looking like God." Hence, Richard concludes that creation in the image and likeness of God "does not mean what it has often been taken to mean in recent interpretation."

I am not persuaded by this argument. Much hinges on the conditional sentence "if this very distinctive phrase ['in his likeness,' 'according to his image'] is used consistently." Given the few times this phrase appears, it is perilous to make such an assumption. Furthermore, what does it mean to say that being made in God's image means that we look like God? What does it mean to say that "visible resemblance is only analogical"? Richard himself admits that creation in the image and likeness of God points "not merely to an office or task," yet he also claims that "it does not confer an office or task on humans." So, which is it? And what does it mean to say that being made in God's image is "a relatively open concept"? In sum, while Richard Bauckham's case is interesting, I remain persuaded that Richard Middleton's interpretation is more plausible.

I agree with Richard Bauckham that the usual suspects for answering the question of what constitutes the *imago Dei*—rationality, self-consciousness, moral awareness, capacity for knowing God—are problematic. And I agree that nonhuman creatures exhibit many of the attributes we once thought were unique to humans.[77] A much more scientifically, philosophically, and theologically informed approach is to grant that while there are no differences of kind between humans and animals, there are vast differences in degree such that, to use Richard's words, "human uniqueness results from the aggregation of such differences of degree." This perspective acknowledges our kinship with other creatures while also recognizing our genuine distinctiveness. I, too, like Westermann's notion that we humans are "counterparts" to God,[78] with certain capacities, such as "altruistic care for creatures other than our own species" and

77. See, for example, David Clough, *On Animals*, 2 vols. (London: T&T Clark, 2012).
78. Claus Westermann, *Genesis 1–11: A Commentary* (London: SPCK, 1984).

the ability "to share God's own appreciation of and love for all his creatures," that allow us to serve and protect the earth and its creatures.

I also agree that the primal human transgression is our aspiration for divine status. We want to be "like God" in all the wrong ways. Richard puts it well: sin is "the desire to escape the limits of being creatures among other creatures." So he rightly warns against the tendency to inflate our collective human self-image and role on God's good earth, for example, by speaking of humans as cocreators with God or the priests of creation. All creatures worship God (Pss. 19; 96; 104; 148), each in its own creaturely way, whether we humans are there or not. I wonder, however, whether Richard doesn't downplay too much the role we humans have, given that because of us the whole creation is groaning in travail (Rom. 8). Perhaps more could be said about how we humans "can take up the praise of other creatures into our own, giving it voice in language."

In his conclusion, Richard focuses on Colossians 1:15–20.[79] His insightful reading highlights the cosmic scope of this poem. Reconciliation through Christ is as wide as creation itself. God's salvation includes much more than humans. How do we proclaim, in word and deed, this gospel? How do we bear witness to this all-embracing vision of shalom? How do we live to the glory of God and for the love of the world?

From John F. Haught

With Richard I want to ground our Christian ecological vocation in a thoroughly biblical sense of human dignity. For this reason, I deeply appreciate his unusually lucid and careful exegetical study of the Bible's *imago Dei* theology and its important anthropological and ecological implications. Such scholarship is an essential part of any specifically Christian response to the question of our human role in the conservation and healing of nature.

I would only add, along with Pierre Teilhard de Chardin (1881–1955), that a Christian theological appreciation of human dignity requires our becoming

79. For a legendary interpretation, see Joseph Sittler, "Called to Unity," in *Evocations of Grace: Writings on Ecology, Theology, and Ethics*, ed. Steven Bouma-Prediger and Peter Bakken (Grand Rapids: Eerdmans, 2000), 38–50.

aware of the place and extent of human creativity in the context of an unfinished universe. Human creativity, especially in the application of technology, has generally been more destructive than preservative of nature, and so it is tempting ecologically to scorn it and maybe even seek to suppress it. But developments in geology, evolutionary biology, astronomy, cosmology, and other sciences have now demonstrated that the universe of which we are a part has always been an epic of emergent, ceaseless creativity. What, then, may our own moral self-understanding, sense of dignity, and creative vocation be like in the context of our current awareness that we humans, with our passion for research and development, are part of a world that is still coming into being? It seems to me that Christian theologians and moralists until now have had little sense of our organic linkage to the creative story of life on Earth and, beyond that, of our having been given birth recently by a 13.8 billion-year-old, big bang universe that has never settled indefinitely for the status quo.

I doubt, then, that good exegesis, indispensable though it may be, is enough to shape the kind of moral and religious character—and sense of human dignity—needed now to deal with the fact of life in an unfinished universe. On the other hand, the ancient Abrahamic-anticipatory vision of reality may have something refreshing to offer as we seek inspiration for moral responsibility in the ongoing creation of the universe. Here again I believe a Teilhardian cosmic religious vision, as I draw on it in my own chapter, can contribute to an ecologically appropriate sense of human creativity—and along with it a fresh understanding of human dignity—as we face the challenges of our current ecological predicament.

By anybody's standards, to be more specific, something of considerable importance has been going on during the billions of years that have preceded human evolution. Ecological theology, I have been arguing, must be attentive to this prehistory. The universe has not just slopped around without any axis of consistency in its general movement from past to future. As Teilhard and others have observed, the cosmic story has moved in the direction of *increasing* physical complexity and, along with that, has produced an overall *intensification* of consciousness. Moreover, as Alfred North Whitehead, probably more than any other modern philosopher, has noticed,[80] the cosmic process has

80. Alfred North Whitehead, *Adventures of Ideas* (New York: Free Press, 1967), 252–72, 283–95.

taken on a dramatic mode of becoming simply by virtue of having an overall aim toward the *intensification of beauty*, a quality whose inherent value makes nature worthy not only of preservation but also of enhancement.

As I reflect upon Richard's justifiable concern to understand rightly the meaning of *imago Dei*, I wonder if we may not speculate reasonably, in the light of both scientific cosmology and biblical theology, that awareness of our human dignity now enjoins on us not only the vocation of conservation but also that of the *enhancement* of life, consciousness, and beauty. Obviously, there are risks and dangers in making practical application of such an awareness, but the deeper we look into what has already happened in cosmic history, the more reason we have here and now to turn our attention toward the cosmic future. Perhaps we have a legitimate, though limited and morally disciplined, role to play in bringing that future about.

Christian faith, in its current search for a scientifically congenial religious motivation for ecological responsibility, may interpret the dramatic quality of natural process—and especially its past generosity in giving rise to life, consciousness, and other instances of beauty—as carrying the promise of "fuller being" yet to come. Nature, interpreted in an anticipatory way, is full of promise. It may not have been mechanically designed, but it harbors the finer quality of being a promise.

The cosmic process has been promising from the start. Recent astrophysics, for example, has demonstrated that even the earliest physical conditions and constants, during the first microseconds of cosmic beginnings, already held the promise that nature would eventually become alive and conscious. Scientists wonder why matter was charged so early with such potential—especially since alternative initial physical patterns not so promising are theoretically possible. What scientists do know is that the initial cosmic conditions and constants (for whatever reason) were restricted to the narrow range of numerical values that alone would make ours a life- and mind-bearing universe.

Theologians should probably hesitate to conclude that this improbable arrangement is the result of divine "design," since this term conjures up a host of problems that have led to questionable theological results. But it does not seem rash, either scientifically or religiously, to conclude that our universe—and perhaps a multiverse (if it exists)—has always been seeded with the *promise* of becoming alive and conscious. This quality of promise, it seems to me, calls for a new way of valuing the entirety of nature theologically. It opens up room for an Abrahamic, anticipatory ecological sensitivity.

Coming back to Richard's exegetical interests, then, the imprint on human nature of God's image not only disposes us to look for hints of promise even in the most desperate of situations but also moves us to expect something *surprising* in the promise's fulfillment. True faith does not insist that a promise's fulfillment will fit our own expectations. It disciplines us instead to be ready for results that will surpass our paltry images of future satisfaction. Consequently, a contemporary Christian faith that is informed by scientific cosmology acknowledges that the actual shape of the world's future is presently a mystery hidden in God. Faith and hope may inspire visions of the cosmic future, but these involve much more than planning and predicting. Instead, faith's visions of what is to come must be committed to *waiting* attentively, not passively, in harmony with the universe's own deliberate pace, for surprising things to happen up ahead in the cosmic process, outcomes that correspond not to our desires but to our hopes.

Educated readers, however, might ask here whether an anticipatory way of reading the story of the universe is compatible with the natural sciences. I believe it is. Science itself has now shown that the cosmos is put together in a narratively developmental, and not simply a mathematically ordered, fashion. Rather than being an immobile state of affairs whose intelligibility geometry alone can disclose, as Albert Einstein liked to think, the cosmos is also a dramatic production whose coherence requires on our part the virtue of patience: we simply have to wait for its meaning to emerge. We cannot expect to discover what a play is all about if we walk out of the theater after the first act. So also, we are not in a position to understand what a dramatic universe is all about if we decide to leap out of time and into eternity, or if we decide with the cosmic pessimists that there is no drama at all and that life is destined to collapse altogether in a state of final nothingness.

Contrary to such perspectives, the anticipatory vision is aware that grasping the meaning in any narrative requires patience. So, if nature is narrative to the core, it is not foolish for our species to adopt the biblical posture of patience—and to pass this discipline on to our offspring. In this respect, I would suggest, in line with Richard's concern for a right understanding of our being created in the image of God, that the sense of human dignity requires the cultivation of a "courage to create" that is deeply intertwined with the virtue of patience, one of the main qualities of the infinite beneficence we attribute to Abraham's God.

In any case, Einstein's discovery of the inseparability of matter and time has in principle rendered the notion of "promise" consistent with what science is now telling us about nature. If the universe were eternal, having no origin and no end, it would be difficult for us to interpret it as the carrier of a promise. It is ironic that Einstein—whose field equations mathematically establish that the universe is an unfinished story—personally preferred throughout his life the ideal of an eternal cosmos, one whose intelligibility can be grasped only and exclusively in the language of geometry. As far as he could tell, no promise of a surprising new cosmic future leapt out of his numbers. Other physicists and mathematicians, however, were finally able to convince him (although never with complete success) that the universe is changing dramatically over the course of time and that Einstein's own mathematics had already predicted the narrative quality of nature.

A universe that is static, eternal, and storyless—as Einstein wanted it to be—would not be going anywhere, so it could easily be thought of as devoid of drama, meaning, and promise. In a storyless universe, such as the one most traditional theologians and modern scientific thinkers had taken for granted, human history might seem to have a rather localized kind of meaning, and human persons would have the opportunity to express the dignity of their lives in the practice of virtues, but the cosmos itself would be little more than a stage for these performances. It could not have been understood as the main repository of either meaning or promise.

In spite of Einstein's own preferences, however, the big bang cosmology based on his general theory of relativity has demonstrated that the universe is not eternal, that it is tied inextricably to time, that time moves from past to future irreversibly, and that the universe may even have had a beginning. Consequently, nature now appears to have a dramatic rather than purely geometric constitution. Nature's narrative patterning is such that it may even carry a meaning, an intelligibility or coherence that for now lies mostly out of range. It is not scientifically silly to suppose, then, that nature is a promise for whose fulfillment it is part of our dignity and duty as human beings to wait—attentively but creatively.

Even if, as most cosmologists believe, the universe is heading toward a final death by heat or cold, in the meantime it has a dramatic quality—and hence the capacity to carry a meaning. Christian hope and faith, in that case, have room to trust that this dramatic meaning, invisible to science, is everlastingly saved in the compassionate heart of the God who calls the universe into being, the God who makes and keeps promises, the God who creates out of nothing and who is able therefore to pull the world forward into fuller being from its teetering now on the edge of nonbeing.

In responding to Richard's concern to understand the meaning of *imago Dei*, I have been arguing for a dramatic rather than purely geometrical understanding of the universe. The main scientific reason for doing so is because of the overwhelming acceptance in the scientific community of standard big bang cosmology. Astronomers have now shown that the universe overall is still expanding. After Einstein, astronomers soon began to reason that if we follow the lines of expansion backward into the past, we will arrive at a discrete point, now estimated to lie 13.8 billion years in the past, from which the universe commenced its irreversible journey.

After becoming acquainted with the outlines of Einstein's science, Teilhard never tired of emphasizing the unfinished, narrative quality of nature, and this understanding allowed him to conclude that the universe has a future that should grab our interest and help instill in us a new sense of human dignity. Long before most other scientific thinkers in the twentieth century had become aware that the universe is still coming into being, Teilhard had suggested, in his own way, that nature is seeded not with design but with promise.[81] Nature is not shaped by a prefabricated plan but by a dramatic disposition that allows it to be the carrier of a meaning hidden from science.

As we study new cosmological accounts of nature, we cannot suppress the question that readers of any great story would ask. Toward what ending is the drama moving? What is it all about? Are there hints in past cosmic history of a directionality to the story as it has already unfolded? No doubt there have been vast periods of seemingly unpromising silence, entire epochs in which not much seems to have happened. And there have been aeons of apparently

81. See, for example, Pierre Teilhard de Chardin, *The Heart of Matter*, trans. René Hague (New York: Harcourt Brace, 1978); *Human Energy*, trans. J. M. Cohen (New York: Harcourt Brace Jovanovich, 1962); *The Future of Man*, trans. Norman Denny (New York: Harper & Row, 1964).

pointless experimentation, both before and after the origin of life 3.8 billion years ago. At the same time, however, it is undeniable that in the long run matter has gradually become alive. Then, over the past several million years, due to the complexity of the human brain, the universe has begun to think, look for meaning, aspire to right action—and even to pray.

Hence the new scientific cosmic story, with its picture of billions of years of fermentation prior to the emergence of life, and many more millions of years preparatory to the recent emergence of mind, instructs us that here and now, during the present epoch of cosmic awakening, the universe has yet to ripen. I would argue that the fact of an awakening universe is a necessary condition for the existence and exercise of human freedom and creativity, possibilities whose actualizing is essential to our own sense of special dignity in the scheme of things.[82]

While its invariant regulations seemed until recently to make nature seem completely deterministic, inimical to freedom, and incompatible with hope, determinism is not the only way to make sense of nature's underlying lawfulness. For if we allow that the universe is fundamentally dramatic rather than mechanical, the inviolable rules essential for its continuity and consistency over the course of time seem less like ironclad "laws" than like grammatical constraints. If we acknowledge that "drama" is a more appropriate metaphor for nature than "machine," then we need a correspondingly fresh metaphor to represent the unchanging physical habits that keep the universe from going completely off the rails. I propose that of "grammar" instead of "law."

If nature is dramatic rather than mechanical, then nature's unbending "laws" are comparable to syntactical rules. And so, just as adherence to inviolable grammatical regularities is essential to the telling of a good story, so also if nature is to have an intelligible history, it has to follow unbending rules. But just as adherence to rigorous grammatical rules does not determine the content or meaning of a story, neither do the "laws" of physics tell us what is *really* going on in the universe. To declare, with scientific materialists, that life is "just physics" or that mind is "just chemistry" is like claiming that Melville's *Moby Dick* is just syntax.

82. To be consistent with both the Bible and cosmology, whatever creativity we deploy needs always to be constrained by the virtue of patience. Again, this is because the natural world has a dramatic rather than mechanical constitution.

But scientific thinkers today will persist: Isn't the universe, as it exists presently, simply the product of inevitable, impersonal, and invariant laws? And isn't human dignity "a stupid idea," incompatible with science, as the esteemed materialist linguist Steven Pinker has recently declared.[83] I suggest, in reply, that the notion of "law" is a metaphor too anthropocentrically rooted in juridical experience to let us appreciate the dramatic, promissory quality of natural process. The idea of a law-bound universe usually conjures up the image of a body of objects hopelessly imprisoned by impersonal physical forces. Over the past several centuries, unfortunately, numerous philosophers have cooperated with materialists by incarcerating living and thinking organisms inside the same imaginary lockup that classical physics had constructed for purely physical objects. Abandon hope, all you who enter there. Accordingly, the materialist sequestration of life and mind has allowed several centuries of modern thought to toy with the idea that, since human organisms are part of law-bound nature, human freedom and dignity cannot really exist.

Nature does not deserve such diminishment, nor do human persons. And, as it turns out, the juridical interpretation of nature's habitual routines is misleading. For after Darwin and Einstein, science is gradually revealing the overall narrative quality of the universe, allowing us therefore to interpret and reevaluate the epochs of matter, life, mind—and faith too—as episodes in a cosmic drama about which our philosophical, scientific, and religious ancestors knew almost nothing.

Located within the context of an unfinished *story*, the predictability characteristic of the preliving, physical, and chemical epochs of natural history can be understood as the laying out of a grammatical latticework around which an indeterminate drama of life and mind is now being wound. The grammatical metaphor for nature's strict rules allows us to value the whole of nature in a new way. Yes, the "laws" of physics and chemistry are inviolable and unforgiving, but so too are grammatical rules. Yet, just as grammatical rules do not determine in advance the content or meaning of a story you may be writing, so also the rigor of physical "laws" at work in nature does not determine the meaning of the drama weaving itself into the invariant routines of physics, chemistry,

83. Steven Pinker, "The Stupidity of Dignity," *New Republic*, May 28, 2008, http://www.ub.edu/valors/Estilos%20UB/imatges/Documents/The%20stupidity%20of%20dignity.pdf.

and natural selection. Understood in this way, the picture of nature as the carrier of a promise discernible by faith is, I believe, completely compatible with science. It is also a way of thinking about nature that allows us to embrace, without the slightest contradiction, the world of science on the one hand and a theological understanding of the universe as the matrix of meaning, dignity, creativity, and freedom on the other.

2 ~ Love Incarnate

Hope and Moral-Spiritual Power for Climate Justice

Cynthia Moe-Lobeda

Incarnate love is the breathtaking centerpiece of Christian faith. The incarnation story begins with God's infinite love. Creation unfolds embraced by a Love that can be deterred by no force in heaven or earth. More magnificent than we can imagine, this love of God is both intimately personal—for everyone without exception, embracing our very being—and expanding vastly beyond the person to envelop creation as a whole. Christian traditions hold that this Spirit of love—the creating, liberating, healing, sustaining Source—is at play in the world. It is luring creation toward the reign of God, a world in which justice, compassion, and joy are lived in their fullness by all and in which creation flourishes in the light of God. We human creatures are created and called to recognize this gracious and indomitable love—to receive it, relish it, revel in it, and trust it.

But that is not all. After receiving and trusting God's love, we are to embody it in the world. We are beckoned to be the body of God's justice-making, Earth-relishing Love working through us, in us, and among us to bring healing from all forms of sin that would thwart God's gift of abundant life for all. According to widespread understanding of the Christian story, this is the human vocation, our life's work.

I am haunted by the contradiction between this reason for being—to love as God loves—and the relatively hidden realities of our collective lives. "Our" and "we" herein refer to the world's high-consuming people. Through climate change and the economic practices and policies undergirding it, our ways of life are destroying Earth's God-given capacity to generate life. Moreover, climate change is wreaking death and destruction first and foremost on economically impoverished people, those who are least responsible for the greenhouse gas emissions currently causing climate to change. In this sense we are defying God's primary calls to the human creature—to serve and preserve garden Earth (Gen. 2:15) and to love neighbor.

Where will we find the moral-spiritual agency for a dramatic and rapid reversal, a turn to ways of living that care for the earth and enable all to have the necessities for life in its fullness? This is a crucial question of faith facing climate-privileged sectors and societies at this moment in history. Urgency to pursue it and to engage others in that quest is the motivating passion behind this essay.

"The Word of God wherever it comes, comes to change and renew the world."[1] The speaker here is Martin Luther. Christian traditions hold profound resources for faithful work to change and renew the world. This chapter explores one such resource for faithful moral agency—love incarnate. A few pages can only begin to unearth the infinite hope and agency inherent in the call to embody God's love. May the reader, therefore, carry this quest beyond these pages, moving more deeply into it.

Two crucial clarifications are in order. First, when I speak of the call to love with God's love, I am at times misinterpreted as implying that doing so is for the purpose of winning God's favor for the sake of personal salvation. Nothing could be further from the truth as I understand it. I am convinced that God's love for each of us cannot be won, increased, or diminished by anything that we do or fail to do, or by our way of being; God gives us God's eternal presence and embrace regardless of what we say or do. Said differently, a fundamental faith claim grounding my life and the work in this essay is that God's forgiving grace infinitely outweighs and outlasts all our failings in love, now and forever, without exception. This is my faith conviction. While the reader need not share it, the reader must know that I am not suggesting we are to love *in order to* win God's favor or salvation.

The second clarification will unfold in this essay but bears noting at the outset, lest the reader be misled in the beginning. "Love" as a biblical norm does not mean most of what is normally associated with this word. It does not necessarily imply the feeling of sympathy, kindness, or goodwill that is implied

1. Martin Luther, "The Bondage of the Will," in *Luther's Works*, American ed., 55 vols. (St. Louis: Concordia; Minneapolis: Fortress, 1900–1986), 33:52.

when people say things like "all we need is love" or "we just need to love everyone." The biblical call to love is not primarily a feeling at all. What love, as a gift and call from Jesus and the God he revealed, does imply is explored herein.

The Paradox of the Human

The apostle Paul writes, "I do not understand my own actions. . . . For I do not do the good I want, but the evil I do not want is what I do" (Rom. 7:15, 19). This wrenching, pervasive challenge of being human—hungering for the good yet swayed to betray it—catapults us in our day into unprecedented peril, unimaginable climate catastrophe in which those least responsible for the disaster suffer first and foremost from it.

The paradox of the human species stuns. Capable of beauty, creativity, and goodness beyond imagining, we also engender brutality unspeakable. Now, the species that creates music to heal the soul, risks life to save others, spins pure joy through laughter and compassion, and engenders so much more that is good and beautiful is bent on destroying the delicate conditions necessary for life as we know it to continue on Earth.

The paradox is manifold. First, many of the seemingly good things in our lives, things that build joy, strength, understanding, character, and health, and that improve people's lives depend upon (1) a petroleum orgy in which US citizens guzzle oil with mindless abandon in our plastics, fabrics, industrial agriculture, air and auto travel, transportation of goods around the globe, and militarization, and (2) a global finance-driven economy that displaces, devastates, and destroys people and communities the world over while generating vast material wealth for a minority of the world's people. They include me and most of you, the readers. Yes, activities and products assumed to be good or not harmful—air travel to see distant relatives; packaging for medical instruments, meat, and other food produced by industrial agriculture; plastic materials that enable sanitation and convenience; the minerals that go into our electronics and our infrastructures; family vacations; "good buys" on consumer goods; and on and on—are built on death and destruction due to climate change and the exploitation of people and their lands.[2]

2. To illustrate: many vacation hotels and mineral extraction sites displaced the people who had occupied the land for centuries; inexpensive goods may be inexpensive due

In this way, climate change brings the intertwining of good with evil in human life to unprecedented heights. Both evil's seductive parade as good and the actual intertwining of good and evil become deadly on a scale unseen in human history. That is, truly decent people, good people, live in ways that render good in some senses while spelling death, displacement, or devastation for countless people. Science reports that three-quarters of known fossil fuel reserves must be kept in the ground if we are to avoid more than a 2-degree Celsius rise in average global surface temperature.[3] And even that level of increase will devastate low-lying regions, populated largely by low-consuming and economically impoverished people. Yet carrying on with much of the "good" activity in our lives (e.g., the examples in the previous paragraph) requires extracting significant fossil fuel reserves.

The paradox goes deeper. Many of us who begin to recognize the damaging consequences of life as we live it tend to *carry on with it,* despite our knowledge of the damage done. Chains of "the way things are" seem to bind our imagination and our movement. A magnet sucks us toward a future that mirrors the present. We experience apparent limits imposed by fears, insecurities, ego needs, rituals, habituated patterns. Moreover, very real practicalities of life make radical change truly difficult: many people do not have public

to sweatshop production and other forms of terrible exploitation as well as ecological degradation. See Pamela Brubaker, *Globalization at What Price?* (Cleveland: Pilgrim, 2007), and Cynthia Moe-Lobeda, *Resisting Structural Evil: Love as Ecological-Economic Vocation* (Minneapolis: Fortress, 2013).

3. "The Earth Statement," developed by the Earth League, a network of seventeen leading climate scientists, together with the Global Challenges Foundation. The statement summarizes the synthesis of the global research on climate change. See https://www.the-earth-league.org/075863/index.php.en. The Earth League includes, among others, the economist Nicholas Stern and Hans Joachim Schellnhuber, a climate scientist and adviser to Angela Merkel. Johan Rockström, the statement's lead author, reports that "From a scientific perspective, 2015 is a decisive moment. The window to navigate ourselves free from a 'beyond 2C future' is barely open. It's the last chance to navigate ourselves towards a desired future. . . . It's so frustrating, because it's the choice of moving down a business-as-usual route with devastating outcomes for humanity and, at the same time, we have this almost unprecedented opportunity, we can transform the world economy to a fossil fuel-free one and moreover do it in a way that is security and health-wise more attractive." Quoted in Adam Vaughan, "Earth Day: Scientists Say 75% of Known Fossil Fuel Reserves Must Stay in Ground," *Guardian*, April 22, 2015, https://www.theguardian.com/environment/2015/apr/22/earth-day-scientists-warning-fossil-fuels-.

transportation, bike access, or the money to travel by electric car in their daily efforts to get to work and meet dependents' needs; hours and energies may be consumed by caring for children, parents, and others, leaving little time to organize for necessary shifts in public policy; the agro-food industry makes it nearly impossible for some people and institutions to access locally or regionally produced food. This list of obstacles is daunting, to say the very least. Yet, while finite and fallible in these and other ways, we also are—according to the Christian story—called and claimed by God's love for the world, and sent to embody it. And that includes living in ways that dismantle systemic injustice and build more equitable and ecologically sustainable alternatives. Paradox, then, is the color of the human as moral being, and it reaches new intensity for the human complicit in climate catastrophe.

To grapple with this paradox, hear two eloquent voices. The first is theologian Peter Pero discussing the global economy, and the second is Christopher Rajkumara, executive secretary of the National Council of Churches in India.

> In ecclesiological terms, if the church is the one universal body of Christ, this body of Christ is divided among active thieves, passive profiteers, and deprived victims.[4]

> Climate change and global warming are caused by the colonization of the atmospheric commons. The subaltern communities are denied of their right to atmospheric common and the powerful nations and the powerful within the developing nations continue to extract from the atmospheric common disproportionately. In that process they . . . have emitted and continue to emit greenhouse gases beyond the capacity of the planet to withstand. However, the subaltern communities with almost zero footprint are forced to bear the brunt of the consequences of global warming.[5]

God help us! Hear us in our plea! Lend thine heart to our plight, that we might live! Amidst the horror that we have wrought, enliven our vision, our

4. Albert Pero Jr., "The Church and Racism," in *Between Vision and Reality: Lutheran Churches in Transition*, ed. Wolfgang Greive (Geneva: Lutheran World Federation, 2001), 262.

5. Christopher Rajkumara, executive secretary of the National Council of Churches in India, in conversation.

courage, that we might see and that, even seeing, we might know hope and power, power to arise, arise from complicity and complacency, arise from privatized morality, fly into the subversive moral power of your love that we might not drown in despair at what we have wrought. Grant courage of vision that we might see those unbearable things from which we daily flee, and that—even seeing such horror—we might live as the body of your justice-seeking, Earth-relishing, live-saving love.

I suspect that we have been given what we need. If God is creating, saving, and sustaining this astoundingly magnificent creation; and if we are called to love God and serve God's activity on Earth; and if God does not call us where God does not give us the resources to go, then we have been given or are being given what we need to serve and preserve garden Earth and to build more socially just economies and societies. Said differently, God gives us what we need to orient our lives around God's call to love neighbor as self and to care for garden Earth. This includes forging ways of life that do not purchase overconsumption for a few at the cost of exploiting many and the earth.

The gifts given to the human to heed our vocation are many. They include our intelligence and capacity to reason, our ability to look to the past and future for solving problems of the present, our emotional depth, and our finely tuned bodies. This essay explores another of these gifts: the gift of divine love and its embodiment in humans as neighbor love.

We begin by identifying the question of this essay as it stems from a central question of Christian faith today. We then identify roots of moral inertia that may be uprooted by incarnate love. From there we acknowledge a few methodological challenges inherent in exploring love as a biblical and theological calling. The body of the chapter then unfolds in three sections. The first uncovers eleven world-altering features of love and how they might play out as moral agency for choosing life in the context of climate catastrophe. The second focuses more fully on four of these features. And the third builds on these features of neighbor love to generate guideposts for embodying love in the context of climate violence.

However, what we discover herein about love will make sense and bear weight only in light of the climate catastrophe bursting upon us with powers of death and destruction unparalleled in human history. Therefore, before following the path of question and exploration outlined above, we must look first at the climate crisis—focusing on its theological and moral dimensions—not only because it is the reason for this inquiry into love but also because honestly facing "what is going on" is a vital step in following Jesus and in faithful living.[6]

Climate Catastrophe: Theological and Moral Crisis

Being among the world's people most responsible for the climate disaster presents a number of theological and moral crises. All may be seen as manifestations of structural sin, in this case climate sin. One of these crises—betraying the call to love neighbor—has three layers.[7] First, the people who "suffer most acutely [from climate change] are also those who are least responsible for the crisis to date."[8] To fully acknowledge this is to be tormented by it; others are dying from how we live. Second, "climate-privileged"[9] societies and sectors may respond to climate change with policies and practices that protect us to some degree from the ravages of climate change while deserting others—the most "climate vulnerable"—to death or devastation. And the final layer? Measures to reduce carbon emissions designed by privileged sectors may further endanger climate-vulnerable sectors. A team of Indian scholars points out, for example, that "poor and marginalized communities in the developing countries often suffer more from . . . climate mitigation schemes than from the impacts of actual physical changes in the climate."[10]

The situation screams white privilege, class privilege, and environmental racism. Caused overwhelmingly by descendants of Europe, climate change is wreaking destruction first and foremost on impoverished people who also are

6. Elsewhere, in introducing the tasks of Christian ethics, I explain that a probing inquiry into "what is going on" or "what is the case" precedes asking "what ought be" or what one ought to do in response to "what is going on." See Bruce Birch, Jaqueline Lapsley, Cynthia Moe-Lobeda, and Larry Rasmussen, in *The Bible and Ethics: A New Conversation* (Minneapolis: Fortress, 2018).

7. This and the following two paragraphs draw heavily on Cynthia Moe-Lobeda, "Climate Change as Climate Debt: Forging a Just Future," *Journal of the Society of Christian Ethics* 36, no. 1 (Spring 2016).

8. Maxine Burkett, "Climate Reparations," *Melbourne Journal of International Law* 10 (2009): 2.

9. I use "climate-privileged" to indicate nations and sectors most able to adapt to or prevent the negative impacts of climate change.

10. Soumya Dutta et al., *Climate Change and India* (New Delhi: Daanish Books, 2013), 12.

disproportionately people of color. The island nations and coastal peoples of Bangladesh, China, parts of Africa, and elsewhere forced to flee their flooded lands; subsistence farmers whose crops are undermined by climate change; and impoverished people who cannot compete in the free market economy when food prices are driven up by decreased yields of rice, wheat, and corn due to climate change are not the people largely responsible for greenhouse gas emissions. Nor are they, for the most part, white.

Many voices of the Global South recognize this as climate debt or climate colonialism and situate it as a continuation of the colonialism that enabled the Global North to enrich itself for five centuries at the expense of Africa, Latin America, indigenous North America, and parts of Asia.[11] "Climate violence" seems, to me, an accurate descriptor. It is wed to economic violence.[12]

Within the United States, too, economically marginalized people—who are also disproportionately people of color—will remain most vulnerable to ongoing suffering from the extreme storms, as well as the respiratory illness, food insecurity, and disease, brought on by climate change.[13] This is to suggest not that some people are exempt from climate change impacts but rather that some are vastly more vulnerable than others.[14]

11. See, for example, Angelica Navarro, then climate negotiator for Bolivia, at the Climate Summit in Copenhagen, in "'We Are Not Begging for Aid'—Chief Bolivian Negotiator Says Developed Countries Owe Climate Debt," *Democracy Now!*, December 9, 2009, http://www.democracynow.org/2009/12/9/we_are_not_begging_for_aid, and in Joseph Huff-Hannon, "Bolivia Steps Up: Interview with Climate Negotiator Angelica Navarro on the Eve of Cochabamba Climate Summit," *Huffington Post*, last updated May 25, 2011, http://www.huffingtonpost.com/joseph-huffhannon/bolivia-steps-up-an-inter_b_536312.html. See also "Climate Debt, Climate Credit," accessed December 2, 2019, https://sites.google.com/site/climatedebtclimatecredit/.

12. The economic practices and policies that transfer(red) riches of Africa and Latin America to Europe and North America (and more recently to Asia) result(ed) in exploitation of people and in climate change.

13. *A Climate of Change: African Americans, Global Warming, and a Just Climate Policy for the U.S*, by Nia Robinson and J. Andrew Hoerner (Environmental Justice and Climate Change Initiative, 2008), shows that "global warming amplifies nearly all existing inequalities," "African Americans are dis-proportionately affected by climate change," and some approaches to reducing greenhouse gas emissions have disproportionately adverse impacts on African Americans.

14.As early as 2001, the third annual report of the Intergovernmental Panel on Climate Change (IPCC) maintained that "the impacts of climate change will fall dispro-

The problems of climate sin extend beyond this betrayal of the call to love neighbor.[15] A second aspect of climate sin concerns the ancient faith claim, present in multiple streams of Christian tradition, that God dwells within the earth's creatures and elements. If so, then the earth now being "crucified" by human ignorance, greed, and arrogance is, in some sense, also the body of Christ. Are those of us most responsible for global warming, poisoned rivers, the extinction of tens of thousands of species per year, and ocean acidification crucifying Christ?

Yet another moral and theological problem inherent in climate sin concerns revelation. Christian traditions hold that God reveals Godself in creation. It is the "first book of revelation." If to do and be as God would have us we must receive God's self-revelation, then God's self-revelation is necessary for the life of faith. Yet, humankind is pelting headlong down a trajectory of destroying essential features of God's "first book of revelation." What do we make of endangering the first and enduring "book of revelation"?

Finally, Christians claim that human beings are created "in the image of God." Yet, if global warming continues unchecked, we may be an endangered species. We are endangering the existence of the creatures crafted "in the image of God."

This earth crisis as climate sin and all its theological and moral implications is the context of our inquiry into love. What does the call to love neighbor as self mean for the "powerful nations and the powerful within the developing nations" if they "continue to extract from the atmospheric common disproportionately"? What does it mean (in Pero's words) for the "active thieves" and "passive profiteers" to claim neighbor love for their "deprived victims"?

The Question of this Chapter

How will love, given by God and incarnate on Earth, enable us—the world's high-consuming minority—to choose life abundant in the face of climate disaster?

---

portionately upon developing countries and the poor persons within all countries, and thereby exacerbate inequities in health status and access to adequate food, clean water, and other resources." https://www.ipcc.ch/report/ar3/syr.

15. See Moe-Lobeda, *Resisting Structural Evil*, chap. 3, for a deeper discussion of the following.

All theology is tested now. Can it stand up to the reality in which we are terribly implicated, the crucible in which we live—the reality that life as we know it is killing people through climate change, displacing people, destroying communities, and endangering Earth's life-sustaining capacity?

Two biblical passages conflate to form a central problem for Christian faith in our day: "I call heaven and earth to witness against you today that I have set before you life and death, blessings and curses. Choose life so that you and your descendants may live" (Deut. 30:19), and Jesus's words in John 10:10: "I came that they may have life, and have it abundantly." The central questions are these: *Will* Christian faith enable us to choose life for the earth community, to live toward abundant life for all? And *how* will faith in the God whom Jesus loved enable us to stop endangering the conditions for life on Earth and killing people through climate change? If faith enables me merely to have a sense of ease and comfort, inner peace, retreat from turmoil and uncertainty, then it is not the faith to which Jesus calls us.

In the resurrection, God promised and demonstrated that, by the power of God's love, life triumphs over death and destruction. God's saving love is stronger than all else. Death and devastation are not the last word. In some way that we do not grasp, the last word is life raised up out of death. God "will not allow our complicity in . . . evil to defeat God's being for us and for the good of all creation."[16] We have heard the end of the story. In the midst of suffering and death—be it individual, social, or ecological—the promise given to the earth community is that abundant life in God will reign. So speaks the resurrection.

If this is true, then by the power of God's love at play in life on Earth, life can triumph over the death and destruction that we now engender in climate change and economic exploitation. From this claim arises the question pursued in this essay. *How will incarnate love as known in and given by this God enable the world's high-consuming minority to choose life abundant for all in the face of climate disaster?* Can "love" do this? How might love help to save us from our woundedness, our fear, our malformation by societal forces that condone profit at almost any cost and privilege people with economic status and white people over oth-

16. Christopher Morse, *Not Every Spirit: A Dogmatics of Christian Disbelief* (Valley Forge, PA: Trinity Press International, 1994), 249.

ers? What can we learn from faith forebearers about the power of love given by the God of Jesus—power, that is, for resisting climate injustice and seduction into ways of life that betray God by betraying both neighbor and Earth?

From Moral Inertia to Moral Agency

Choosing life rather than continuing in the trajectory of injustice and ecological devastation is an act of moral agency. "Moral agency" refers to the dual movement of (1) seeking to discern what is good, right, and true, and then (2) acting in that direction. Moral agency is the opposite of moral inertia. In this discussion moral inertia is manifest as complicity with ways of life that contribute to and rationalize injustice and ecological devastation. (By "ways of life" I mean everything from daily practices to public policies, worldviews, and corporate and institutional policies and practices.)

Conversion from a culture of relative moral inertia vis-à-vis the magnitude and urgency of the earth crisis to a culture of moral agency requires carefully figuring out the roots of that moral inertia. The moral inertia of US society in the face of climate change has multiple roots. Elsewhere I have discussed many of them.[17]

This essay addresses three roots of moral inertia that may be uprooted by divine love incarnate on Earth. One is inadequate formation in the arts of discerning God's love at play in the world. Many contemporary Christians of the Global North are not connected to faith communities that focus on discerning what God's love is doing in the world in relationship to social structures. This is a tremendous loss and obstacle *if* we claim that our vocation in life is to align our lives with that love's activity.

A second root of moral inertia is a highly privatized sensibility of what is neighbor love—as in Jesus's call to "love neighbor as self." The challenge of systemic injustice calls forth a political-economic-ecological understanding of

17. See Moe-Lobeda, *Resisting Structural Evil*, chap. 4; Cynthia Moe-Lobeda, *Healing a Broken World: Globalization and God* (Minneapolis: Fortress, 2002), chaps. 2 and 3; Cynthia Moe-Lobeda, "Climate Debt, White Privilege and Christian Ethics as Political Theology," in *Common Good(s): Economy, Ecology, Political Theology*, ed. Catherine Keller, Melanie Johnson-DeBaufre, and Elias Ortega-Aponte (New York: Fordham University Press, 2016).

love as a biblical norm. Love is not only a calling and norm for interpersonal relationships, as it often is conceptualized; love also is a calling and norm for the systemic dimensions of our lives. That is, it pertains to us as corporate or collective actors, not only as individual actors. We will, in this essay, explore neighbor love as an ecological-economic-political vocation.

Third is the problematic set of assumptions regarding who we are as moral beings. The socially constructed moral self of modernity/postmodernity is not adequate to the task of resisting collective or structural evil. Steeped in the elevation of the individual over the collective, the individual moral self of modernity is socialized to perceive moral culpability and agency in an individualized sense. Thus acquiescence to *collective* moral wrong goes unacknowledged, and thereby it becomes normalized and acceptable. Moreover, the self of postmodernity and therefore of advanced global capitalism is socialized to perceive self as powerless in the face of global corporate power. Hence, we are morally formed to acquiesce to its mandates and the moral wrong that it does. The mandates of global corporate power take on a mask of *inevitability*. Love, if it is to save us, will need to help reconstruct us from this individualized moral identity to an awareness of collective moral culpability and agency, and from selves prone to accept systemic evil to selves that resist and rebuild as a part of loving God and neighbor.

Early church communities offer clues to overcoming this third problem, the need to reconstruct moral identity. Margaret Miles argues that early Christian communities were able to create a self alternative to and critical of the socialized self of the broader society. While she explores the role and practice of worship in enabling the construction of "a consciously chosen alternative [self] to the socialized self" and the "practices by which it is formed and strengthened," we will explore the role of love in that reconstruction of moral identity.[18]

Methodological Integrity

Exploring with integrity the gift and calling to love is fraught with complexity and problems.[19] First is the inadequacy of the term "love" to depict the depth,

18. Margaret R. Miles, *Practicing Christianity: Critical Perspectives for an Embodied Spirituality* (New York: Crossroad, 1988), 111.

19. See Moe-Lobeda, *Resisting Structural Evil*, chap. 7.

breadth, and varied meanings of the biblical terms that it is used to translate. To the extent possible, we will separate love as a biblical and theological reality from the word "love" in English. The term "love" is far too domesticated, and it bears endless connotations and denotations that distract from the power and mystery of divine love and the call to "love neighbor as self." The love I have for butterscotch, or the love I had in a madly attractive summer romance, is different from the love to which God calls the people in Leviticus or the love known in Jesus's words and deeds. Even love for neighbor in religious discourse summons images of kindness, warm feelings, and inoffensiveness that may have little to do with love as a biblical and theological reality in the image of God's love. We hear "love" and bring to it assumptions of meaning that may dilute or even betray whatever is meant by the love that the God of Jesus bears for creation and calls us to embody.

To avoid as much as possible this reduction and domestication of love, we will occasionally add "*ahav*" or "*agapē*" to the word "love" as a reminder that we are not using "love" to signify the meanings commonly attached to it in English. *Ahav* is the word in the Hebrew Scriptures most frequently translated as "love" in English; it is used to designate love for neighbor (Lev. 19:18) and for God (Deut. 6:5), and God's love for God's people (Deut. 5:10; Hos. 3:1). *Agapē is* the Greek word used in Jesus's injunctions to love neighbor as self as recorded in the Synoptic Gospels.[20]

A second problem in exploring love as a biblical and theological norm is the magnitude of the corpus of writings regarding the meaning and moral implications of love (*ahav/agapē*) in Christian and Jewish traditions. That body of writings—in Christian traditions alone—is vast. The Bible, early Greek and Latin church "fathers," the medieval mystics, the reformers, later theologians

20. "Love" also is used occasionally in English translations of the Hebrew Bible to translate the Hebrew Bible's *hesed*—"steadfast love." *Hesed* bears similar but not the same connotations as *ahav.* Three different words of New Testament Greek are translated into English as "love": *agapē, erōs,* and *philia*. Most frequently used is *agapē,* to translate *ahav* and *hesed* in the Septuagint. See Gerhard Kittel, ed., *Theological Dictionary of the New Testament,* vol. 1 (Grand Rapids: Eerdmans, 1964), 39, and Bernard V. Brady, *Christian Love* (Washington, DC: Georgetown University Press, 2003), 53. While *agapē* is indeed the Greek word used in Jesus's injunctions to "love neighbor as self," Jesus, as far as we know, may not have used the word because he spoke primarily Aramaic and not Greek. "Love," then, is a translation of a translation.

and people of faith all illumine the vast beauty, challenge, and danger in the gift and calling of love. Which sources then ought we to choose, and by what criteria ought we to decide? For this brief essay, I have drawn upon those who seem most rich with potential to provide insight into our question: "How will love, given by God and incarnate on Earth, enable us to choose life abundant in the face of climate disaster?"

Third, we acknowledge that the nature of neighbor love grounded in divine love is beyond full comprehension. As "God is love," and as God is both intimately knowable and infinitely beyond our knowing, so too is love. This inquiry will only glimpse the depth and breadth of the love given by God.

Next, to claim, as I will, that receiving the love of God and embodying it in the world is the heart of Christian faith is not to claim the perfectibility of human love. Nor is it to deny the ubiquitous nature of sin, both individual and corporate. I cannot emphasize this enough. If I know anything, it is that human love is fallible and finite. I am fully aware, for example, that my love is always limited by my own brokenness manifest in habit, addictive tendencies, physical wants, fears, anxieties, laziness, ego needs, and more. Love's limitations glare even more in the face of structural sin. We are "in bondage" to—and many of us benefit from—systemic injustice every moment of our lives. As a white woman, for example, I am the historic "beneficiary" of a five-hundred-year legacy of white supremacy on this land. Much as I seek to be a traitor to white racism, I still participate in it through the systems that privilege whiteness over blackness or brownness and that penalize the latter two (the purpose of this acknowledgment is decidedly not to shame me as a white person but rather to invite me more fully into the faithful struggle for racial equity). In the words of Joseph Sittler, "Evil is a thing we always fight but never destroy."[21] Nevertheless, I am equally convinced that by God's grace, love—as an interpersonal vocation and a political-economic-ecological vocation—still can and does grow and work within us. And, at play imperfectly in our lives, love seeks a world in which systemic injustice is no more.

21. Joseph Sittler, "Nature and Grace in Romans 8," in *Evocations of Grace: Writings on Ecology, Theology, and Ethics*, ed. Steven Bouma-Prediger and Peter Bakken (Grand Rapids: Eerdmans, 2000), 214.

Love (*Agapē/Ahav*): Wellspring of Moral Power

Love—as given by God—makes claims that shake the foundations of life as we know it.[22] We note eleven key claims about love as a biblical and theological reality, and then return to focus more fully on four of them. The hope is that love (*agapē/ahav*), understood in this sense, bears power for uprooting the roots of moral inertia noted above. (They were: lack of preparation for discerning the Spirit at work in the world, a privatized sense of neighbor love, and an individualized sense of who we are as moral beings, powerless in the face of structural sin.)

First is the breathtaking claim that God—the creating, liberating, healing, sustaining Source—loves this world and each of us with a love that will neither cease nor diminish, a love more powerful than any other force in heaven or earth. That is the beginning point. Here I am tutored by the Lutheran tradition in which I stand both critically and appreciatively, and by its emphasis on a magnificent gift to the world from God. It is that each person personally, humankind as a whole, and the entirety of creation are beloved with a love that cannot be escaped, a love that will not cease or lessen regardless of whatever we do or fail to do. In short, we are beloved by an unconditional and infinite love. This will be a piece in the puzzle of reconstructed moral identity.

And the second claim? This God is at play in the world, breathing life into it, saving. In building ways of life to replace ways of climate sin, we do not depend on human power alone. We are carried collectively in the stream of God's life-transforming power actively engaged in the world. Again, the privatized moral self is replaced.

Next, the biblical call to love God is a call to place ultimate trust in God. We human creatures are created and called to recognize God's gracious and unstoppable love, receive it, relish it, revel in it, and—most important of all—to trust it. God's love is infinitely trustworthy and will bring abundant life for all. This is a third life-giving claim. I speak very personally here. I am tempted toward despair when I acknowledge the insidious nature of climate injustice and its consequences. A subtle voice within me whispers that things

22. This section and the following draw heavily on Moe-Lobeda, *Resisting Structural Evil*, chap. 7.

will continue as they are despite our best efforts. However, the story of God's love manifest in cross and resurrection defies that voice and promises otherwise. That story became very real to me as a young person who had fallen into despair regarding the pernicious presence of structural injustice woven into our lives. I realized that I needed to talk with someone who was deeply aware of structural injustice and the massive suffering it causes, and yet who maintained hope, active efforts at social transformation, and a sense of joy in living. I thought of one person, a Lutheran pastor who was a leader in religious resistance to the Trident nuclear submarines that were stationed in Puget Sound. (I was living in Seattle at this time.) He—along with his eighty-five-year-old mother!—had been in one of the small boats that was trying to block passage of the submarines across the sound. When I poured out to him my pain and despair, and asked him how he maintained his hope and laughter, his response was life-changing for me. He said, "You know, Cindy, I know the end of the story." Instantly I knew what he meant: God's life-saving, justice-seeking love is stronger than all else. In some way that we do not grasp, the last word is life raised up out of death. God "will not allow our complicity in . . . evil to defeat God's being for us and for the good of all creation."[23] We have heard the end of the story. In the midst of suffering and death—be it individual, social, or ecological—the promise given to the earth community is that abundant life in God will reign. So speaks the resurrection. A startling element of hope gushes forth from this third claim. It—together with the first feature of love noted above—is the source of my life's hope.

The astonishing reality of divine love swirls yet deeper, to a fourth claim. Having received God's love, we are then to embody it in the world by loving neighbor as self and by loving as God loves (Matt. 22:39; Eph. 5:1).[24] We are summoned to join with God's Spirit of justice-seeking Love in its steadfast commitment to gain fullness of life for all. We are called to "love as God loves," and to do this with the love of God given to abide in and among us. Christian faith offers to the world the wild notion that the God who creates and saves all that is becomes incarnate—takes on fleshly form; this God is embodied in matter, in earthy material stuff, and in a particular way in the human mammal. God as human has been understood variously by Christian communities

23. Morse, *Not Every Spirit*, 249.
24. See also Mark 12:38–44 and Luke 10:25–28.

throughout the last two millennia. This essay works with the understanding that God took on human form as Jesus of Nazareth and continues since Jesus's time to abide in human creatures through the power of the Holy Spirit. Another piece of a reconstructed moral identity appears—humans are the body of God's love. Shortly we will explore the related claim that God is incarnate also in other creatures and elements.

Fifth, love as a biblical norm is not primarily a good feeling for the person loved. While love may entail kindness, affection, attraction, protectiveness, delight, and other good feelings, these are not essential ingredients of love as a biblical and theological norm. Love your neighbor, in either Testament, does mean serving your neighbor's well-being and is active, but it does not necessarily entail good feelings. This will be important shortly in our discussion of love as a political-economic-ecological vocation.

Sixth, Jesus's love takes many distinct forms; it responds differently to different people and situations. Neighbor love, modeled on Jesus's love, thus is manifest in varied ways. "Love . . . changes form and brings new forms into being. . . . The forms of love's expression cannot be identified with only one pattern or motif."[25]

Next, according to the biblical witness, God's love seeks to transform injustice into ways of living and organizing social life that nourish dignity, freedom from oppression and from oppressing, and right relationships. Love is justice-seeking. The images of kindness, inoffensiveness, and meekness often invoked by "love thy neighbor" misrepresent love as a biblical and theological reality in the heritage of the Hebrew prophets. "Justice," writes Daniel Maguire, "is the love language of the Bible."[26]

Eighth is the assertion—present in Christian theology since its beginning—that God abides not only in the human creature but within all creation. Fascinating to me and relevant here are the implications for moral power. If "the Word of God wherever it comes, comes to change and renew the world," and if God is present within winds and waters, trees and creatures, then God is at play within our earthy kin to change and renew the world. We are called

25. Daniel Day Williams, *The Spirit and the Forms of Love* (New York: Harper & Row, 1968), 4–5, 9.

26. Daniel Maguire, *The Moral Core of Judaism and Christianity: Reclaiming the Revolution* (Minneapolis: Fortress, 1993), 211.

to hear the healing, liberating, and transforming Word of God in the creatures and elements of this earth. How will we prepare ourselves to learn from a cosmos animated by the Spirit of the living God? How will we—who may never have sought God's saving presence in the trees and waters—cultivate that capacity? For now let us say this: If God indwells the earth, then our hope and power for the work of radical love may be fed by God incarnate in the created world.

The next three features we note here briefly and then return to them more fully in the following section.

- "Love your neighbor" is not in the first place a commandment; it is a statement of what will be.
- Neighbor love is both interpersonal and social-structural; it is an economic-political-ecological vocation.
- The embodiment of Christlike neighbor love is not only an individual matter but also communal—perhaps primarily communal.

These eleven world-shifting claims about divine love are central to Christian traditions.[27]

Four Features of Love (*Agapē/Ahav*)—a Deeper Look

A single essay cannot begin to uncover the implications that all eleven of the above claims bear for moral agency. So we focus on four—the first one noted in the previous section and the last three.

Beloved with a Love That Will Neither Cease Nor Diminish

"For God so loved the world . . ." You and I, all who have ever lived or will live, and all of creation are beloved with a love that will not cease or diminish regardless of what we may do or fail to do. We are beloved. This promise is at the heart of Christian faith.

Common wisdom holds that human beings grow in our capacity to love by being loved. Perhaps the most important gift of the parent to the young child

27. None of them is held by all Christians. This is the case with all Christian faith claims.

is the gift of knowing self to be loved, to be of infinite worth, a worth that does not need to be proven or won.

Yet, the ubiquitous message to the socially constructed self in contemporary US society is "I am fully worthy and I am beloved *only* if I get good grades, if I am a terrific athlete, if I am hot, if I am popular, if I get into a good university, if I have a good job, if I earn a lot and have expensive stuff, if others respect me, if, if, if." The advertising industry, the wind in the fire of overconsumption, utterly depends on this pervasive inner refrain: "I am fully worthy of others' love, esteem, respect, attention *if*. . ."

How much of our overconsumption, need to maximize profit, and compulsion to get good deals on the market (and therefore, how much of our greenhouse gas emissions) is a product of believing that we are fully worthy of love and respect *if* we accumulate, consume, own, or control ever more socially applauded "stuff" that makes us "look good" in the eyes of those whose respect and applause we seek? What radical reversal of overconsumption and therefore of greenhouse gas emissions would be possible for people who knew in their very bones that "I am splendidly, lavishly, wildly beloved as I am, and this state of belovedness is absolutely independent of what I own, acquire, accumulate, control, or achieve"?

Here we step back some seven to nine centuries to learn from the Beguines, a heterogeneous movement of northern European women religious that rose, flourished, and then was suppressed from the late twelfth through the mid-fourteenth century. The movement is relevant for the startling degree of moral agency that it manifested for transgressing cultural norms, including economic norms and allegiance to dominant power structures. Medieval convention bound religious life to specific rules and church-recognized orders that remained detached from secular life. Beguine communities, in contrast, lived dedicated religious lives while remaining engaged in worldly life and relatively unaccountable to male authority figures. Moreover, while the religious power structure of the day claimed to be the sole locus of God's authority on Earth, in stark contrast many Beguines professed to be authorized by God, trusted the truth of their own experience, and engaged in public theological discourse unauthorized by religious officials.

They were, therefore, seen as challenging the exclusive authority of the church hierarchy in its roles as singular medium of redemption, exclusive source of theological truth, and regulator of discourse. The strength of Beguine moral-spiritual power cast fear into the heart of hegemonic power. While some Beguines were burned at the stake, others were forbidden to spread their teachings, speak publicly, travel, or join the movement before the age of forty. The words of Beguines' persecutors reveal the power of these women's agency in spite of efforts to repress it. The "way of life" of the Beguines, wrote the General Council of Vienne in 1312, "is to be permanently forbidden and altogether excluded from the Church of God. Because they . . . promise no obedience to anyone and do not profess an approved Rule."[28]

These women did not perceive themselves as "moral agents" or as leaders undermining hegemonic power structures of their day (such assertions would be anachronistic). Yet, many of them were both.[29] Wherein lay their moral-spiritual power to exercise such agency despite the threat of death, even death by fire?

That moral agency had many roots. It derived in part from the lens through which they perceived themselves. The Beguines, at least as we know them through their surviving literary works, saw themselves as they believed that God saw them—as beloved by God. The extraordinary extent to which these women were moral agents and subjects of their lives seems to lie in a perception of self and each other derived directly from knowing themselves as *in* God, *beloved* by God, and *lovers* of God. Hadewijch of Brabant, a thirteenth-century Beguine poet and mystic, declares: "I entreat you . . . open the eyes of your heart (cf. Eph 1:18) to see clearly and contemplate yourself in God."[30] Whereas the dominant culture proclaimed these women to be "unworthy," they understood themselves to be of infinite worth.[31] This way of knowing self

28. See the reinstated declarations of Boniface VIII, in *Council of Vienne 1311–1312 AD*, section 16, online at https://www.papalencyclicals.net/councils/ecum15.htm.

29. The Beguines, as most movements undermining systems of domination, are riddled with paradox in their relationship to those systems, in some senses undermining but in others underwriting them. Excellent secondary sources include Emilie Zum Brunn and Georgette Epiney-Burgard, *Women Mystics in Medieval Europe* (Chicago: University of Chicago Press, 1989); John Milhaven, *Hadewijch and Her Sisters* (New York: SUNY Press, 1993); and various works by Carolyn Walker Bynum. Two primary sources for Beguine writings are *Hadewijch: The Complete Works*, trans. Mother Columba Hart (Mahwah, NJ: Paulist, 1980), and Margurerite Porete, *The Mirror of Simple Souls*, trans. Ellen L. Babinsky (Mahwah, NJ: Paulist, 1993).

30. *Hadewijch: The Complete Works*, "Letters," 1.

31. For example, in late twelfth-century Liege, the priest Lambert was accused of delivering Scripture "to the unworthy" when he translated it into the vernacular for small

issued in a way of doing and being—that is, a form of moral life—characterized by nearly irrepressible agency, especially for doing what they understood to be loving as God loved. They understood themselves to be "subject to no one save Love alone doing service and performing the works of Love . . . day and night in all liberty, without delay of fear and without counting the cost."[32]

We note an incredible wealth of what moderns call moral subjectivity and agency—awareness of self, strength of self-expression, and power to act with a purpose based on conviction. It was grounded in seeing God as Love itself and seeing self as primarily God's beloved, in whose veins Godself coursed and was poured out to others. This vision found self to be good and able to act because of who they understood themselves to be in the eyes of God: "And then you will be Love, as I am love . . . go forth and live what I am," declared God's voice to Hadewijch.[33]

To see oneself through the eyes of God, to see what God sees, is to see a human creature loved beyond all comprehension. Our socially constructed identities and our "need" to maintain them may give way to a primary and primal identity, the beloved. Seeing self through the eyes of God—seeing self as beloved before all else—may engender the compassion and deep love for self that flow into justice-seeking love for others. Moreover, to see others through the eyes of God is to see them first and foremost as precious beloved creatures of God. The construction of other people into others whom we must impress, or be better than, or for whom we must "measure up" may give way to the construction of others as neighbors who are, before all else, beloved.

Walter Wink notes that "The obstacle between us and God is not what is imperfect in us . . . but our belief that we are unworthy of being loved . . . people of little value, power, or gifts."[34] The moral power inherent in perceiving self as beloved called to embody love is beyond full human knowing. It may draw one away from serving the needs of self alone where so doing damages others, and may evoke deep compassion for the pain and needs of others. And, if the witness of the Beguines holds true, then believing self to be primarily God's beloved engenders moral-spiritual power to serve God and to love self and

---

pious communities of women. Herbert Grundmann, *Religious Movements in the Middle Ages* (Notre Dame: University of Notre Dame Press, 1995), 193.

32. *Hadewijch: The Complete Works*, "Letters," 18.

33. *Hadewijch: The Complete Works*, "Verses," 3.

34. Walter Wink, *Engaging the Powers* (Minneapolis: Augsburg Fortress, 1992), 319.

others regardless of the risks entailed. In the context of climate colonialism, seeing self as beloved may evoke power to love through crafting ways of living that build climate justice.

"Love Your Neighbor"—a Statement of What Will Be

A *commandment* to love is not adequate to bring about radical change in human beings, at least in many cases. Too easily we know the good we ought to do (are "commanded" to do) but do it not. "For I do not do what I want, but I do the very thing I hate" (Rom. 7:15, 19). Love, as the antidote to sin, must be something *more than commandment.*

For this reason, I was engulfed by hope upon learning that Jesus's "You shall love your neighbor as yourself" is not primarily a commandment regarding what people *should* do. Jesus is declaring what we *will* do. The verb, *agapaō* (shall love), is in the future indicative. This is the case in all three Synoptic Gospels (Matt. 22:37–39; Mark 12:31; Luke 10:25–28). Likewise, in the Pauline epistles, "you shall love" is expressing, in the words of New Testament scholar Matthew Whitlock, "assurance in the fulfillment" of this declaration.[35] This is true also of the Leviticus text. Essentially, we are promised that this justice-making love will be and is becoming. It is in the future tense with 100 percent claim on the present; it is a promise fulfilled, yet still to be unfolded. This assurance is profoundly hope giving, particularly as heard by contemporary people caught up in webs of climate injustice from which it is hard to imagine escape. In seeking to align our lives with the call to love neighbor as self and as God loves, we are not merely heeding a commandment and invitation; we are claiming a promise made by God.

Neighbor Love Is Structural: An Economic-Political-Ecological Vocation

An egregious moral atrocity for contemporary Christians in positions of privilege relative to race, class, gender, and climate is our astounding willingness to ignore the impact we have on neighbors through social systems. That dangerous moral oblivion leads to a second moral atrocity—the tendency to address

35. Matthew Whitlock, in conversation. Whitlock goes on to explain that Paul, in Gal. 5:14, sees Lev. 19:18 as a promise fulfilled in Christ and in the church.

structural injustice with privatized solutions. Doing so perpetuates structural injustice and may breed a sense of moral righteousness.

Recall the haunting words with which we began.

> In ecclesiological terms, if the church is the one universal body of Christ, this body of Christ is divided among active thieves, passive profiteers, and deprived victims.[36]

> Climate change and global warming are caused by the colonization of the atmospheric commons. . . . The powerful nations and the powerful within the developing nations continue to . . . emit greenhouse gases beyond the capacity of the planet to withstand. However, the subaltern communities with almost zero footprint are forced to bear the brunt of the consequences.[37]

Soul-shaking questions cry out. What does the call to love neighbor as self mean for the "powerful nations and the powerful within the developing nations [who] continue to extract from the atmospheric common disproportionately"? What does the call to "love your neighbor as yourself" mean for the "active thieves" and "passive profiteers"? Systems (ways of organizing society) that we did not actively choose shape our relations with neighbors and with Earth. These relations include deadly ecological and economic violence that we tend not to see if we are not immediately victimized by them. For people benefiting from those systems, how does love call us to respond?

God's justice-making love is both intimately personal and "structural." It pertains not only to interpersonal relationships but also to the social structures that shape our relations with neighbors both near us and around the globe. That is, neighbor love (as our embodiment of God's love) is both an interpersonal vocation and a political-economic-ecological vocation.

Why? The call to love neighbor is a call to serve the neighbor's well-being. And as a biblical norm, a neighbor is whomever my life touches. Through systems that enable our material wealth, the world's high consumers (including me and many of my readers) have tremendous impact on others far and near. Jesuit priest Jon Sobrino, speaking to a delegation of US elected officials whom I was

36. Pero, "The Church and Racism," 262.
37. Christopher Rajkumara, in conversation.

coleading on a trip to El Salvador, articulated this reality with stunning impact. "In El Salvador," he declared, "poverty means death. And our people are not poor due to their own fault or bad luck. They are poor because the economic systems that create your wealth make them poor." My life touches people the world over through systemic links—especially economic, political, and ecological links. In fact, the moral impact of our actions as individuals pales next to the moral impact of our collective lives through the social systems in which we are players.

What happens when Christian neighbor love encounters suffering that is caused by the sin of unjust social structures in which we participate and from which we benefit, albeit often unknowingly? The response of Christian love in the context of slavery was not simply to bind up the wounds of the beaten slaves. It was to expose, resist, and dismantle the structural sin, the social system of slavery, even though it provided economic "benefits" to slave owners, industrialists, and consumers who could purchase relatively cheap cotton and sugar due to slave labor. Likewise, in the face of contemporary institutional racism, the call of neighbor love is not only to develop strong interpersonal relationships across racial lines, but it is also to dismantle the structural sin of racism. If "theft" is done through political-economic systems, then love, as response, also works through political-economic systems. If climate change is wrought through political-economic systems, then so too must response include change in those systems. In short, if we do tremendous harm through the systems that generate our material wealth, then neighbor love calls us to seek to change those systems for the good.

Yet, in stark contrast, we are socialized to ignore and thereby not to address these broad structural sins. I easily see the impact that I have on people with whom I interact personally—my students, family members, and friends, strangers on the street or on the Web. Yet I do not readily see the impact that I have on neighbors whose lives I touch by participation in systems that hurt them while benefiting me. These neighbors include, of course, the people displaced or killed by climate change as well as countless others—sweatshop workers who make my clothing, those who labor in fields exposed to toxic chemicals, those whose communities are destroyed by hotel chains coming into their coastal villages, those whose lands or water supplies are destroyed by extractive industries and who may be killed in efforts to resist those industries on their lands, homeless people who work full time but are not paid enough to maintain a roof over their heads, Walmart employees who earn a pittance while Walmart keeps its prices low for people like me. And on and on.

Feelings of caring for the neighbor are relatively meaningless if we are stamping on the neighbor's back or helping to destroy her children's water supply and making a profit from her terrible loss. I write this in a coffee shop. It sells bottled water, encouraging customers to buy the bottled water because a few cents from each sale go to a water project in Africa. Yet, unacknowledged are the children of India, Latin America, and elsewhere whose water supply was destroyed by the bottled water company that uses many gallons of the local community's precious water to fill the plastic bottles of water sold in the United States. Unacknowledged are the mountains of "recycled" water bottles from the Global North accumulating in huge piles in countries of the Global South. Mutual funds invested in the bottled water company are gaining from the devastation of those children's water supply.

The customer in front of me in line today happily added a bottle of water to his coffee order, glad to be supporting the water project in Africa. Privatized response to systemic injustice can be deadly. So too is moral oblivion. Love calls for a moral commitment to see—what I call moral vision—and for systemic response to systemic injustice.

The claim that neighbor love pertains to our structural relationships radiates complexity and impossibility. These may lure us to ignore love as a structural calling and retreat into privatized morality. Instead, let us delve into the complexity, seeking pathways through the fog, and let us delve into the apparent impossibility, looking for the possible.

Complexity

Complex is the contradiction between the *public or collective* moral impact of our lives, on the one hand, and pervasive perceptions of the moral life as a *private* matter, on the other. Our privatized sense of morality stems in part from modernity's "turn to the individual" as the primary unit of existence. The modern individualized moral consciousness allows us to assume that because I am not *individually* culpable in another's suffering, I am innocent. A structural sense of morality, in contrast, recognizes that what I do as part of a larger body of people has enormous moral consequences for which I am, to some extent, accountable. What we eat, how we heat our homes, what we purchase, what legislation we actively or passively support, who we elect to office—all have moral impact even if my individual piece, in isolation, does not. Never has this been clearer to me than when I was listening to a Mexican strawberry picker speaking to a delegation of elected officials from the United States that I was leading on a travel seminar. "Our children go hungry," she declared, "because this land which should grow beans and corn for them, grows strawberries for your tables." Love as a structural vocation (a political-economic-ecological vocation), then, calls not only for awareness of the structural connections between me and others the world over, but also for awareness of the moral weight of those links.

To illustrate, the culture of the automobile—generated over decades through many forms of corporate persuasion, including legislative lobbies, campaign financing, and intense marketing—is a central feature of public life in the United States. The ecological consequences of the automobile obsession are infinitely *public* and costly because of its immense contribution to climate change. Yet we hold the absurd assumption that driving a large vehicle that produces enormous quantities of greenhouse gases is a matter of *individual* freedom, and that the move not to do so must depend upon individual conscience rather than on public policy aimed at limiting global warming. Laws regulate the amount of toxins that can be dumped into a river but not necessarily the amount of greenhouse gases that can be dumped into the atmosphere.

A reconstructed sense of the moral self (moral identity) would confront the contradiction between the impact of our collective actions and decisions and our privatized sense of moral response. This is crucial if we are to see more clearly the roots and consequences of ecological and economic violence. While the social structural dimension of neighbor love is indeed complex, that complexity is not insurmountable and is eased by naming and facing illustrations such as these.

Apparent Impossibility

What of the impossibility of love as a structural gift and calling? For many reasons, love as a political-economic-ecological (structural) calling seems impossible.

- It would be impossible to know about all the impacts that we have through social systems—the impacts of tax policy, trade treaties, collective consumer practices, energy policy, military decisions, laws governing corporate practice, legal systems, decisions about public funding, legislation regarding the criminal (in)justice system, and more—on local, national, and global levels.

- We cannot address all those impacts.
- Moreover, structural relations are often rife with contradiction and ambiguity. What might bring justice to one group of people might devastate another. How is one to know amidst the complexity and ambiguity of public matters what will best serve the well-being of the vulnerable?
- Even regarding matters that we do seek to impact, often our efforts seem futile. We may struggle for more just legislation regarding trade policy, energy policy, health care, incarceration, and funding to meet public needs, only to find our efforts thwarted.
- The current form of global capitalism (finance and corporate driven, fossil fuel dependent, consumption maximizing, profit maximizing) developed over decades; changing it also will take decades. Yet Earth does not have decades left before climate change caused by this system renders unimaginable disaster.

Yes, impossible it would be to love completely and perfectly. However, a great truth of Christian faith is that we are *not* called to love completely and perfectly this side of death. Nor are we promised that our efforts in love toward the good will be successful. Rather, we are called to accept, trust, and live out the love that is incarnate in us though interpersonal relations and as parts of social structures. That is, we are to allow our lives to be aligned with the justice-seeking, Earth-honoring, life-giving love of God. We are called to ways of life that best approximate this love, despite the impossibility of doing so fully or perfectly.

In essence, where the wrong that we do is done collectively—for example, climate change—and where individual repentance or change is not adequate to undo or repair it, then we are called to reunderstand love as lived out in action that shapes our collective life, even though that action will be imperfect and inadequate! This understanding is crucial.

The social structural dimension of neighbor love does not lessen the truth that love is also an interpersonal vocation. Love, as a biblical and theological reality, is not reducible to either the individual or the structural. It is both. "God's will is the transformation of people and society."[38]

38. Wink, *Engaging the Powers*, 85.

Love as Mystical Communion

We have said that collective or structural sin calls for the collective or structural response of neighbor love. However, both the biblical texts and biology compel us further in this direction. They suggest that embodying the love of God as revealed in Jesus Christ and given in the Spirit may be inherently a communal matter. This communal embodiment on Earth—or rather, our fallible movement into this communal embodiment—may be a foretaste of the destiny into which God, working through the things of Earth (including human creatures), is saving creation.

"The *basileia* of God is among you," we learn from Jesus. He does not say, "The *basileia* of God is in you" (singular). When Jesus addresses the disciples soon before his arrest, for example, even when responding to individual disciples' queries, he responds in the plural. "You know the way to the place where I am going" (John 14:4) contains a plural "you." "Let not your hearts be troubled" (John 14:1 RSV) refers to the community's heart; the "your" is plural. "In my Father's house there are many dwelling places" (14:2). I go "to prepare a place for you" there. Wes Howard-Brook notes that "my father's house" in John is not a building. It is rather "a relationship among those who hear God and do God's will"—the community. Likewise, when the Spirit comes at Pentecost, she comes to a body of people.

Jesus and the Spirit are calling into being an unshakable reality that the disciples do not yet perceive; they do not realize that it exists. Nor do we, except in glimpses. It is a communal reality—in the words of the ancients, a union and communion.[39]

The call to love in the context of climate sin/climate violence may be a call to embody love as communities. These would be communities of resistance and rebuilding. In the Norwegian film *As It Is in Heaven,* a musician who creates life-transforming music remarks that in creating music that brings life to deadened hearts he is calling down the music that already exists. Likewise, communities of faith living into climate justice are perhaps "calling down" the communion (the music) that already exists but that we only glimpse dimly.

39. As we learn elsewhere in the biblical witness, especially in the First Testament, that communion extends—in ways that we do not fully grasp—to all people and indeed to all of creation.

From a sacramental perspective this all makes sense. In baptism, Christians claim to be woven into a body, a communion, a mystery beyond our ken. We rise from and against death-dealing ways of life and embody love not as individuals, but as a body. The Eucharist too transforms people from primarily individuals to primarily "we." Hear Martin Luther: "The sacrament has no blessing and significance unless love grows daily and so changes a person that he *is made one with all others*."[40] "Christ has given his body for this purpose, that the one thing signified by the sacrament—the *fellowship*, the change wrought by love—may be put into practice."[41]

It may well be that as moral beings we are not primarily an "I"; we are a "we." Thus, "What does it mean for 'me' to love neighbor as self in the context of climate sin?" may be a misleading question. Perhaps we are to ask instead: "What does it mean for 'us' to love neighbor as self in the context of climate sin?" My strong hunch is that we will know more fully the meaning of love in the age of climate violence as we learn to know it communally, and as we re-experience the moral self not first and foremost as an "I" but as a "we." We are, I sense, called to resist and rebuild in a mode of being that is vastly foreign to contemporary US Christians formed by the individualism of modernity and the privatization of neoliberalism. It is a communal mode of being, being as "we"—a cloud of witnesses spanning ages and continents, seeking more just and sustainable ways of living on Earth.

Biology confirms that "I" am not primarily an "I." I am part of a "we." I would not take my next breath without the collaborative work of thousands of small communities of organisms living in my guts, in my tear ducts, and on my skin and hair and other parts of my body; without the Amazon forest providing oxygen; without the four thousand microorganisms in the square foot of soil that grew the apples that I munched for lunch.

Theologically and biologically, I am a "we." Therefore, I embody love as a "we." Love is a collaborative, collective, communal reality. I am only beginning to discover what this might mean for moral agency. What it means may be key to forging a future that yields social equity and ecological regeneration.

40. Martin Luther, "The Blessed Sacrament of the Holy and True Body and Blood of Christ, and the Brotherhoods" §13, in *Martin Luther's Basic Theological Writings*, ed. Timothy Lull (Minneapolis: Fortress, 2005), 251 (emphasis added).

41. Luther, "Blessed Sacrament," §19 (emphasis added).

Consider two inklings about the implications of embodying love as a "we." Wise voices in theology and climate science call for communities to shift rapidly toward carbon neutrality, turning first to local and regional resources for sustainable food, water systems, energy, and other goods. The "transition town" movement begun in England illustrates these principles. Likewise, Larry Rasmussen calls for anticipatory communities, "places where people collaboratively develop ways of life that are ecologically sustainable and socially just, places in which eco-social virtues are consciously cultivated and embodied in community practices."[42] Imagine such communities strengthened by a firm grounding in incarnate love understood in the sense unfolding herein, as a communal embodiment. Commitment to such love and experience of it might nourish power for weathering the strife and stark demands inherent in building such communities.

A second inkling grows from my experience of searing grief and the healing power of lament. Grief—knowing it, expressing it, and living it—is essential to individual healing from terrible loss. It is an ingredient of going forward in life-giving ways. If this is true, then the same may be true for communal loss and healing. On some level, we must be howling with anguish—to know that our grandchildren may never know the utter beauty of vast forests and livable outdoor temperatures, to realize that hundreds of thousands of people will be flung from their homelands, to glimpse the horror of climate-intensified hurricanes terrorizing entire nations. Perhaps communal lament is integral to unlocking our moral power to repent of climate sin. In a powerful sermon on the book of Joel, Christian womanist ethicist Emilie Townes claims that social healing begins with communal lament.[43] Communal lament, she explains, is the assembly crying out in distress to the God in whom it trusts. It is a cry of sorrow by the people gathered, a cry of grief and repentance and a plea for help in the midst of social affliction. Deep and sincere "communal lament . . . names problems, seeks justice, and hopes for God's deliverance." "When Israel used lament as rite and worship on a regular basis, it kept the question of justice visible and legitimate."[44] Perhaps for us, too, communal lament is integral

42. Larry Rasmussen, *Earth-Honoring Faith: Religious Ethics in a New Key* (Oxford: Oxford University Press, 2012), 227.

43. This portion of this paragraph appears previously in Moe-Lobeda, "Climate Change as Climate Debt."

44. Emilie M. Townes, *Breaking the Fine Rain of Death* (New York: Continuum, 2001), 24.

to social restoration. Might the church be called to provide public space for communal lament for the ways in which our lives endanger Earth's web of life and vulnerable neighbors far and near? Perhaps communities of resistance and rebuilding, rooted in Christian claims, could remind people that we can lament without drowning in despair because sacred power for healing the world is present with it and incarnate within it.

These two—communal lament and love-strengthened communities shifting to carbon neutrality—are but two of infinite possibilities for love embodied as communities of resistance and rebuilding. Human communities' movement toward communally embodying love—despite that movement's ubiquitous fallibility—may be a foretaste of the destiny into which God, working through the things of Earth (including human creatures), is saving creation. That destiny, or "feast to come," while not fully knowable by limited human capacities, is glimpsed when joy and flourishing are deep and shared. It is signified by the ancient claim, heard in the second-century theologian Irenaeus of Lyons, that God is molding us, through God's two hands of Word and wisdom, into union and communion with all and with God.

If Irenaeus is right that this communion we are called to embody is our home, may we discover ever more fully what it means to live into this union and communion with divine love that ultimately will overcome all forms of death and destruction, including the many realities of systemic oppression and ecological degradation that eat away at our hearts and societies, destroying the very people we are called to love and the garden we are called to tend.

Incarnate Love's Transformative Power: Guideposts

We set out to explore a question: How will love given by God and incarnate in life on Earth enable humans in the high-consuming world to choose life abundant in the face of climate disaster? Noting features of love as a reality given by God yields no certain formula. However, if God's incarnate love bears the qualities noted above, then love may indeed bear power to transform moral inertia into moral agency, even if only partially. Moreover, these features of love issue in invaluable guideposts for embodying love or for faithful living in the face of climate catastrophe. Here we offer a set of suggestive guidelines to be ever deepened and refined.

First Guidepost: Lovers will trust "the end of the story"—resurrection seen in life abundant for the earth community—and live toward it.

Second Guidepost: Lovers will rise each day remembering who they are and who everyone is. We will see ourselves and one another as beloved beyond all comprehension; wildly, lavishly, magnificently loved; creatures who cannot shake off that divine love. We will, that is, defy the society's corrosive myth that "you are worthy only if you buy this, look this way, accomplish this, win this, are better than the others, etc." Spiritual practice will include reminding one another of who we are, and seeing ourselves through God's eyes.

Third Guidepost: Lovers will practice a form of moral vision that enables seeing structural brutalities *in order to change them,* while also maintaining hope. If our calling in life is to be the body of God's love active in the world, then a vital art of faithful living is the art of discerning—or seeking to see—where God's love is betrayed and where God's love is at play in the world so that we may participate in it. Catherine of Siena illumines: "Unless you see you cannot love. The more you see, the more you will love. Once you love you will follow, and you will clothe yourself in God's will."[45]

Many of us are ill equipped in this art of discernment. Cultivating moral vision that sees the world through three lenses at once may be a key to discerning where God's healing, liberating love is under way. What are these three lenses?

1. Seeing "what is going on." We have said that love seeks to change social systems that cause grave suffering for some while giving privilege and power to others. Doing so requires at least beginning to recognize such systems and to see how they work. Yet, those who benefit from systemic injustice are the last to recognize it. Nothing is more hidden from people of privilege than the ways in which our advantages are linked to others' suffering. Therefore, few things are more vital to discerning God's love at work in the world than learning to perceive "what is going

45. Catherine of Siena, final words of Prayer 19, circa 1379, in Mary O'Driscoll, ed., *Catherine of Siena* (Hyde Park, NY: New City, 2005), 85.

on" that may be veiled by the blinders of privilege. Lovers will develop a keen social analysis skill that asks what I call "reality-revealing questions"—questions that uncover the dynamics of power and privilege behind suffering. These include: "Who has the power in this situation to decide what will happen?" "Whose voices are heard and whose are not?" "Who benefits and who loses in the long-term from this situation?" The effort is to pierce through the myths rationalizing prevailing distributions of power and resources.[46] It is to unmask evil where it parades as good, and to see the brutality often hidden behind the cloak of apparent beauty.

2. Seeing "what could be and is in the making." Seeing "what is going on" may breed despair if our moral vision stops there. Lovers, therefore, will cultivate a second form of vision. It is awareness of "what could be and is in the making"—more just and sustainable practices, policies, and worldviews at the levels of household, institutions, businesses, and government. "Until we see what is possible," cautions Jean Piaget, "what is appears necessary."
3. Seeing the Spirit's life-restoring presence at play in the world luring us toward what could be. Even while we watch with one eye "what could be and is in the making," at times it seems that injustice, suffering, brutality, death, and destruction (recognized by the first form of vision above) will prevail. The horror of climate change set in motion to date even if we became carbon-neutral tomorrow, the ongoing killing of black men in the United States, abject poverty, and similar social atrocities may seem insurmountable. Therefore, a third lens perceives that God's love is at work in the world, actively luring us from "what is" toward "what could be." This third mode of vision sees that we human creatures are not alone in the quest for more just and sustainable ways of living. The sacred life-giving, life-saving Source of the cosmos—the Spirit—is with and within Earth's elements and creatures to bring life abundant (John 10:10) to all. This Spirit is enabling life and love ultimately to reign over death and destruction.

46. By myths I mean assumptions such as the following: that people in the United States have equal opportunities across class and racial lines; that fossil-fuel-driven, finance-oriented global capitalism is sustainable; that economic growth is inherently good; and that maximizing profit is a human right.

Moral power for living toward climate justice may grow from the soil of these three forms of vision held together. I refer to this three-eyed vision as "critical mystical vision." It is subversive because it reveals a future in the making and breeds hope for moving into it. "Mystical" here does not refer to an esoteric experience available to a few. It means experiencing or trusting in a reality behind the material and social reality of life.[47] It means trusting that the power of sacred energy for healing the world works in us and through us, in spite of us and beyond us. And it means choosing to trust that this power, divine love, is greater than all else.

Fourth Guidepost: Lovers will move toward two epistemological shifts. Both seek to develop capacities foreign to many of us. One is the capacity to hear, learn from, heed, and be nourished by the presence and voice of God in the creatures and elements of Earth. The other is to hear and learn from social movements of people who are damaged by the systems that bring material benefits to many of us in positions of privilege by color, economic standing, etc. This calls for participating in coalitions across class lines, racial lines, and national borders. Hearing and learning in this sense enable critical mystical vision.

Fifth Guidepost: Lovers will voice the need for honest public deliberation and innovative public policy moves—at national, local, and international levels—that take seriously the moral call to climate reparations. If love as a biblical norm seeks justice, and if love pays close attention to "what is going on," then the realities of climate debt (described earlier) come crashing in with inescapable urgency. What will justice-making love do in the lives of the high-consuming few, given the horrible consequences of our lifeways for millions of climate refugees and others damaged by the storms, droughts, and diseases brought on by climate change? The idea of climate reparations opens a door.

While the connotations and denotations of the term "reparations" are fluid and shifting, depending in part on context, the concept bears tremendous

47. I have used the words "experiencing or trusting" pointedly. "Mystical vision" does not depend upon experiencing the sacred. The choice to trust God's presence does not require experiencing it. As Luther so adamantly insisted, God is hidden in God's apparent absence. The nonexperience of God is no less a reality of God's presence than is heartfelt experience of it.

moral weight and possibility as a framework for addressing climate debt.[48] Lawyer Maxine Burkett argues that if reparations become a persistent presence in climate change discourse, the idea of climate reparations could make visible the profound moral dimension of climate change and could galvanize moral accountability and moral agency for change. Bringing climate reparations into the public discourse will be a "step in revealing the enormity of the harm and injustice faced by the climate vulnerable—and lay bare the speed and scale of the remedy needed."[49]

Angelica Navarro, while serving as Bolivia's climate negotiator at Copenhagen, explained what form climate reparations could take. "Climate debt," she declared, is "basically that developed countries have over-consumed . . . common atmospheric space. . . . As a result, we [developing countries] are suffering."[50] "In the South, countries like Bolivia that don't produce much CO2 . . . we're the ones seeing the negative effects of what others have produced, their economies, their way of life, and they don't see that our countries are bearing the cost. . . . In Bolivia our glaciers are melting. Tuni Condoriri, one of the glaciers that supplies water to La Paz (the capital), has decreased by 40–45% in the last twenty years. We are talking about a shortage of water for one to two million people."[51] "We have extended droughts. We have in the lowlands more flooding. . . . And what we are asking is repayment. We are not asking for aid. We are not asking—we are not begging for aid. We want developed countries to comply with their obligation and pay their debt. . . . How are they going to pay it? The first part is to pay it through reduced emission domestically. . . . And the second part of the climate debt is adaptation debt."[52] She goes on to call for

48. See Pable de Greiff, "Repairing the Past: Compensation for Victims of Human Rights Violations," in *The Handbook of Reparations*, ed. Pable de Greiff (Oxford: Oxford University Press, 2008), 13.

49. The quotations in this paragraph are from Burkett, "Climate Reparations," 3.

50. Angelica Navarro, interviewed by Amy Goodman, in "'We Are Not Begging for Aid'—Chief Bolivian Negotiator Says Developed Countries Owe Climate Debt."

51. Angelica Navarro, in Huff-Hannon, "Bolivia Steps Up."

52. Angelica Navarro, interviewed by Goodman, in "'We Are Not Begging for Aid'—Chief Bolivian Negotiator Says Developed Countries Owe Climate Debt." In a speech at a UN climate conference in 2009, Navarro called for a "Marshall Plan for the Earth. This plan must mobilize financing and technology transfer on a scale never seen before. It must get technology onto the ground in every country to ensure we reduce emissions while raising people's quality of life. We have only a decade." Cited in Naomi Klein, *This Changes Everything: Capitalism vs. the Climate* (New York: Simon & Schuster, 2014), 5.

significant financial contributions and transfer of technology to enable countries of the Global South to adapt to the demands of climate change in ways that countries of the Global North are able to do because of financial and technological resources. Climate reparations can take these two forms as well as a third. It is financial assistance and technology transfer to cover costs of mitigating climate change without sacrificing basic needs and rights of the people.[53]

Sixth Guidepost: Lovers will practice the two complementary movements in the work of justice-making love: resistance and rebuilding. This means resisting ways of life that perpetrate climate change and the economic injustice that accompanies it, and rebuilding alternatives more resonant with the call to love.

Seventh Guidepost: Lovers will recognize multiple fingers on the hands of love as a political-economic-ecological calling.[54] Just as Jesus's ways of loving varied tremendously, so too love's actions to create a more just, compassionate, and ecologically regenerative world take many forms. In discerning one's role in this movement, it is useful to view the range of actions. Moreover, a sense of empowerment and hope flows from realizing that one's efforts in one of these practices actually enable other people's efforts in other practices to bear fruit. The categories in the following typology are not meant to be rigid or exhaustive. Rather, they illumine the multiple forms of love's action and their empowering interdependence.

- Lifestyle changes (housing, transportation, eating, consumption levels, travel, recreation, etc.)
- Economic advocacy (boycotts, shareholder advocacy, socially/ecologically responsible buying, socially and ecologically responsible investing)
- Legislative advocacy and electoral advocacy (local, state, national)
- Community-organizing campaigns
- Education and consciousness raising
- Public witness (public protest and demonstrations, public art, civil disobedience, etc.)

53. See Moe-Lobeda, "Climate Change as Climate Debt."
54. See Moe-Lobeda, *Resisting Structural Evil*, chap. 7.

- Economic alternatives (co-ops; worker-owned business; municipality-owned services such as cable, telephone, and Internet services; local or regional reinvestment banks; community-supported agriculture and farmers' markets; etc.)
- Direct service to people in need
- Worship and prayer (Earth-honoring liturgy, public lament, celebrating religious heritage of resistance, prayers of repentance and for courage and wisdom, etc.)
- Biblical study and theological reflection

These are practical forms of incarnate love in our context. They are means of resisting economic and ecological violence and rebuilding more equitable, sustainable, and democratic economic life.

Eighth Guidepost: For many people in this country, the demands of everyday life do not leave time and energy for extraordinary measures to dramatically lower carbon footprints and resist economic violence in a society structured around fossil fuels and economic exploitation. Love, therefore, will strive to rebuild structures (institutions, public policies, economic norms, etc.) so that they enable people's daily activities to contribute to healthy ecosystems and socially just human relations, without requiring extraordinary risk, sacrifice, time, and effort. To illustrate: if public policy creates safe bike lanes on all streets, more people commute by bike without extraordinary risk of injury; if public policy rewards research and development in renewable energy, it becomes more affordable; if the law forbids maximizing profit where doing so denies worker rights and environmental health, then companies could honor those rights and health without losing market standing relative to companies that do not. Erich Fromm, in his *Art of Loving,* says as much: "Those who are seriously concerned with love as the only rational answer to the problem of human existence must, then, arrive at the conclusion that important and radical changes in our social structure are necessary, if love is to become a social and not a highly individualistic, marginal phenomenon."[55]

55. Erich Fromm, *The Art of Loving* (New York: Harper & Brothers, 1956), 132.

Conclusion

These guideposts are manifestations of love incarnate in the age of climate injustice. They are initial markers on a little-known path toward "choosing life and blessings" over "death and curses" (Deut. 30:19). Readers and their communities committed to forging that path may explore these markers and surely will develop others. Given the reality of climate crisis, the path will pass through perils great. But if the claims about God's love incarnate on Earth are true, then the perilous path will lead only more deeply into Love's embrace.

Christian faith is tested today. Can it help us to repent of the climate sin in which we are so terribly implicated? (Recall that "repent" in the biblical sense is to turn the other direction.) Can it help us to move away from ways of life—individual and societal—that are displacing and killing people, destroying communities, and endangering Earth's life-sustaining capacity?

In this essay, I as a "we" have said yes. Grounded in the biblical witness that God's love is stronger than all else, we have explored the claim that, by the power of God's love incarnate on Earth, life can triumph over the death and destruction that we now engender through climate injustice. "How," we asked, "will the love given by God enable humans to choose life abundant in the face of climate disaster?"

After posing this question, we began by noting roots of moral inertia that may be partially uprooted by love incarnate. Those roots were the following: (1) a lack of formation in the arts of discerning the Spirit at play in the world, (2) a privatized sense of "love neighbor as self," and (3) an individualized sense of who we are as moral beings largely powerless in the face of finance-driven, fossil-fueled corporate capitalism. In response, we noted eleven features of neighbor love that uproot these sources of moral inertia and explored four of the features more fully. Building on these features of neighbor love, we suggested guideposts for embodying love incarnate in the face of climate sin. The features of love held together with the guideposts suggest that incarnate love may indeed counter the forces of moral inertia with which we began. That is, incarnate love and our "guideposts" in concert point to (1) tools for discerning the Spirit's activity of justice-seeking, Earth-honoring neighbor love, (2) a political-economic-ecological understanding of neighbor love, and (3) a collective or communal sense of moral being and agency. In the process we dared to face the daunting question: What does it mean for the "active thieves" and "passive profiteers" of climate injustice to heed Jesus's call to love neighbor as self?

May climate-privileged people and societies dare to face the questions probed herein. May those among us who know the great and intimate mystery of God through Jesus and the Spirit allow God's love to work among us toward a world in which all have the necessities for life abundant and in which garden Earth can flourish.

Responses

From Richard Bauckham

~ Cynthia Moe-Lobeda's eloquent and passionate essay is confined, as far as the ecological issues it addresses go, to climate change, and in that sense it is the most narrowly focused of the essays. This is a problem only if it gives the impression that climate change is the only moral issue of importance in the relationships of humans to other creatures at the present juncture of history. In my view, the magnitude and urgency of climate change cannot be exaggerated, and I agree with Moe-Lobeda's perspective in seeing it as an issue of justice, since it is especially the poor who are suffering from the effects of overconsumption by the more affluent of the world's peoples. But it is not the only issue. We are living through the sixth great age of extinction in the planet's history, in which species of animals and plants are going extinct at a rate not paralleled since the catastrophe that brought the era of the dinosaurs to an end. The process of extinction is aggravated by climate change, but it would still be happening without climate change, since it is the effect of the many ways in which humans have been destroying the habitats of other living creatures and generally taking over almost all the planet for ourselves.

In a rare reference to what is concretely going wrong in the natural world, Moe-Lobeda refers to "global warming, poisoned rivers, the extinction of tens of thousands of species per year, and ocean acidification." The acidification of the oceans is indeed an effect of greenhouse gases, which are also causing climate change, but we are also polluting the oceans and destroying most of their creatures by overfishing and by filling them with plastic. The poisoning of rivers and the extinction of species are largely quite independent of climate change. Moe-Lobeda does not exaggerate when she speaks of "the climate catastrophe bursting upon us with powers of death and destruction unparalleled in human history," but even apart from this climate catastrophe, humans are currently responsible for destroying other creatures—whole ecosystems by the million—on a scale unparalleled in human history and paralleled in the history of the planet only by the effect of the meteorite that destroyed the dinosaurs.

I think it is the exclusive concentration on climate change and climate justice that also makes this essay the most anthropocentric of the essays. Despite occasional references to "the earth" and "the earth community," Moe-Lobeda is overwhelmingly concerned with the human victims of climate change. I guess I find this rather disappointing because I have come to see the issue of *wilderness* as a test of an adequate ecological theology. We do not really care for and about all God's creatures on this planet unless we are concerned to protect as much of the planet as possible from human interference. We must reverse the process of taking over the whole planet for ourselves that has gathered pace in the last few decades and give space again for other creatures to be themselves, because in a theocentric, rather than anthropocentric, world, they have their own value for God and for themselves that we should respect and treasure. An exclusive focus on climate change cannot do full justice to this aspect of ecological concern, although it could bear on it (preserving rainforests helps to mitigate climate change as well as protecting wilderness).

Turning now to Moe-Lobeda's rich and valuable account of the nature and implications of neighbor love, I do have to correct her exegesis of the biblical command "You shall love your neighbor as yourself." Pointing out that in the occurrences of this command in the New Testament the Greek verb "shall love" is future indicative (*agapēseis*), she infers that the words are "not primarily a commandment regarding what people *should* do" but a promise of "what we *will* do." In fact, this is an idiomatic use of the future aspect of the Greek verb (known as the "imperatival future") that expresses a strong injunction or prohibition.[56] It is used largely when commandments of the Torah are quoted (e.g., six of the Ten Commandments in Mark 10:19), following the Greek version of the Old Testament, and reflecting the Hebrew Bible's use of the "imperfect" aspect of the Hebrew verb to express a strong injunction or prohibition.[57] It is

56. F. Blass and A. Debrunner, *A Greek Grammar of the New Testament and Other Early Christian Literature*, trans. and ed. Robert W. Funk (Chicago: University of Chicago Press, 1961), 183 (§362).

57. See, e.g., Bill T. Arnold and John H. Choi, *A Guide to Biblical Hebrew Syntax*, 2nd ed. (Cambridge: Cambridge University Press, 2018), 72.

very common in commandments in the Torah.[58] It is a kind of legal language that evokes a strict obligation to obey the commandment, not an assurance that the commandment will be obeyed. It is a usage that English speakers familiar with the Ten Commandments or with the two great love commandments in English translation readily recognize and understand. In fact, it is also current in everyday English. If a parent says to a child, "You will do as I say," the parent is not predicting the child's obedience but commanding it. Attractive as it might be to understand the love commandment as a promise, this is not what the text means.

I agree with one of Moe-Lobeda's main contentions: that Christian love must be expressed in political-economic-ecological action as well as in the "private" sphere of interpersonal relationships. Against the privatization of Christian ethics in much pietistic Christianity, this does need to be strongly asserted. However, I think we should be careful not to make a sharp and artificial distinction between the "public" and "private" spheres of life. Here Steven Bouma-Prediger's account of virtue ethics may be helpful. The "sorts of persons" we Christians are supposed to be becoming will act lovingly in relationships of friendship and family, in work and daily life, and also in all the opportunities we may have to help overcome structural evils. When such persons become aware of the suffering caused to people in other communities and societies by the systems in which they participate, they will want to act on that awareness just as they will if a neighbor on the same street is in need. If they are not the sorts of persons who easily neglect the neighbor on the street, then, even if they are involved in social and political activism, the latter will likely be unloving.

Moe-Lobeda is rather dismissive of the notion of neighbor love in religious discourse that "summons images of kindness, warm feelings, and inoffensiveness." I'm not so sure that something like these aspects of love, properly understood, is not needed in the works of love in the political-economic-ecological spheres. There is such a thing as hard-hearted activism that deals in cold and abstract ideals of justice. It has marred many a political revolution. When aid workers practice sexual abuse of those they are employed to help, they show

58. Lev. 19:18, the source of the love commandment cited in the New Testament, reads, "You shall not take vengeance or bear a grudge against any of your people, but you shall love your neighbor as yourself." The first two verbs are imperfect, but the third ("you shall love") is perfect because it follows the conjunction *vav*. The Septuagint correctly uses the Greek future (*agapēseis*) to translate it.

that they are not "the sorts of persons" who will treat individuals with kindness and respect, and so are not "the sorts of persons" fit to administer aid programs either. The interpersonal is always intertwined with the structural.

In this connection, Paul's great reflection on love in 1 Corinthians 13 may help. It has often been suggested that we could read it as a character description of Jesus Christ. Those who care passionately about structural injustice may fear that the effect of Paul's description is to confine love to the interpersonal sphere. I do not think this is the case. But to me this chapter does suggest that we should not leave aside the qualities that matter in interpersonal relations (patience, kindness, humility, and so forth) when we seek to exercise love in the struggle against structural evils.

From Steven Bouma-Prediger

A sincere thank you to Cynthia for her thoughtful and challenging chapter. I agree with much of what she says, but I also have some questions.

I agree that "incarnate love is . . . the centerpiece of Christian faith." At the heart of our faith are three central claims. First, "the Word became flesh and lived among us" (John 1:14). Second, this incarnate Word, "who, though he was in the form of God, . . . emptied himself, taking the form of a slave, being born in human likeness . . . became obedient to the point of death—even death on a cross" (Phil. 2:6–8). Third, "this Jesus God raised up" (Acts 2:32), and "God, who is rich in mercy, out of the great love with which he loved us even when we were dead through our trespasses, made us alive together with Christ . . . and raised us up with him" (Eph. 2:4–6). Incarnation, crucifixion, resurrection. All because of God's unfathomable love.

The centrality of love is affirmed again and again in the history and theology of the church: Polycarp and Perpetua, Antony and Augustine, Maximus the Confessor and Bernard of Clairvaux, Francis and Clare of Assisi, Richard Rolle and Julian of Norwich, Therese of Lisieux and Dietrich Bonhoeffer, Oscar Romero and Mother Teresa. The list is long of the followers of Jesus whose words and lives speak of the importance of the love of God.[59]

59. For more on love as a reoccuring theme in Christian spirituality, see Bradley Holt, *Thirsty for God: A Brief History of Christian Spirituality*, 2nd ed. (Minneapolis: Fortress,

So, love is central. But Cynthia is right to insist that what the Christian tradition knows as love is quite different from what goes by that name in contemporary culture. Love, in common parlance, "is far too domesticated." Love in the Bible "is not primarily a feeling at all." It is, rather, a habitual disposition to care for the welfare of another.[60] It is what Jesus asks us to do when he calls us to love our enemies and pray for those who persecute us (Matt. 5:44; for the apostle Paul's version, see Rom. 12:14–21).

But as Cynthia insightfully observes, the call to love bumps into the paradox of the human condition. As Pascal notes, we humans are capable of both beauty and ugliness, goodness and brutality, compassion and indifference.[61] This mix of good and evil is especially complex with respect to climate change, since most if not all of us are, to use Cynthia's phrase, "complicit in climate catastrophe." One of the most useful, if difficult, features of Cynthia's essay is her unflinching honesty about moral culpability when it comes to climate change. Hence her plea that God grant us insight and courage.

Climate change is both a theological and a moral crisis. It is true that those who suffer most from climate change are those who are the least responsible for it. "To fully acknowledge this," Cynthia asserts, "is to be tormented by it." That we are not anguished by this inequity is damning evidence that we are blind or indifferent to the plight of our human brothers and sisters, not to mention our nonhuman neighbors and their habitats. So Cynthia courageously calls to our attention the environmental racism, sexism, and classism present in our society today. Colonialism, Cynthia insists, is not dead but has simply taken another form: climate colonialism in which the Global North is enriched at the expense of the Global South (Africa, Latin America, and parts of Asia).

This moral crisis is also a theological crisis, Cynthia avers, because "if God dwells within the earth's creatures and elements," then our degradations of the earth are "crucifying Christ." Furthermore, if creation is a book that reveals who God is, then our ecological degradations are "destroying essential fea-

2005), and Gerald Sittser, *Water from a Deep Well: Christian Spirituality from Early Martyrs to Modern Missionaries* (Downers Grove, IL: InterVarsity Press, 2007).

60. On love as a virtue, see Steven Bouma-Prediger, *Earthkeeping and Character: Exploring a Christian Ecological Virtue Ethic* (Grand Rapids: Baker Academic, 2019), chap. 4.

61. Thomas Morris, *Making Sense of It All: Pascal and the Meaning of Life* (Grand Rapids: Eerdmans, 1992).

tures of God's 'first book of revelation.'" But in what way(s) does the Creator dwell within creation? How is God (Father, Son, and Holy Spirit) present in the world? Is it really true that in our poisoning of the rivers we are crucifying Christ? These claims, at the very least, require more discussion of theology proper (views of God and God's attributes), ontology (theism, pantheism, panentheism), and Christology (the locus of the resurrected Christ and the ubiquity of Christ's body).[62]

The question at the center of Cynthia's chapter is this: How will God's love, made manifest in Christ, enable the world's high-consuming minority "to choose life abundant in the face of climate disaster"? In other words, how will our love-formed faith "enable us to choose life for the earth community, to live toward abundant life for all"? This is, indeed, the central (ethical and practical) question of our age: How does our faith shape our practices and everyday life such that God's good future of shalom is made real for all?

The power of this question, however, often gets diminished by an all-too-common lens we use for viewing the world. If we divide life into the sacred (church, Sunday, prayer) and the secular (work, the rest of the week, politics), then much of life is seen as outside the orbit of faith. The mantras are many. Don't mix religion and politics. Faith and science are at war. You can believe whatever you want, just keep your faith private. However, for Christians, life should not be divided into dual parts (sacred and secular), relegating our faith to some closet. God is not a hobby. Biblical faith is all-inclusive. If God's love triumphs over sin and death, then we need to ask what that means for where we live, what we eat, how we get from place to place, what we do for a living, how we vote.[63]

Asking about how our faith shapes our practices leads to the issue of moral inertia, which is a huge problem Cynthia directly addresses. Among the various environmental issues, climate change most often evokes cries of helplessness. "What can I do?" is a common response from those awakened to the grim

62. For more on these issues, see Steven Bouma-Prediger, *The Greening of Theology: The Ecological Models of Rosemary Radford Ruether, Joseph Sittler, and Jürgen Moltmann* (Atlanta: Scholars Press, 1995).

63. For more on subverting these dualisms, see J. Richard Middleton and Brian Walsh, *Truth Is Stranger Than It Used to Be: Biblical Faith in a Postmodern Age* (Downers Grove, IL: InterVarsity Press, 1995), and Bob Goudzwaard and Craig Bartholomew, *Beyond the Modern Age* (Downers Grove, IL: InterVarsity Press, 2017).

realities of climate change. Cynthia offers a perceptive analysis of the reasons for moral inertia: the inability to discern God's love at work in the world, a privatized sense of love for neighbor, and individualistic assumptions about who we are as moral beings. She points to the urgent need for churches to cultivate "a self alternative to and critical of the socialized self of the broader society" and mentions the role of worship in such a process of identity creation. I could not agree more.[64] And on the topic of fostering agency, we must also provide concrete examples of things we can do simply because they are right and good, regardless of the consequences.[65] In short, we must eschew the dominant de facto ethic of our age, consequentialism, which stipulates that the moral worth of an action is determined entirely by whether it will most likely bring about good consequences.[66] Many things are worth doing simply because they honor the intrinsic value of another creature or shape us into good people.[67]

Cynthia's discussion of love as the "wellspring of moral power" is full of insights, as she succinctly restates many of the basic claims of the Bible and the Christian tradition. God loves all of this world, and this love is unconditional. God's love does not depend on our performance. This loving God has not gone on holiday but is actively breathing life into this world. The cross and the resurrection testify that God loves this world and will not abandon it. Knowing this gives us hope when tempted by despair but calls us to trust in God's promise that love will win in the end. Having faith about the end of the story—that love wins and all things will one day flourish—not only gives us hope but empowers action. We are called to join with God by serving our neighbors, whether we have good feelings for them or not. Jesus is our exemplar in this

64. On the pivotal role of worship in the formation of Christian identity, see James K. A. Smith, *Desiring the Kingdom: Worship, Worldview, and Cultural Formation* (Grand Rapids: Baker Academic, 2009), as well as his two more recent volumes in his Cultural Liturgies series.

65. For more on what we can and should do, see Seth Shulman et al., *Cooler Smarter: Practical Steps for Low-Carbon Living* (Washington, DC: Island, 2012), a book produced by the Union of Concerned Scientists.

66. See Kathleen Dean Moore, *Great Tide Rising: Towards Clarity and Moral Courage in a Time of Planetary Change* (Berkeley, CA: Counterpoint, 2016), and Kathleen Dean Moore and Michael Nelson, eds., *Moral Ground: Ethical Action for a Planet in Peril* (San Antonio: Trinity University Press, 2010).

67. For more on virtues, see Michael Austin and R. Douglas Geivett, eds., *Being Good: Christian Virtues for Everyday Life* (Grand Rapids: Eerdmans, 2012).

calling to love our neighbors. Love, if it is really God's love, necessarily implies justice.[68] God's love envelops the whole of creation, and thus God is at play in all things to renew the world.[69] Our love of neighbor must address structural systems of injustice. Amen and amen.

In a world where love is dished out only if I [fill in the blank], Cynthia emphasizes, as one might expect from a good Lutheran, that God's love does not depend on what we do or don't do. God's love is not conditional. *Sola gratia* comes to mind, and come to mind it should to challenge our quid-pro-quo culture. And from this famous *sola* it follows: "To see oneself through the eyes of God, to see what God sees, is to see a human creature loved beyond all comprehension." However, I wonder, good Calvinist that I am, about the noetic effects of sin. Can I ever, finite and fallen creature that I am, in this life see through the eyes of God? The work of the Holy Spirit in sanctification is not to be taken lightly, as Calvin clearly affirms,[70] but with all due respect to John Wesley and his robust ideas of perfect love and holiness, I am doubtful that we humans will anytime soon see the world or our neighbors through the eyes of God.

I agree that justice making is both personal and structural and that the latter is often omitted or ignored. The various social-political-economic systems that shape our culture benefit some people and harm others. The various isms (sexism, racism, classism, etc.) attempt to name these systemic injustices. Cynthia courageously confronts these "structural sins" while acknowledging their complexity. She cites the culture of the automobile in the United States as one classic example of how individualism and a privatized sense of morality warp our perception of neighbor love. What we need, she argues, is "a reconstructed sense of the moral self" that enables us "to see more clearly the roots

68. For more insight on the relationship between justice and love, see Nicholas Wolterstorff, *Justice in Love* (Grand Rapids: Eerdmans, 2011).

69. It must be stressed that in God's good future the world will be renewed, not destroyed. See Steven Bouma-Prediger, *For the Beauty of the Earth*, 2nd ed. (Grand Rapids: Baker Academic, 2010), chaps. 3–4. See also Barbara Rossing, *The Rapture Exposed: The Message of Hope in the Book of Revelation* (Cambridge, MA: Westview, 2004), and J. Richard Middleton, *A New Heaven and a New Earth: Reclaiming Biblical Eschatology* (Grand Rapids: Baker Academic, 2014).

70. See, for example, Calvin, *Institutes of the Christian Religion*, ed. John McNeill (Philadelphia: Westminster, 1960), 3.1–10.

and consequences of ecological and economic violence." True enough, but we also need people who "can do the difficult things that will be necessary to live within the boundaries of the earth."[71] In other words, we need more than merely insight. We need people (and the families and churches and schools and cities that form such people) who embody the virtues of wonder and humility, self-control and wisdom, justice and love, courage and hope.[72]

We certainly do, as Cynthia argues, need to recapture the communal perspective of much of Scripture and the best of the Christian tradition, whether by noting the plural Greek verbs and pronouns hiding behind the ambiguous English second-person pronoun translations ("you" or "y'all"?) or in recognizing the communal character at the heart of the sacraments of baptism and Eucharist. And given the scope and power of climate change, Cynthia rightly argues that lament (communal and individual) is "integral to unlocking our moral power to repent of climate sin." Only if we can voice the sorrow of our loss will we be able to move toward action animated by genuine hope.[73]

There is much wisdom in Cynthia's guideposts. We must recall that our faith is in vain without the resurrection. We must remember that our true identity is found in being loved by God. We need to cultivate the virtue of discernment in order to see what is really going on in our world and also to foster the virtues of courage and hope in order to imagine and work for a more just future. We must become more ecologically literate—knowledgeable about the world in which we live and its plethora of creatures and systems. And we need to act in multiple ways to change how we live, from eating lower on the food chain to advocating for community-supported agriculture, from offering prayers of repentance in worship to marching for environmental justice in public.

In her conclusion Cynthia observes that "Christian faith is tested today." She is certainly right. And she challenges those of us who are in places of privilege to "allow God's love to work among us" so that all might have what they need and the world might flourish. May we heed these wise words, to the glory of God and for the love of the world.

71. David Orr, *Earth in Mind: On Education, Environment, and the Human Prospect* (Washington, DC: Island, 2004), 62.

72. For more on this, see Bouma-Prediger, *Earthkeeping and Character*, chaps. 2–5.

73. See Soong-Chan Rah, *Prophetic Lament: A Call for Justice in Troubled Times* (Downers Grove, IL: InterVarsity Press, 2015).

From John F. Haught

~ I want to express my admiration and gratitude for Cynthia's fine essay, especially its highlighting—as a condition of ecological responsibility—the importance of our first *attending* carefully to what is really going on. The cognitive imperative to be attentive is not one that we theologians have always obeyed devoutly. In addition to awakening to the harsh facts of climate change and other ecological ills, therefore, I want to suggest that Christian theology may responsibly fulfill the imperative to look at *what is really going on* only if it also takes into consideration, much more attentively than it has so far, what scientific discoveries over the last two hundred years have been telling us about the natural world. Before deciding on what we need to do, morally speaking, in the context of presently disheartening ecological circumstances, theologians need to look much more intently at what was already going on in the universe for 13.8 billion years before humans recently arrived and began to alter the face of the natural world here on Earth.

A contemporary ecological theology or ethics would do well to reflect, therefore, on the specific patterns of cosmic activity that have served in the past to open the universe to emergent new forms of being such as the phenomena of life and mind on our planet. Only by way of an empirically based understanding of natural history can we think and act responsibly to ensure that life, at least in our terrestrial precincts, will have a rich future. Here again, I am convinced that Teilhard was much more closely attuned to what is really going on in the cosmic drama and earth history preparatory to the emergence of life and mind than most other scientists and religious thinkers have been up until now.

This devout Catholic geologist was one of the very first scientists in the last century to have emphasized the fact that the universe is a *story* and not a state. And he was almost alone among Christians of his generation in pointing out the inadequacies of the pessimistic understanding of creation that has been so influential in shaping Christian thought and moral life for centuries. Long before theologians such as Wolfhart Pannenberg and Jürgen Moltmann were recovering the early Christian sense of the future, Teilhard had already done so—and in a way that is still in line with developments in evolutionary biology, geology, and cosmology. Even during the Great War, where he was an intrepid stretcher-bearer in the French army, Teilhard was already beginning to lay out a hopeful, anticipatory way of looking at nature that has not yet caught on either among scientists or among theologians but that is vital, I believe, to a scientifically informed Christian ecological theology.

More explicitly than any other Christian thinker of his day, Teilhard was able to show that Christians must *see* the natural world, and that they can learn to love what they see without having to feel that they are thereby turning their backs on God. Cynthia, I believe, would be impressed by the number of times the verb "to see" appears in Teilhard's writings. Traditional Christian thought, because of world-fleeing assumptions inherited from ancient Platonic and sometimes dualistic worldviews, has failed to follow the empirical imperative in developing an accurate sense of the natural world.

In line with Cynthia's exhortation to attend carefully to what is really going on, I wonder if an anticipatory Christian faith might not discipline our faculties now to look more carefully for signs of promise, not only in human history but also in nature, a region of being that in Israelite culture was never crisply distinguished from that of historical process. The Bible's anticipatory hope even now might train our senses to *see* things in cosmic process that would be invisible to those whose consciousness is shaped by dispositions of neutrality, world escapism, disinterest, or despair.

If there are any present hints of nature's openness to new creation, they would scarcely even show up in an awareness that had not already been shaped by the virtue of hope. Putting on the habit of hope, I suggest, is fundamental to the formation of the kind of Christian empiricism and moral responsiveness that might implement Cynthia's suggestions to be fully attentive to our present ecological situation. Neither the full deployment of our minds nor the opening of our senses to the real world is independent of the life of virtue, not least of which is that of hope.

I wonder, then, if we can ever truly see what's really going on in the universe unless we first learn to *trust* that it has a future, and that this future is in some sense indestructible. If we agreed with the cosmic pessimists that nature is headed toward absolute death, could we experience it as anything more than a transient delight? If the destiny of everything were a reversion to nothingness, what would be the incentives for a truly robust ecological morality? Granted, we may enjoy transient beauty as it lingers briefly for our delight, but do we love it because of its transience, that is, because it teeters defiantly on the edge of nothingness? Or instead, perhaps, because it carries the promise of deeper, wider, and even everlasting beauty? Can we sense and savor the beauties of nature with full appreciation if at the same time we feel forced by fate or scientism to see everything slipping toward an absolute death?

Teilhard, I believe, is right to highlight the enfeebling moral implications of cosmic pessimism. He writes: "The prospect of a *total death* (and that is a word to which we should devote much thought if we are to gauge its destructive effect on our souls) will, I warn you, when it has become part of our consciousness, immediately dry up in us the springs from which our efforts are drawn."[74] I believe this warning applies especially to those interested in finding reasons for ecological morality. As a condition for serious moral action, biblical (anticipatory) hope seeks to develop in us a capacity to *see* promise even in the most unpromising of circumstances. Contrary to assumptions of modern materialists, an anticipatory vision considers hope to be anything but an escape from reality. The kind of metaphysics that corresponds to an anticipatory vision locates what is "really real" in the arena of the future, in the not-yet of what is still coming into being. So, in accordance with an anticipatory epistemology, human knowers cannot plausibly claim to be attentive to or in touch with reality unless their minds and hearts have already been stretched by the virtue of hope toward looking out for the coming of *new* being.

What this means ecologically is that apart from risking hope—and this is my main point here—we are likely to turn our attention away from what is really going on in nature. But if through hope we begin to sense the promise of nature, the tantalizing whiff it gives us of nature's future destiny in God may energize our senses, minds, and moral aspirations, even here and now, to undertake the kind of moral actions—including a responsible exercise of human creativity—that will ensure that the natural world stays open to renewal indefinitely.

We would love nature, in that case, not only because of its intrinsic sacramental goodness but even more because it bears within itself the dawning

74. Pierre Teilhard de Chardin, *How I Believe*, trans. René Hague (New York: Harper & Row, 1969), 43–44.

of a new and indestructible future. We would care for the fragile beauties of nature, therefore, not because of their evanescence, and not only because of their capacity to connect us symbolically to an eternal present, but because their glorious flourishing here and now is an anticipation of a fullness that belongs to the not-yet.

3 ~ The Character of Earthkeeping

A Christian Ecological Virtue Ethic

Steven Bouma-Prediger

In his essay "Christianity and the Survival of Creation," Kentucky farmer, novelist, essayist, and poet Wendell Berry argues that the indictment by conservationists that Christianity is culpable in the destruction of the natural world "is in many respects just." He writes that "Christian organizations, to this day, remain largely indifferent to the rape and plunder of the world and its traditional cultures. It is hardly too much to say that most Christian organizations are as happily indifferent to the ecological, cultural, and religious implications of industrial economics as are most industrial organizations."[1] In the very next breath, however, Berry insists that "however just it may be," the indictment of Christianity by non-Christian conservationists "does not come from an adequate understanding of the Bible and the cultural traditions that descend from the Bible." Critics too often dismiss the Bible, Berry observes, usually without ever reading it. He thus concludes: "Our predicament now, I believe, requires us to learn to read and understand the Bible in light of the present fact of Creation."[2]

Many have taken up this challenge and offered articulate and insightful readings of Scripture in light of the groaning of creation, to use the apostle

1. Wendell Berry, *Sex, Economy, Freedom, and Community* (New York: Pantheon, 1993), 94.

2. Berry, *Sex, Economy, Freedom, and Community*, 94–95.

Paul's metaphor in Romans 8.[3] Indeed, that number happily grows as Christians revisit the Bible, reread its texts, and reconsider their previously held views and practices. More work needs to be done to make the fruit of these reflections on Scripture more widely available via liturgies, sermons, music, prayers, church school instruction, and the like.

Berry himself has clearly presented his understanding of how to read the Bible in light of the present fact of creation.[4] His conclusion on the Bible and what it teaches about humans and the natural world is worth quoting at length.

> The Bible leaves no doubt at all about the sanctity of the act of world-making, or of the world that was made, or of creaturely or bodily life in this world. We are holy creatures living among other holy creatures in a world that is holy. Some people know this, and some do not. Nobody, of course, knows it all the time. But what keeps it from being far better known than it is? Why is it apparently unknown to millions of professed students of the Bible? How can modern Christianity have so solemnly folded its hands while so much of the work of God was and is being destroyed?[5]

Berry's succinct summation bears repeating: we are holy creatures living among other holy creatures in a world that is holy. So, Berry concludes, "we have no entitlement from the Bible to exterminate or permanently destroy or

3. For example, Richard Bauckham, *The Bible and Ecology* (Waco, TX: Baylor University Press, 2010); Richard Bauckham, *Living with Other Creatures* (Waco, TX: Baylor University Press, 2011); William Brown and S. Dean McBride, eds., *God Who Creates* (Grand Rapids: Eerdmans, 2000); William Brown, *The Seven Pillars of Creation* (New York: Oxford University Press, 2010); Ellen Davis, *Scripture, Culture, and Agriculture* (Cambridge: Cambridge University Press, 2009); Terence Fretheim, *God and the World* (Nashville: Abingdon, 2005); J. Richard Middleton, *The Liberating Image* (Grand Rapids: Brazos, 2005); J. Richard Middleton, *A New Heaven and a New Earth* (Grand Rapids: Baker Academic, 2015). In my book *For the Beauty of the Earth*, rev. 2nd ed. (Grand Rapids: Baker Academic, 2010), I also take up Berry's call to read Scripture in light of the present fact of creation.

4. Berry's views are available not only in his nonfiction but also in his novels, e.g., *Jayber Crow*, and in his poetry, e.g., many of his Sabbath poems.

5. Berry, *Sex, Economy, Freedom, and Community*, 99.

hold in contempt anything on the earth or in the heavens above it or in the waters beneath it. We have the right to use the gifts of nature but not to ruin or waste them."[6]

I can only say "Amen." The Bible begins and ends with rivers and trees. The Bible speaks of humans as earthkeepers. The Bible portrays God's good future as earthly and earthy. Furthermore, in the Apostles' Creed we begin with a confession of God as Maker of heaven and earth. In the Lord's Prayer we pray that God's will be done on earth as it is in heaven. In the doxology we sing that all creatures here below praise God. Earthkeeping is woven into the fabric of our faith.[7] We human earth creatures—*adam* from the *adamah*[8] and made *imago Dei*—have the God-given responsibility of caring for the earth and its plethora of creatures. As the prophetic ecological theologian Joseph Sittler put it: "When we turn the attention of the church to a definition of the Christian relationship with the natural world, we are not stepping away from grave and proper theological ideas; we are stepping right into the middle of them. There is a deeply rooted, genuinely Christian motivation for attention to God's creation."[9]

In this chapter I intend to develop this theme of earthkeeping. I will first examine an ongoing debate about stewardship. Is "stewardship," despite its long history of use, the best term to accurately describe our human calling on our home planet? Then I will make a biblical case for humans as earthkeepers. According to the Bible, who are we humans and what exactly are we called to do? Third and last, I will explore earthkeeping in terms of a Christian virtue ethic. If earthkeeping is integral to Christian faith, then what are the character traits of holy creatures living among other holy creatures in a world that is holy? How do we become people who embody virtues such as wonder and humility, frugality and self-restraint, justice and love, faithfulness and wisdom, courage and hope?

6. Berry, *Sex, Economy, Freedom, and Community*, 98.

7. For one creative demonstration of this, see H. Paul Santmire, *Ritualizing Nature: Renewing Christian Liturgy in a Time of Crisis* (Minneapolis: Fortress, 2008).

8. In Hebrew, *adamah* means earth or soil, hence *adam* means human creature of the earth.

9. Joseph Sittler, *Gravity and Grace* (Minneapolis: Augsburg, 1986), 15.

The Debate about Stewardship

The term "stewardship" has long been employed by Christians to denote the proper use of and care for the natural world.[10] In the 1970s through the 1990s, especially in Protestant circles in the United States, "stewardship" was a common term adopted by Christians who were awakening to the biblical call to care for the earth and its various creatures.[11] In American evangelical circles, the jointly authored book *Earthkeeping: Christian Stewardship of Natural Resources,* published in 1980, was a very influential resource for Christians concerned with the relationship between their faith and the health of the planet.[12] This book was put out in a revised second edition in 1991 as *Earthkeeping in the '90s: Stewardship of Creation.*[13]

The shift in subtitle indicates a not-so-subtle shift in understanding. In the words of the authors in the preface to the revised edition: "But the passage of a decade has revealed problems with the book's original subtitle, *Christian Stewardship of Natural Resources.* For to the Christian the earth ought to be neither 'Nature' (which suggests its elevation to divinity) nor 'resources' (which implies its degradation to a mere stockpile of raw material awaiting the action of human industry). Nor is it simply the abstract 'environment.' It is rather 'creation,' a word which reminds us not only of the Creator, but also of our status as creatures and task as stewards."[14]

In chapters entitled "Dominion as Stewardship: Biblical Principles of Earthkeeping" and "Stewardship," the authors argue that humans are both embedded in creation, a part of the created world like all other nonhuman creatures, and also made in God's image and thus unique compared to other creatures. Also, they describe the human calling in terms of dominion, but

10. For background on the biblical and historical meaning of the term, and an argument for its contemporary use, see Douglas John Hall, *The Steward: A Biblical Symbol Come of Age,* rev. ed. (Grand Rapids: Eerdmans, 1990).

11. See, e.g., Fred VanDyke et al., *Redeeming Creation: The Biblical Basis for Environmental Stewardship* (Downers Grove, IL: InterVarsity Press, 1996).

12. Loren Wilkinson et al., *Earthkeeping: Christian Stewardship of Natural Resources* (Grand Rapids: Eerdmans, 1980).

13. Loren Wilkinson et al., *Earthkeeping in the '90s: Stewardship of Creation,* rev. ed. (Grand Rapids: Eerdmans, 1991).

14. Wilkinson, *Earthkeeping in the '90s,* x.

dominion is understood to mean care and preservation, not domination. In other words, humans are earth creatures who are responsible stewards, called to exercise care-full dominion over the earth as a form of service rather than, as is often thought, an exercise in domination. This view is derived from a reading of the first chapters of Genesis and is supported by the New Testament, most especially in the words and deeds of Jesus Christ, who models a type of dominion most clearly characterized by a life of serving others, even to the point of a cross. In a summary of sorts, the *Earthkeeping in the '90s* authors write: "If stewardship is indeed dominion as service—as the whole Christian gospel suggests—then stewardship (used or misused) is an inescapable condition of human existence. All humans exercise dominion over things and people. Most often, that dominion is used only to increase their own glory and does not seem like 'stewardly' behavior. But the basic question is not *whether* we are stewards; the fact of dominion, and the possibility of using it for service, decides that. The question is *how* we are to exercise our stewardship."[15]

This is not the place for an extensive discussion of these issues. I merely note that the tradition of describing the Christian responsibility to care for creation in terms of stewardship has both advocates and critics. One of the most articulate advocates is Robin Attfield, who convincingly shows how stewardship, as a way of stressing human responsibility for the natural world, is rooted in the Christian tradition. He rightly argues that "whatever the causes of the [ecological] problems may be, our traditions offer resources which may, in refurbished form, allow us to cope with these problems."[16] One of those resources is the stewardship tradition, with roots going back to Chrysostom, Augustine, and Calvin. This tradition affirms that humans are "the stewards of the earth" and thus "responsible for its conservation, for its lasting improvement, and also for the care of our fellow creatures, its nonhuman inhabitants."[17]

Among the critics, the most eloquent and persuasive is Paul Santmire. Santmire cogently argues that it is best "to retire" the words "dominion" and "stewardship," "so that we do not have to explain constantly to others and to ourselves what they really mean."[18] These terms, according to Santmire, "still

15. Wilkinson, *Earthkeeping in the '90s*, 308.

16. Robin Attfield, *The Ethics of Environmental Concern*, 2nd ed. (Athens: University of Georgia Press, 1991), 34.

17. Attfield, *Ethics of Environmental Concern*, 45.

18. H. Paul Santmire, *Nature Reborn: The Ecological and Cosmic Promise of Christian*

carry too much baggage from the anthropocentric and indeed androcentric theology of the past; they are still too fraught with the heavy images of management, control, and exploitation of persons and resources."[19] In a later essay Santmire levels an even more trenchant critique. He argues that the term "stewardship" has such a broad meaning that it is too easily co-opted to mean nothing more than "wise use"; that its meaning is too anthropocentric; that the term connotes a managerial mode of exploiting the earth; that it is most often understood in terms of fund-raising for the church; and that "the Scriptures in fact teach us something richer and more complex."[20] In sum, the term "stewardship" is beyond redeeming.

While Attfield and others insist that "stewardship" is a valuable term worthy of continued use today, I find Santmire's critique compelling. Neither Santmire nor I disagree with Attfield's main claim, namely, that the Christian tradition has rich resources for addressing the ecological crisis before us. Our quarrel has to do with the usefulness of the term "stewardship" in today's discussions and debates. Simply put, the term carries too much baggage—it connotes exploitation and, for most people, primarily refers to giving money to the church—and the Bible teaches us something much richer and more compelling. In short, the term "stewardship" should be replaced.

In contrast to the language of stewardship, Santmire articulates our responsibility by way of four callings: the calling to cooperate with nature righteously, the calling to care for nature sensitively, the calling to wonder at nature blessedly, and the calling to anticipate the reign of God joyfully.[21] To cooperate with nature righteously means "intervening in the systems of nature, yes, but doing

---

Theology (Minneapolis: Augsburg/Fortress, 2000), 120. See also his books *The Travail of Nature: The Ambiguous Ecological Promise of Christian Theology* (Philadelphia: Fortress, 1985); *Ritualizing Nature,* mentioned above; and his most recent volume, *Before Nature: A Christian Spirituality* (Minneapolis: Fortress, 2014).

19. Santmire, *Nature Reborn,* 120.

20. H. Paul Santmire, "Partnership with Nature according to the Scriptures: Beyond the Theology of Stewardship," *Christian Scholar's Review* 32, no. 4 (Summer 2003): 381–412. I was the guest editor of this edition of *CSR,* which focused on "The Fate of the Earth" and included essays by Cal DeWitt, Joe Sheldon and Dave Foster, Loren Wilkinson, and Kenneth Peterson, along with this essay by Paul.

21. Santmire, *Nature Reborn,* chap. 8. In his *CSR* essay a few years after *Nature Reborn* was published, Santmire sets forth "three fundamental expressions or emphases" in his biblical theology of partnership with nature: creative intervention in nature, sensitive

so respectfully and creatively, attentive to nature's own God-given structure and processes, and attentive to the divinely mandated claims of social justice." So "we contemplate nature before we seek to change it. We live with the trees before we seek to cut them. And when we do intervene, we then do so for good reasons."[22] Santmire is here assuming, if not explicitly using, the language of virtues such as respect, attentiveness, and justice.

To care for nature sensitively means "serving nature as an end in itself, loving nature not for what it can do for us but for what it is and what it needs. This also means caring for the whole garden, in appropriate ways, the so-called useless plants and animals, as well as the productive ones."[23] So Santmire argues that sensitive care for nature implies three different kinds of engagement with nature—wild, cultivated, and fabricated. Wilderness, farmlands, and urban architecture each calls for a different kind of human intervention. This calling, too, assumes the presence of virtues—virtues such as self-control, love, and wisdom.

To wonder at nature blessedly asks us to contemplate the marvels of the world, like the psalmist in Psalm 104 admiring the cedars of Lebanon or the wild asses. Here, too, various virtues are implied, for example, wonder, attentiveness, humility.

And, finally, to anticipate the reign of God joyfully means to celebrate the good news of the consummation of creation inaugurated by the resurrection of Christ. We do this by believing that God's good future includes bodily renewal, a transfigured life, and a redeemed heaven-on-earth—all acts of hope in an age of despair.[24] Once again the language of virtue—faithfulness, courage, and hope—is prominent.

---

care for nature, and awestruck contemplation of nature, correlated respectively with the priestly creation story of Gen. 1, the Yahwist creation story of Gen. 2, and the book of Job.

22. Santmire, *Nature Reborn*, 120–21.

23. Santmire, *Nature Reborn*, 122.

24. Santmire's suggestive alternative represents one option in contemporary ecological theology, namely, the revisionist response, to use his three-part typology (*Nature Reborn*, 6–10). Santmire describes his own work in the theology of nature as falling into "that orthodox but innovative revisionist tradition which stands over against the sometimes heterodox religious expressions of the reconstructionist position, on the one hand, and the often thoughtful, but typically conventional traditionalism of modern ecumenical theology, on the other" (9). If I had to, I would locate my own work in the

The Case for Earthkeeping

In my view, Santmire's approach suggests a better way (than stewardship) to describe the Christian calling to care for our aching earth. My shorthand for such an approach is the term "earthkeeping." This term is biblically rooted. It focuses on our home planet (earthkeeping) rather than all of creation (creation care). It captures our human identity as earthy and earthly creatures. It reminds us that we are not owners but users and conservers of a world we hold in trust from God, who made and sustains it. It acknowledges that we humans have an important calling to serve the earth and its creatures so that all will flourish. What follows is a brief presentation of the biblical case for earthkeeping. Needless to say, there is much more that could be said.[25]

First, Genesis chapters 1 and 2 speak about both who humans are and what humans are to do. They speak both of human being and human doing. With respect to being, Genesis 1:26 clearly distinguishes between human creatures and nonhuman creatures by speaking only of the former as created *imago Dei*—in the image (*tselem*) and likeness (*demut*) of God. We humans are distinct in some important sense—unique among all the creatures to come from God's hand.

The story of the naming of the animals in Genesis 2:19–20, among other things, likewise points to human uniqueness. The human creature has the responsibility of giving names to the other creatures—no small task, given the significance of names in the Bible, for names signify identity. Abram becomes Abraham, ancestor of a multitude. Jacob becomes Israel, one who wrestles with God. Saul the persecutor becomes Paul the apostle. To name properly implies personal knowledge. To get the name right, one must intimately know the creature named. But naming also indicates a kind of authority. To name is to

---

same category of orthodox but innovative revisionism, exemplified by Joseph Sittler, Jürgen Moltmann, and Denis Edwards, to name but a few others.

25. My own views are more fully set forth in various places, most especially in the revised second edition of my book *For the Beauty of the Earth: A Christian Vision for Creation Care*. Another scholar whose views resemble my own is my friend Norman Wirzba; see, e.g., his excellent books *The Paradise of God: Renewing Religion in an Ecological Age* (Oxford: Oxford University Press, 2003) and, more recently, *From Nature to Creation: A Christian Vision for Understanding and Loving Our World* (Grand Rapids: Baker Academic, 2015).

have power. Clearly, therefore, humans are unique in important ways. Animals are sentient, and some show elements of moral thought, language, and puzzle solving, but humans as a package are still unique. To use modern language, only humans are persons. We are response-able and responsible persons. That is an inescapable part of who we are.

But what is often ignored or intentionally overlooked is that humans are not only distinct from but also similar to nonhuman creatures. We are, all of us, embedded in creation. For example, in the Genesis 1 narrative, the creation of humans does not occur on a day different from the creation of other animals. There is no separate day for humans. On the sixth day, as Genesis 1:24–31 tells it, all kinds of living creatures came forth: domestic animals and wild animals and creeping things. Humans and other animals of the earth, the text implies, have something in common. And as Genesis 2:7 indicates, the human earth creature (*adam*) is made from the earth (*adamah*). Humans are made of dirt or soil. To carry the Hebrew wordplay into Latin, we are humans because we are from the humus. We are earthy creatures. Other creatures, to take seriously the language of Joseph Sittler, are our sisters and brothers.[26] In sum, these texts indicate that we humans are not only different from but also similar to our nonhuman neighbors. We are both responsible persons and earthy creatures.

With respect to doing, the Hebrew verbs in Genesis 1:26–28 indicate that one dimension of the human calling is dominion. The earth creature is called to subdue (*kavash*) and have dominion over (*radah*) other creatures. But what does this mean? Does dominion, as is often assumed, necessarily mean domination? A larger canonical perspective sheds light on this important question. For example, Psalm 72 speaks most clearly of the ideal king—of one who rules and exercises dominion properly. The psalm unequivocally states that such a ruler executes justice for the oppressed, delivers the needy, helps the poor, and embodies righteousness in all he does. In short, the proper exercise of dominion yields shalom—the flourishing of all creation. This is a far cry from dominion as domination. And Jesus, in the gospel accounts, defines dominion in terms clearly contrary to the way it is often understood. For Jesus, to rule is to serve. To exercise dominion is to suffer, if necessary, for the good of

26. See, e.g., Joseph Sittler, "Ecological Commitment as Theological Responsibility," *Zygon* 5 (June 1970): 175.

the other. There is no question of domination, exploitation, misuse. Humans, therefore, are called to rule, but ruling must be understood rightly.

But once again this is only part of the picture. Yes, we are called to exercise dominion, but we are also called to service. For example, Genesis 2:5 speaks of humans serving the earth (*adam* is to *avad* the *adamah*). And Genesis 2:15 defines the human calling in terms of service: we are to serve (*avad*) and protect (*shamar*). We are to serve and protect the garden that is creation—for its own good, as well as for our benefit. Taking seriously both of these aspects of human doing implies that dominion must be defined in terms of service. We are called to dominion as service. In short, to focus only on the dominion texts and then to interpret them as necessarily entailing domination is faulty exegesis. It is a selective and tendentious reading of Genesis 1–2. With respect to the argument that Genesis 1:28 gives unconditional permission to humans to use and abuse the world, Wendell Berry puts it well:

> Such a reading of Genesis 1:28 is contradicted by virtually all the rest of the Bible, as many people by now have pointed out. The ecological teaching of the Bible is simply inescapable: God made the world because He wanted it made. He thinks the world is good, and He loves it. It is His world; He has never relinquished title to it. And He has never revoked the conditions, bearing on His gift to us of the use of it, that oblige us to take excellent care of it. If God loves the world, then how might any person of faith be excused for not loving it or justified in destroying it?[27]

We are earthkeepers. We are called to serve and protect this world that God made and loves and sustains. If this is true, then how could we be justified in abusing it?

Virtue and the Virtues

In order to be earthkeepers, we need to emphasize character as well as conduct—virtue in addition to rights, duties, and consequences. This is the main point of this chapter. To the questions "What are my duties?" and "What are

27. Wendell Berry, *What Are People For?* (New York: North Point, 1990), 98.

the consequences?" we need to add "What kind of person should I be?"[28] In other words, what kind of people should we human earthkeepers be if we are members of the community that is creation? Indeed, while obligations and consequences are important in ethics, I think concern for the virtues is even more important. I realize that this emphasis on virtue goes against the grain of much ethical theory, which typically focuses on duties or consequences.[29] Nevertheless, my claim is that areteology is more basic than deontology or teleology—that character is more fundamental than conduct.

The reason, in brief, for adopting a virtue-based approach to ethics is quite simple: what we do depends on who we are. Doing is contingent on being. To a large extent our actions arise from our desires and affections, our dispositions and inclinations—in short, our character. James K. A. Smith captures this point well: "Much of our action is not the fruit of conscious deliberation; instead, much of what we do grows out of our passional orientation to the world—affected by all the ways we've been primed to perceive the world. In short, our action emerges from how we *imagine* the world. What we do is driven by who we are, by the kind of person we have become."[30] What we do is driven by who we are. And who we are—the kind of person we have become—is best described by traits of character such as virtues and vices. This approach implies a critique of much contemporary ethics as too intellectualistic, too focused on rational principles and conscious deliberation. Such ethical theory has failed to notice or understand the prereflective and preconscious basis of (moral) action. While rational reflection is important, the simple fact is that most of our actions are prereflective, a result of having an intuitive, embodied feel for the world—a kinesthetic way of being in the world shaped over time by habits and routines.[31]

28. For a masterful combination of all three, see Lewis Smedes, *Choices: Making Right Decisions in a Complex World* (San Francisco: Harper & Row, 1986).

29. As Charles Taylor, among others, notes: "The dominant philosophical ethics today, divided into the two major branches of Utilitarianism and post-Kantianism, both conceive of morality as determining through some criterion what an agent ought to do. They are rather hostile to an ethics of virtue or the good, such as that of Aristotle." Charles Taylor, *A Secular Age* (Cambridge, MA: Harvard University Press, 2007), 282.

30. James K. A. Smith, *Imagining the Kingdom* (Grand Rapids: Baker Academic, 2013), 31–32.

31. For more on this, see James K. A. Smith, *Desiring the Kingdom* (Grand Rapids:

Furthermore, the kind of person we have become depends on the stories we identify with. We are, to use the words of Jonathan Gottschall, "the story-telling animal."[32] What does this mean? Barbara Kingsolver puts it well: "Storytelling is as old as our need to remember where the water is, where the best food grows, where we find our courage to hunt."[33] Contrary to what many believe, stories are useful beyond mere entertainment. Indeed, stories are, according to Kingsolver, "as persistent as our desire to teach our children how to live in this place that we have known longer than they have."[34] Narratives engage that part of us that most shapes our desires, namely, the imagination. Stories, including "legends, myths, plays, novels, and films," best speak to this imaginative core of our being because they paint a "more affective, sensible, even aesthetic *picture*" than do lectures or textbooks.[35] As many biblical commentators have remarked, Jesus was on to something in using parables for the instruction of his followers.

As an example, imagine two young students introduced to issues of ecological degradation.[36] John is given a pamphlet about deforestation in the Amazon. He reads about the importance of these rainforests to global environmental health, looks through the predictions, and even memorizes statistics. Meanwhile, Joanna is given Dr. Seuss's *The Lorax*. She may not be able to spout statistics, but she understands the impacts of human greed on the voiceless. The story gives her a sense that some things matter beyond their economic value—that there is much to lose by "biggering and biggering" our bottom line. Both of these students are introduced to the same topic, though in different ways. Both methods have value, and taken together provide a student

---

Baker Academic, 2009), part 1, and Smith, *Imagining the Kingdom*, part 1. On this point see also the insightful and important work of Mark Johnson, e.g., *The Meaning of the Body: Aesthetics of Human Understanding* (Chicago: University of Chicago Press, 2007) and *Moral Imagination: Implications of Cognitive Science for Ethics* (Chicago: University of Chicago Press, 1993).

32. Jonathan Gottschall, *The Storytelling Animal: How Stories Make Us Human* (New York: Houghton Mifflin Harcourt, 2012). As Gottschall succinctly puts it, "Our life stories are who we are. They are our identity" (161).

33. Barbara Kingsolver, *Small Wonder* (New York: Harper Perennial, 2003), 40.

34. Kingsolver, *Small Wonder*, 40.

35. Smith, *Desiring the Kingdom*, 53.

36. This example is from my research student Lauren Madison.

with a more thorough understanding of the matter. But taken alone, most of us would wager that Joanna is more likely to "speak for the trees."[37]

So stories shape our character, and thus all human action is shaped in terms of narratively formed character. Smith, again, articulates well the central insight: "And that shaping of our character is, to a great extent, the effect of stories that have captivated us, that have sunk into our bones—stories that 'picture' what we think life is about, what constitutes 'the good life.' We live *into* the stories we've absorbed; we become characters in the drama that has captivated us."[38] In the succinct words of Alasdair MacIntyre: "I can only answer the question 'What am I to do?' if I can answer the prior question 'Of what story or stories do I find myself a part?'"[39] In other words, a founding story is not a husk that can be shucked to get to the kernel inside, but is indispensable to knowing who we are. As Stanley Hauerwas reminds us, "We do not tell stories simply because they provide us a more colorful way to say what can be said in a different way, but because there is no other way we can articulate the richness of intentional activity—that is, behavior that is purposeful but not necessary."[40] There is, in short, a "narrative quality" to human action.[41]

So a virtue is a narratively formed, praiseworthy character trait. In addition, virtues are shaped by practices. As Hauerwas and Burrell put it, "in allowing ourselves to adopt and be adopted by a particular story, we are in fact assuming a set of practices that will shape the ways we relate to our world and destiny."[42] With the indwelling of a particular story comes a particular set of practices—of communal, embodied rhythms and routines—that shape and mold our dispositions. In other words, the metanarratives or big stories we hear and with which we identify—of manifest destiny, of material prosperity,

37. Dr. Seuss, *The Lorax* (New York: Random House, 2012).

38. Smith, *Imagining the Kingdom*, 32.

39. Alasdair MacIntyre, *After Virtue*, 2nd ed. (Notre Dame: University of Notre Dame Press, 1984), 216.

40. Stanley Hauerwas, *Truthfulness and Tragedy* (Notre Dame: University of Notre Dame Press, 1977), 76.

41. See Stephen Crites, "The Narrative Quality of Experience," in *Why Narrative? Readings in Narrative Theology*, ed. Stanley Hauerwas and L. Gregory Jones (Grand Rapids: Eerdmans, 1989), 65–88. See also the seminal work of Paul Ricoeur, *Time and Narrative*, vols. 1–3 (Chicago: University of Chicago Press, 1990).

42. Stanley Hauerwas and David Burrell, "From System to Story: An Alternative Pattern for Rationality in Ethics," in Hauerwas and Jones, *Why Narrative?*, 186.

of an eccentric carpenter from Nazareth—shape our character by enlisting us to engage in certain practices—reciting the Pledge of Allegiance, shopping at the mall, saying the Lord's Prayer. These practices shape the kind of person we become—our virtues and vices—and hence the actions we engage in.

And sometimes we see practices embodied in a person who displays for us what a life of virtue concretely looks like, for example, a well-known saint such as Mother Teresa or a well-loved if unknown relative such as Uncle Peter. Such people are models of virtue who inspire us to live such a life ourselves. So we alter our own life narrative by cultivating the virtues of our most admired exemplars. When it comes to matters ecological, Aldo Leopold and Rachel Carson are some of the most commonly mentioned exemplars of an ecological virtue ethic.[43]

So stories and practices and exemplars shape character. But, furthermore, our practices over time color the way we see ourselves and the world. There is a connection between virtue and vision. As Gilbert Meilaender states, "What duties we perceive—and even what dilemmas—may depend upon what virtues shape our vision of the world."[44] We see the world differently, depending on how we have been formed by the virtues that constitute our character. C. S. Lewis captures this point well in *The Magician's Nephew*, book 6 of *The Chronicles of Narnia*. The creation of Narnia by Aslan looks and feels very different for wicked Uncle Andrew than it does for the children. While the children find Narnia alluring and understand the words spoken by the animals, Uncle Andrew shrinks back in fear and hears only barking and howling. Because of his evil character, he is blind to what the children see and misconstrues both Aslan the creator and what is created. As the narrator comments, "For what you see and hear depends a good deal on where you are standing; it also depends on what sort of person you are."[45]

43. See, for example, Philip Cafaro, "Thoreau, Leopold, and Carson: Toward an Environmental Virtue Ethic," *Environmental Ethics* 23, no. 1 (Spring 2001): 3–17; Philip Cafaro, "A Virtue Ethics Approach to Aldo Leopold's Land Ethic," *Environmental Ethics* 19, no. 1 (Spring 1997): 53–67; Philip Cafaro, "The Naturalist's Virtues," *Philosophy in the Contemporary World* 8, no. 2 (Fall–Winter 2001): 85–99; Kathleen Dean Moore, "The Truth of the Barnacles: Rachel Carson and the Moral Significance of Wonder," *Environmental Ethics* 27, no. 3 (Fall 2005): 265–77.

44. Gilbert Meilaender, "Virtue in Contemporary Religious Thought," in *Virtue—Public and Private*, ed. Richard John Neuhaus (Grand Rapids: Eerdmans, 1986), 9.

45. C. S. Lewis, *The Magician's Nephew* (New York: Macmillan, 1978), 125.

In summary, a virtue is a story-shaped, praiseworthy character trait formed by practices over time that disposes us to act in certain ways. It is a habitual disposition to act with excellence, molded by the narrative(s) we identify with and in which we dwell. We know what is truly good and how to live well by soaking in certain narratives of particular communities, with their corresponding practices, and by looking to people of virtue as role models.

Ecological Virtue Ethics

In the last three decades, significant work has been done on ecological virtue ethics. It began with Thomas Hill's pivotal 1983 essay "Ideals of Human Character and Preserving Natural Environments."[46] In this essay Hill describes a new neighbor who destroys his bushes and trees and paves over his flourishing yard with asphalt. Hill asks: What kind of person would do something like that? And his answer is: Only someone whose character is malformed, someone who lacks the proper virtues. Hill goes on to argue that such a focus on character is sorely needed in contemporary environmental ethics.

With subsequent work by Bill Shaw, Geoffrey Frasz, Ronald Sandler, and Philip Cafaro, to name only a few of the principal contributors, the field of environmental virtue ethics is now well established. Evidence for this includes the publication of anthologies such as *Environmental Virtue Ethics,*[47] by Sandler and Cafaro, and monographs such as *Character and Environment: A Virtue-Oriented Approach to Environmental Ethics,*[48] by Sandler. One sign that the field has developed its own identity is that it now has its own acronym—EVE.

The contributors to the new field of EVE develop and explicate various virtues. For example, Geoffrey Frasz speaks of benevolence as an environmental virtue.[49] This virtue is the active and consistent concern for the flourishing

46. Thomas Hill, "Ideals of Human Character and Preserving Natural Environments," *Environmental Ethics* 5 (1983): 211–24.

47. Ronald Sandler and Philip Cafaro, eds., *Environmental Virtue Ethics* (Lanham, MD: Rowman & Littlefield, 2005).

48. Ronald Sandler, *Character and Environment: A Virtue-Oriented Approach to Environmental Ethics* (New York: Columbia University Press, 2007).

49. Geoffrey Frasz, "Benevolence as an Environmental Virtue," in Sandler and Cafaro, *Environmental Virtue Ethics,* chap. 8.

of both humans and nonhumans. The expansion of the sphere of concern to include whole species and particular places, large ecosystems and local watersheds is what distinguishes benevolence as an environmental virtue from benevolence as such. Following Aldo Leopold, Frasz expands the concept of community to include nonhuman entities, both living and nonliving. He also argues that the environmental virtue of benevolence implies the related virtues of proper humility, patience, and perseverance, as well as the character traits of imagination and attentiveness.

On his list of environmental virtues, Philip Cafaro lists care, patience, persistence, self-control, humility, respect, and self-restraint.[50] Along with these moral virtues, Cafaro also lists intellectual virtues such as attentiveness and wonder, aesthetic virtues such as appreciation and creativity, physical virtues such as stamina and hardiness, and what he calls "overarching virtues" such as wisdom and humility.

In one of the few explicitly Christian forays into EVE, Louke van Wensveen speaks of care and compassion as ecological virtues.[51] In a more recent essay she develops a set of ecological virtues she calls "virtues of care," which include humility, friendship, attentiveness, benevolence, and love.[52] These "cardinal environmental virtues" sensitize us to the needs of all creatures—human and nonhuman—and thus widen the scope of what counts morally.

A more recent effort to develop a Christian environmental virtue ethic comes from Kathryn Blanchard and Kevin O'Brien.[53] They articulate an explicitly Christian approach based on the seven cardinal virtues of prudence, courage, temperance, justice, faith, hope, and love. Each of these virtues is paired with a particular contemporary challenge, for example, prudence with

50. Cafaro, "The Naturalist's Virtues," 85–99.

51. Louke van Wensveen, "The Emergence of Ecological Virtue Language," in Sandler and Cafaro, *Environmental Virtue Ethics*, chap. 1. This is adapted from chap. 1 of her book *Dirty Virtues: The Emergence of Ecological Virtue Ethics* (Amherst, NY: Humanity Books, 2000). See also Celia Deane-Drummond, "Environmental Justice and the Economy: A Christian Theologian's View," *Ecotheology* 11, no. 3 (2006): 294–310; Michael Northcott, *The Environment and Christian Ethics* (Cambridge: Cambridge University Press, 1996), 314–16.

52. Louke van Wensveen, "Cardinal Environmental Virtues: A Neurobiological Perspective," in Sandler and Cafaro, *Environmental Virtue Ethics*, chap. 11.

53. Kathryn Blanchard and Kevin O'Brien, *An Introduction to Christian Environmentalism: Ecology, Virtue, and Ethics* (Waco, TX: Baylor University Press, 2014).

species extinction, temperance with food insecurity, faith with climate change. Their treatment of ecological virtue ethics from a Christian point of view is a creative contribution to this important area of study.

In my book *For the Beauty of the Earth*, I set forth fourteen ecological virtues, for example, respect and receptivity, self-restraint and frugality, humility and honesty, wisdom and hope, patience and serenity, benevolence and love, justice and courage.[54] These are crucial dispositions if we are to properly care for the world in which we live, especially in these times.[55] This is not the place to rehearse all those virtues and vices, but let me merely illustrate this approach with one pair of virtues: wonder and humility.[56]

Wonderings about Wonder

When it comes to literature on wonder and the natural world, the first name that comes to mind for many people is Rachel Carson. Though best known for her last and most famous book, *Silent Spring*, published in 1962, Carson wrote many other books, including *A Sense of Wonder*. Originally published under the title *Help Your Child to Wonder*, this slim volume, as the original title suggests, is designed to help parents foster wonder among their children. Reflecting on her interactions with her nephew, Carson comments:

> A child's world is fresh and new and beautiful, full of wonder and excitement. It is our misfortune that for most of us that clear-eyed vision, that true instinct for what is beautiful and awe-inspiring, is dimmed and even lost before we reach adulthood. If I had influence with the good fairy who is supposed to preside over the christening of all children, I should ask that her gift to each child in the world be a sense of wonder so indestructible that it would last throughout life, as an unfailing antidote against the

54. Bouma-Prediger, *For the Beauty of the Earth*, chap. 6.

55. For more on this, see Steve Bouma-Prediger, "Eschatology Shapes Ethics: New Creation and Christian Ecological Virtue Ethics," in *Rooted and Grounded: Essays on Land and Christian Discipleship*, ed. Ryan Harker and Janeen Bertsche Johnson (Eugene, OR: Pickwick, 2016), 144–54.

56. This is from my book *Earthkeeping and Character: Exploring a Christian Ecological Virtue Ethic* (Grand Rapids, MI: Baker Academic, 2020).

> boredom and disenchantments of later years, the sterile preoccupation with things that are artificial, the alienation from the sources of strength.[57]

So, wonder is the antidote to boredom and disenchantment, the contrary to what is sterile and artificial. Continuing on, Carson observes: "I sincerely believe that for the child, and for the parent seeking to guide him, it is not half so important to know as to feel. If facts are seeds that later produce knowledge and wisdom, then the emotions and the impressions of the senses are the fertile soil in which the seeds must grow. . . . Once the emotions have been aroused—a sense of the beautiful, the excitement of the new and the unknown, a feeling of sympathy, pity, admiration or love—then we wish for knowledge about the object of our emotional response."[58] Wonder has to do with a sense of the beautiful, an excitement for the novel and unknown, a feeling of sympathy and admiration and even love for the object of one's attention.

So what exactly is wonder? "Wonder," as a noun, is anything that causes astonishment. A wonder is some event or place or thing that evokes amazed admiration. "It's a wonder you weren't killed," we may say after a miraculous escape from a dangerous automobile accident. Or "Iguazu Falls is one of the wonders of the world," we exclaim after visiting this spectacular series of waterfalls on the border of Argentina and Brazil. As a verb, "wonder" denotes a state of amazement or astonishment evoked by that which is beyond what we expect or think possible. As in "She wondered at the virtuosity of the musicians" or "He marveled at how effortlessly the dolphins swam and frolicked together." Wonder is rapt attention in the presence of something awesomely mysterious or new to our experience. Hence wonder often includes a sense of surprise: "She was amazed at how many seeds came out of that small sequoia cone."

This is all well and good, you may be saying, but is wonder really a virtue? Is wonder not an ability given at birth and thus not in need of cultivation over time? If so, then wonder is not a virtue but what Aristotle calls a "faculty" given "by nature."[59] While it is true that wonder seems to be an innate capability given at birth and particularly present in children of a certain age, wonder is also a disposition cultivated by practice over time. It is this adult disposition

57. Rachel Carson, *A Sense of Wonder* (New York: Harper & Row, 1965), 42–43.

58. Carson, *A Sense of Wonder*, 45.

59. Aristotle, *Nicomachean Ethics* 2.5.1105b.20–25.

of attentiveness and awareness to what is new and beyond one's expectations that I refer to when speaking of wonder. In short, the virtue of wonder is the cultivated capacity to be astonished.

Without using the language of virtue, Rachel Carson nevertheless assumes that wonder is a virtue. For example, she observes that "exploring nature with your child is largely a matter of becoming receptive to what lies around you. It is learning again to use your eyes, ears, nostrils and finger tips, opening up the disused channels of sensory impression."[60] How do we become more receptive? How do we learn again to open up our senses? Carson offers specific advice on how to proceed. She notes how a hand lens or magnifying glass can bring a new world into sight, how powerful the sense of smell is in evoking long-lost memories, and how touch is a potent if too-little-used sense. And she more than hints at the need to cultivate our abilities to perceive the world around us when, for example, she says, "Hearing can be a source of even more exquisite pleasure but it requires conscious cultivation."[61] As any novice birder painfully knows, it takes time and practice to learn to distinguish and identify bird calls. The point is that "conscious cultivation" is the language of virtue.

Annie Dillard also has her eye on wonder as a virtue. Her award-winning book *Pilgrim at Tinker Creek* is, among other things, a treasure trove of musings on wonder. For example, after she happens upon the sight of a mockingbird making a steep vertical descent, only at the last second to land upright on the grass, she writes, "Beauty and grace are performed whether or not we will or sense them. The least we can do is try to be there."[62] So, she remarks, "I'm always on the lookout for antlion traps in sandy soil, monarch pupae near milkweed, skipper larvae in locust leaves," and so understanding one's surroundings is "a matter of keeping eyes open,"[63] of taking care to notice small things like cone flowers and field mice. But there's more to it: Dillard makes a concerted effort not just to see, but to alter the way she sees. Usually "I see what I expect,"[64] she muses ruefully. So she attempts to open her eyes to the possibilities of beauty and intricacy around her. Trying to be there with eyes

60. Carson, *A Sense of Wonder*, 52.

61. Carson, *A Sense of Wonder*, 68.

62. Annie Dillard, *Pilgrim at Tinker Creek* (New York: Harper Perennial Modern Classics, 2007), 10.

63. Dillard, *Pilgrim at Tinker Creek*, 19.

64. Dillard, *Pilgrim at Tinker Creek*, 20.

open and always being on the lookout is Dillard's shorthand for the virtue of wonder. This requires attentiveness and diligence, both necessary to develop the capacity for wonder.[65]

These ruminations prompt further reflection on wonder as a character trait. What kind of person seeks out and is able to perceive the amazing inhabitants and astonishing places in this world of wonders? And how is wonder related to humility? What exactly is humility, and is it a necessary condition for the cultivation of wonder? Let us turn to a discussion of wonder's close cousin.

Musings on Humility

"I'm humble and proud of it." So goes the one-liner about humility. Being humble is not something about which you can be proud, lest you run afoul of what philosophers call a performative self-contradiction: the very claim to be proud of your humility proves that you are not, in fact, humble. But what exactly is humility, and is pride its corresponding vice?

It seems that Aristotle was not big on humility. Like most Athenian men of his status in his time, he believed that pride was a virtue. Great men (and it was only males) who are worthy of great things can and should be proud. That is, they should exhibit a justifiable self-respect and self-esteem based on the honor due them. Great men who do great things merit honor and thus justifiably exhibit pride. Indeed, pride "seems to be a sort of crown of the virtues."[66] However, Aristotle's views are more nuanced than this, for he acknowledges that pride, to be proper, must be commensurate with greatness. That is, pride must be proportionate to accomplishments. In his words, "the proud man . . . claims what is in accordance with his merits."[67] So, according to Aristotle, there are two vices correlative to the virtue of pride. The person who "thinks himself worthy of great things, being unworthy of them, is vain," while the person "who thinks himself worthy of less than he is really worthy of is unduly humble."[68] Vanity is inordinate or unjustified self-esteem while undue humility

65. Dillard observes, however, that although the secret of seeing "comes to those who wait for it, it is always, even to the most practiced and adept, a gift and a total surprise." *Pilgrim at Tinker Creek*, 35.

66. Aristotle, *Nicomachean Ethics* 4.3.1124a.1.

67. Aristotle, *Nicomachean Ethics* 4.3.1123b.13–14.

68. Aristotle, *Nicomachean Ethics* 4.3.1123b.8–10.

is insufficient or unjustifiably low self-esteem. So for Aristotle, proper pride is the mean between the extremes of vanity and undue humility.

For the desert fathers and mothers in the early centuries of the church, humility was the foundation of the spiritual life. To Abba Anthony, who began living in the Egyptian desert in AD 285, humility was the antidote to the snares of the devil.[69] Abba Poeman compares humility to the air we breathe, that without which we cannot survive: "As the breath which comes out of his nostrils, so does a man need humility and the fear of God."[70] Augustine, as is well known, found pride to be the primal sin, and thus humility the preeminent virtue.[71] For him humility was having a proper sense of one's creatureliness and brokenness, and thus dependence on God. Benedict of Nursia devotes the longest chapter of his influential *Rule of St. Benedict* to humility and thereby lays the foundation for centuries of monastic life centered around humility, which is, in sum, acknowledging that we are not gods but sinful creatures. Following in Benedict's footsteps, the great twelfth-century French mystic and abbot Bernard of Clairvaux wrote a whole book on humility, *The Steps of Humility and Pride,* in which humility is defined as that "virtue by which man has a low opinion of himself because he knows himself well."[72]

Medieval theologian Thomas Aquinas very carefully takes the insights of Aristotle and reframes them in light of the Christian faith. Aquinas describes humility as the virtue that "temper[s] and restrain[s] the mind, lest it tend to high things immoderately." Humility prevents us from becoming conceited or self-important. According to Aquinas, a humble person "restrain[s] himself from being borne toward that which is above him" since "he must know his disproportion to that which surpasses his capacity."[73] Humility is the habitual disposition that prevents us from thinking we are worthy of something we are not. Hence the vice of deficiency, contrary to humility, is pride. Those lacking in humility exhibit arrogance based on an inflated and false sense of self.

But Aquinas, like Aristotle, warns against another vice—the vice of excess—namely, self-deprecation. In this case, a person fails to recognize and

69. *Sayings of the Desert Fathers* (Kalamazoo, MI: Cistercian Publications, 1975), 2.

70. *Sayings,* 173.

71. See, e.g., Augustine, *City of God* 19.

72. Bernard of Clairvaux, *The Steps of Humility and Pride* (Kalamazoo, MI: Cistercian Publications, 1980), 30.

73. Thomas Aquinas, *Summa Theologiae* II-II, q. 161.

accept his or her proper worth. This is the vice Aristotle names undue humility. This vice was clearly exemplified for me when I complimented a college student of mine who had won a national championship in swimming, only to have her respond with "It's no big deal." Instead of owning her accomplishment, she downplayed this significant achievement. I was expecting her to say something like "Thank you. This is a big deal. I worked long and hard to achieve this goal, and I am grateful to my coach, to my teammates, and to God for the opportunity to swim at this elite level." In short, self-flagellation is not a virtue. Humility is not to be confused with low self-worth.[74] To gain even greater understanding of wonder and humility, let's take a brief look at the Bible.

Biblical Insight into Wonder and Humility

Many biblical texts come to mind when thinking of wonder, for example, Psalms 104 and 148, but one perhaps not often mentioned is the book of Job. Recall the story. Deprived of wealth, posterity, and health, Job refuses to follow his wife's advice that he curse God and die. He is, he insists, a blameless man. He does not curse God, but he does curse the day of his birth. He laments. And then his friends—Eliphaz, Bildad, and Zophar—come to offer consolation. They sit with him in silence for a week, and then they offer their own explanations for why he is suffering. Divine discipline for sin. Retribution for the wrongdoings of his children. Punishment for past iniquity. Job responds to these third-rate theodicies, attacking his interlocutors' presumption to speak for God and his inscrutable way with the world. Job reaffirms his innocence and (again) voices his lament. Finally, he lodges his own complaint directly with God: I'm innocent, he says. I am a just and blameless man.

74. In either form—arrogance or self-deprecation—the vices contrary to humility share a common preoccupation with the self. Being constantly focused on oneself, even in terms of self-judgment, promotes the notion that the self is of the upmost importance—more important than God or the rest of creation. Lisa Gerber identifies such self-absorption as the underlying malady, regardless of whether it results in arrogance or self-criticism. In contrast, the truly humble person honestly assesses his or her own abilities and acknowledges both accomplishments and limitations, but without the self-centeredness of either arrogance or self-deprecation. See Lisa Gerber, "Standing Humbly before Nature," *Ethics and the Environment* 7, no. 1 (2002): 39–53.

Often overlooked in this tale of human misfortune is the very end of the story. Here are some slices from the last few chapters.[75]

> At long last, God addresses Job. Speaking from a whirlwind, with an onslaught of questions piled one on the other, God responds to Job's lament and his complaint. But God's response is strange and seemingly not to the point. God's first response is all about cosmology and meteorology and hydrology and animal husbandry and ornithology.
>
> First, earth and sky. "Where were you, Job, when I laid the foundation of the earth? Who was it, Job, who marked the boundaries of the sea? Have you, Job, commanded the morning to come? Were you around, O Job, when the primordial waters were fixed in place? Have you journeyed to the underworld or traveled the expanse of the earth? Did you separate light from darkness? And what about the weather? Do you, Job, know where the snow and hail are stored? Have you knowledge of where lightning comes from or whence the east wind roars? And what, O Job, of the rain? Have you brought it to the desert? Do you provide water to the wasteland? Is it you who begets the ice and frost and snow? Have you, Job, placed the Pleiades in the sky, or fixed Orion and the Great Bear in their celestial circuit?"
>
> Then, animals and birds. "Can you, Job, provide food for the hungry lion? Do you provide for the raven its prey? Do you, Job, know when the wild mountain goats give birth or the wild deer have their young? Is it you, O Job, who let the wild ass go free or made the ox forever wild? And what of the ostrich? Was it your design that it leave its eggs on the earth and deal cruelly with its young? Was it according to your wisdom, Job, that the hawk soar south or the vulture suck the blood of the slain?"
>
> After this cascade of questions, God demands an answer: "Anyone who argues with God must respond." Job has publicly reproached God, and now God awaits his answer. Job simply states, "I am small." And so he places his hand over his mouth. Having spoken once, of things he claimed to know but really did not, he will not make the same mistake twice. He has forcibly been shown the limits of his knowledge and power. And so after declaring that he would approach God "like a prince," Job engages in an act of self-humiliation. He now knows his place, and it is not at the center of things.

75. This translation is from Bouma-Prediger, *For the Beauty of the Earth*, 93–96.

While much could be said about this fascinating text, especially about the enigmatic creatures Behemoth and Leviathan, one main point is germane for our purposes here: we live in a world of wonders, and one of our tasks (and privileges) is to nurture the ability to appreciate such wonders.[76] This text prods us to a disciplined attentiveness in order to cultivate a capacity to wonder. Before he is commanded to act, Job is asked to behold and appreciate—even that which is repugnant and dangerous. Carol Newsom's observation is apropos: "There are probably not many ethics courses in colleges or seminaries that spend the first three days in silence—one day in the forest, one day at the shore of the sea, and one night in a field gazing at the stars. Yet something like that is what God requires of Job as the starting point for a new moral understanding."[77] Conduct flows from character, actions from basic attitudes. This text nudges us to cultivate certain virtues such as wonder (and humility)—precisely the kinds of habitual dispositions required of those called by God to be earthkeepers.

What, then, is the virtue of wonder? The virtue of wonder is the settled disposition to stand in rapt attention and amazement in the presence of something awe-inspiring, mysterious, or new. People who exhibit this virtue have the cultivated capability to stand in grateful amazement at what God has made and is remaking. Those full of wonder never lose their childlike ability to see and appreciate and be amazed by features of the world often invisible to the rest of us.

The vice of deficiency is hard to name, but we know it when we see it. It is the inability to perceive and be amazed by the wonders of the world. Taking Aristotle's cue, I call it insensibility. To be insensible is to lack proper sensory perception and emotional response, sometimes bordering on indifference. Aristotle describes something similar when he speaks of the vice of deficiency with respect to the virtue of temperance or self-control. "People who fall short with regard to pleasures and delight in them less than they should," Aristotle declares, "are hardly found, for such insensibility is not human." He continues: "If there is anyone who finds nothing pleasant and nothing more attractive

76. From the song "World of Wonders" by Bruce Cockburn, on the album *World of Wonders*, High Romance Music, 1985.

77. Carol Newsom, "Job," in *New Interpreter's Bible: A Commentary in Twelve Volumes*, ed. Leander Keck et al. (Nashville: Abingdon, 2005), 4:626.

than anything else, he must be something quite different from a man; this sort of person has not received a name because he hardly occurs."[78] While that may have been true in ancient Greece, it is, sadly, not true in twenty-first-century America. The virtue of wonder is, alas, often in short supply.

The vice of excess is also difficult to name but nevertheless real. This person is always in awe, and about the most trivial or unamazing things. Even when the circumstances are, by the most agreed-upon standards, anything but wonder evoking, this person is amazed. He has yet to meet a person, experience an event, or encounter a place that isn't "awesome." Absent a better label, I call this vice hyperastonishment. It is the disposition toward indiscriminate amazement. Similar to self-indulgence, Aristotle's term for the vice of excess with respect to the virtue of temperance, this vice overdoes it when it comes to wonder. Those who exhibit this vice live in a perpetual state of astonishment, but in a way that cheapens or falsifies true wonder.

What insight does Scripture provide about humility? While many passages speak of humility, for example, Psalm 90 and Proverbs 1:7, let's look again at the end of the book of Job. As indicated above, the deluge of questions asked by God about cosmology and hydrology and meteorology and zoology pounds into Job's head that he isn't as smart as he thinks he is. Job has not commanded the morning or entered the storehouses of the snow or provided prey for the ravens. He does not know when the mountain goats give birth or who lets the wild asses go free. That the hawk soars and the eagle mounts up is not Job's doing. Job is forcibly reminded of his finitude. Job's power and knowledge are finite. He is a creature. As with Job, so also with us: we are undeniably finite, and thus have good reason to be humble.

It might seem that this rather obvious point needs no special attention. However, we have a penchant for forgetting this central feature of our existence. Indeed, we have a deep desire to avoid looking our finitude, especially our temporal finitude or mortality, straight in the face.[79] To acknowledge the limited nature of our existence produces anxiety and raises the question of whether death is the end of life or whether there is Someone who is sufficiently

78. Aristotle, *Nicomachean Ethics* 3.10.1119a.5–10.

79. For a powerful and insightful analysis of the human tendency to deny mortality and in so doing create and perpetuate evil, see Ernest Becker, *Denial of Death* (New York: Macmillan, 1973) and *Escape from Evil* (New York: Macmillan, 1975).

able and willing to preserve our life beyond biological death and in whom we can rest in spite of our anxiety.[80]

The book of Job is not the only place in the Bible that speaks of human finitude. As indicated previously, the narrative in Genesis 2 tells us that the human creature is formed out of the ground and made alive by God's life-giving breath (v. 7). We are *'adâm*—earth creature—because we are clumps of earth—*'adâmâh*—animated by the Spirit of God. And lest we forget, the text reminds us that "to dust [we] shall return" (3:19). We, like all of God's creatures, are finite. Even Psalm 8, which speaks of humans as having been created a little lower than God (or angels) and crowned with glory and honor, reminds us that we are creatures and hence finite. We have a God-given dignity and calling, but we are nevertheless limited. Only God is infinite. Only God is the one whose name is majestic in all the earth, and thus worthy of praise.

But we are not just finite; we are faulted. Though often confused, these two are not the same. Finitude is a good feature of human existence. It is simply how God made us—a feature of our humanity to accept joyfully. Faultedness, however, is not God's intention. The brokenness we know in ourselves, and the effects of which we see all around us, is something we acknowledge with regret and seek with God's grace to overcome.

This feature of human existence is also powerfully depicted in the Genesis narrative. In chapter 3 we learn that Adam and Eve desire to transcend their creaturely finitude and become, like God, omniscient. But in this attempt they fail to trust in God and thus become estranged. Their relationship with God is broken. They become estranged from each other (they attempt to pass the blame). They lose touch with their own true and best self (they hide and conceal their actions). And they become out of joint with the earth (working the earth becomes burdensome). In these four ways they and we are alienated. In short, our lives are interwoven with a contagion called sin, which we knowingly and unknowingly perpetuate. The Bible confirms what we know in our hearts: the world is not the way it is supposed to be.[81]

In these and many other biblical texts we find these theological motifs

80. Perhaps the classic presentation of this question is Leo Tolstoy's short story "The Death of Ivan Ilych."

81. Two books that illuminate the phenomenon of sin very clearly are Ted Peters, *Sin: Radical Evil in Soul and Society* (Grand Rapids: Eerdmans, 1995), and Neal Plantinga, *Not the Way It's Supposed to Be: A Breviary of Sin* (Grand Rapids: Eerdmans, 1995).

of human finitude and human faultedness. We are finite—limited in power and knowledge as well as space and time. We are humans from the humus. We are not God. And we are faulted—alienated from God, other humans, ourselves, and the earth. Though we are not God, we all too often think and act as if we were. From these theological motifs comes the ethical principle of responsibility. Given the limitations of our knowledge and power, we must be circumspect and exercise forethought, and given our stubborn unwillingness to admit such limitations, we must be unflinchingly honest and aware of our veiled self-seeking.

Given these biblical insights, what is the virtue of humility? Humility is the disposition to properly estimate one's abilities or capacities. It is the fitting acknowledgment that we humans are earth creatures. The virtue of humility thus implies self-knowledge and knowing the limits of one's knowledge. Aware of their ignorance, humble folk do not pretend to know more than they really know. Aware of their brokenness, humble people do not pretend to be perfect.

The vice of deficiency is hubris—exaggerated self-confidence or overweening pride. Hubris is the failure to acknowledge one's own limits, often resulting in tragic consequences for all concerned, as famously evident in the plays of Euripides and Shakespeare. Overestimating their abilities, prideful people are vain and boastful. Thinking themselves in control, they make foolish decisions that wreak havoc for themselves and for others.

The vice of excess is self-deprecation. People who display this vice play down their abilities and speak disparagingly of their legitimate achievements. They are unable to acknowledge their actual gifts and abilities or they refuse to properly assess their genuine strengths. As we have seen, Aristotle speaks of those who disclaim or belittle their authentic accomplishments as exhibiting undue humility or mock modesty.[82]

82. As I argue in *For the Beauty of the Earth*, chap. 6, with the recognition of our finitude and faultedness, and an acknowledgment of the corresponding ethical principle of responsibility, comes not only the virtue of humility but the virtue of honesty. Honesty is the disposition to tell the truth. It is the refusal to deceive or be duplicitous. Ecological honesty brings with it this kind of transparency. With respect to the earth, there is no need for cover-ups or slush funds or secrets. Ecological honesty promotes telling the truth. The two vices are deception (vice of deficiency) and false honesty (vice of excess).

Ecological Wonder and Humility

With this background, let's focus more precisely on how and why the virtues of wonder and humility are *ecological* virtues.[83] For Ronald Sandler, wonder is an ecological virtue because it is one of the habitual dispositions required for human excellence and flourishing. Following the human excellence approach of generating ecological virtues, Sandler lists wonder as one of his "virtues of communion with nature." The other eco-virtues in that category are openness, aesthetic sensibility, attentiveness, and love.[84] With reference to Rachel Carson, Sandler argues that "wonder is a gateway to love, gratitude, appreciation, and care for that which is found wonderful," and thus wonder is "environmentally informed, environmentally responsive, and environmentally productive."[85] Sandler also includes humility on his list of ecological virtues, in the category of "virtues of sustainability."[86] Indeed, ecological humility is crucial for Sandler, especially given what he calls the modern Western penchant to control and dominate, found, for example, in the case of genetically modified crops. Sandler argues that "humility in our environmental and agricultural practices is justified because it is more conducive to promoting and preserving goods necessary for and conducive to human and environmental flourishing."[87]

Philip Cafaro employs the human exemplar approach to generate his list of ecological virtues. He looks to Henry David Thoreau and Rachel Carson, among others, to find the dispositions needed to enable us to care for the world. Thoreau embodies many of the traits associated with wonder, for example, curiosity, imagination, alertness, sensibility to beauty, while Carson exemplifies humility, among other things. Indeed, Cafaro argues that humility is one of the most central ecological virtues since it inspires the cultivation of other ecological virtues.[88] A properly humble understanding of our place in the world—individually and collectively as humans—necessarily precludes

83. There are five main approaches for developing a list of explicitly ecological virtues: exemplar, extensionist, agent benefit, human excellence, and means/ends.

84. Sandler, *Character and Environment*, 50.

85. Sandler, *Character and Environment*, 50–51.

86. Sandler, *Character and Environment*, 48–49.

87. Sandler, *Character and Environment*, 134.

88. Cafaro, "The Naturalist's Virtues," 85–99. See also Philip Cafaro, "Thoreau, Leo-

greed, wastefulness, and many other vices stemming from hubris. Put positively, ecological humility sets us on a path toward cultivating other virtues—such as frugality, simplicity, and wisdom—that are essential for becoming responsible earthkeepers.

Geoffrey Frasz develops specifically ecological virtues, for example, benevolence, by using the extensionist approach.[89] Applying that approach in this case, he extends the interhuman virtues of wonder and humility to other-than-human ethics to generate ecological virtues that are not fundamentally different from the virtues as such but simply include more than the human world in their purview. The scope of what counts morally or the sphere of moral concern is extended such that wonder and humility now include more than only the human.

Each of these approaches, in my view, has its merits. Some ecological virtues emerge when clarifying the human dispositions required for creational flourishing. Some are evident when describing the moral exemplars among us. And some eco-virtues are identified simply by extending the scope of what counts morally to nonhuman creatures. In all three approaches, wonder and humility appear, only further cementing the centrality of these ecological virtues as virtues that include the whole *oikos*—all of God's good earth.

Thus, building on my previous definition, the virtue of ecological wonder is the settled disposition to stand in rapt attention and enthralled amazement in the presence of the awe-inspiring natural world—its inhabitants and habitats, landscapes and ecosystems. This ecological virtue names the capability of grateful amazement at the world of wonders God has made, sustains, and is remaking. The ecologically wonder-full have the ability to see and be amazed by features of the natural world: the astounding vastness of the Grand Canyon and the quiet closeness of a dense forest trail, the breathtaking beauty of a giant sequoia and the remarkable biochemistry of a pitcher plant, the seemingly harsh world of red-tailed hawks eating black squirrels and the apparently intimate world of nursing seal pups.

The vice of deficiency, as indicated above, is ecological insensibility. This names the inability to be amazed by the wonders of the world. No night sky,

---

pold, and Carson: Toward an Environmental Virtue Ethic," chap. 2 in Sandler and Cafaro, *Environmental Virtue Ethics*.

89. Frasz, "Benevolence as an Environmental Virtue."

however beautiful, can move the insensible person to slack-jawed wonder. No orchid display, no dancing sandhill crane, no acrobatic dusky dolphin can bring this person to marvel and be amazed. To the insensible, the world is flat, uniform, monochrome. The acids of modernity or the suspicions of postmodernity have drained all wonder, and the ability to wonder, from those who exhibit this vice.

The vice of excess is hyperastonishment. This person is always in awe about everything. Granted, we live in a world of wonders that we all too often do not perceive or acknowledge, and the normalcy of the mundane is OK. Are we to be amazed always about everything? Indeed, actually being in a state of perpetual amazement is hard to envision, let alone promote. And to be honest, all of life is not "awesome." Are there not circumstances in which wonder is not appropriate? Is wonder the proper response to leaching landfills or saturating smog? How do we cultivate and express amazement, but in a way that does not falsify true wonder?

What then of ecological humility? The virtue of ecological humility is the settled disposition to act in such way that we know our place and fit harmoniously into it, whether our local community, our bioregion, or our home planet. Eco-humility is the disposition to act as the earth creatures we are—finite, embodied, embedded. If we are ecologically humble, we have an accurate estimation of our abilities and capacities (for good and ill) and thus act in ways that neither overplay nor undervalue our worth. This requires not only self-knowledge and knowledge of the world in which we live, but also awareness of the limits of our knowledge. We frankly acknowledge our limited ability to know the future consequences of our actions, and we have an honest awareness of our penchant for self-deception. Hence we act cautiously. Before making decisions, we survey as many consequences as possible. This implies neither having a God's-eye view of things nor an unrealistic expectation of perfection, but it does mean exploring alternatives, seeking out blind spots, and considering worst-case scenarios.

The vices corresponding to ecological humility are ecological arrogance and ecological self-deprecation. The ecologically arrogant always assume they know best. Ecological hubris puts humans at the center of the universe, cocky and confident. Hence, despite the manifest evidence of both unforeseen and unintended consequences, the ecologically arrogant go too fast and cut corners. Thinking they know everything, they ignore opposing points of view.

Always in a hurry, they do not exercise caution or go slow. And the natural world, of which we humans are an integral part, suffers.

Ecological self-deprecation diminishes the role of humans as earthkeepers on the earth. Those who exhibit this vice undervalue the important place of humans as responsible agents of change for the good. They fail to see how humans have a legitimate and significant role to play—cooperating with nature righteously and caring for nature sensitively, to use Santmire's terms. They sometimes talk as if the world would be better off without us—that humans are a virus, a plague, a scourge upon the earth.[90]

Following the cue from Philip Cafaro and the human exemplar approach, let me briefly give an example of someone who embodied both ecological wonder and ecological humility. In the mid-1920s, a young US Forest Service ranger, newly assigned to the Gila National Forest in New Mexico, was on patrol with his coworkers. Eating lunch high up on the edge of a river valley, they spotted what they thought, from a distance, was a female deer fording the river down below. When the animal emerged on the other side, they realized it was not a doe but a wolf. Our friend writes: "A half-dozen others, evidently grown pups, sprang from the willows and all joined in a welcoming melee of wagging tails and playful maulings. What was literally a pile of wolves writhed and tumbled in the center of an open flat at the foot of our rimrock." He continues: "In those days we had never heard of passing up a chance to kill a wolf. In a second we were pumping lead into the pack, but with more excitement than accuracy: how to aim a steep downhill shot is always confusing. When our rifles were empty, the old wolf was down, and a pup was dragging a leg into the impassible slide-rocks."[91]

And so begins the story told by Aldo Leopold in the essay "Thinking like a Mountain," from his seminal work *A Sand County Almanac and Sketches Here and There.* As he indicates, wolves were then known as dangerous predators of the deer that hunters prized, and so Leopold and company shot at the wolves unthinkingly, hitting one adult and a pup. Excited and impressed with themselves, the group hurried down to the river to examine their target. In now famous prose, Leopold describes his experience of watching the adult wolf die:

90. See, e.g., the Voluntary Human Extinction Movement.

91. Aldo Leopold, *A Sand County Almanac and Sketches Here and There* (New York: Oxford University Press, 1949), 129–30.

"We reached the old wolf in time to watch a fierce green fire dying in her eyes. I realized then, and have known ever since, that there was something new to me in those eyes—something known only to her and to the mountain. I was young then, and full of trigger-itch; I thought that because fewer wolves meant more deer, that no wolves would mean hunters' paradise. But after seeing the green fire die, I sensed that neither the wolf nor the mountain agreed with such a view."[92]

Wonder and humility, lament and remorse, a recognition of error and a resolution that things must change.

As a professor at the University of Wisconsin in Madison, Leopold would go on to found the field of wildlife management, write the very first textbook on "game management," teach and mentor countless students and future leaders, work to change state laws and federal regulations, and begin his own experiment in land restoration at his famous "Shack."[93] Writing some thirty years or so later in his *magnum opus*, Leopold reflects on this pivotal experience of shooting and killing the wolf:

> Since then I have lived to see state after state extirpate its wolves. I have watched the face of many a newly wolfless mountain, and seen the south-facing slopes wrinkle with a maze of new deer trails. I have seen every edible bush and seedling browsed, first to anaemic desuetude, and then to death. I have seen every edible tree defoliated to the height of a saddlehorn. Such a mountain looks as if someone had given God a new pruning shears, and forbidden Him all other exercise. In the end the starved bones of the hoped-for deer herd, dead of its own too-much, bleach with the bones of the dead sage, or molder under the high-lined junipers.
>
> I now suspect that just as a deer herd lived in mortal fear of its wolves, so does a mountain live in mortal fear of its deer. And perhaps with better cause, for while a buck pulled down by wolves can be replaced in two or three years, a range pulled down by too many deer may fail of replacement in as many decades.

92. Leopold, *Sand County Almanac*, 130.

93. For more on the life and legacy of Leopold, see the fine work of Curt Meine, *Aldo Leopold: His Life and Work* (Madison: University of Wisconsin Press, 2010).

> So also with cows. The cowman who cleans his range of wolves does not realize that he is taking over the wolf's job of trimming the herd to fit the range. He has not learned to think like a mountain. Hence we have dustbowls, and rivers washing the future into the sea.[94]

Amazed and humbled, Leopold learned to "think like a mountain." We today need to learn to think ecologically, with greater foresight, with more knowledge of and respect for the earth and its many creatures. In short, to be better earthkeepers, we need to cultivate the ecological virtues of wonder and humility.

Conclusion

The day was picture perfect. A brilliant sun was shimmying up a clear blue sky, birds were singing to their hearts' content, and the temperature was in the low fifties. My group of hikers—five Hope College students and one other instructor on a ten-day canoeing and backpacking expedition in the Adirondacks of upstate New York, as part of a May Term course called "Ecological Theology and Ethics"—broke camp and hit the trail toward our evening's destination. Later that day, as we rounded the bend in the rocky trail, we could not believe what met our eyes. The campsite by the trail was trashed. Litter was everywhere. Half-burned wood from the fire ring was strewn hither and yon. Large pieces of metal, hard to recognize, were leaning up against an old log lean-to that was thoroughly inscribed with knife carvings. Birch trees were stripped of their bark all the way around. After a long silence, one of my students uttered the words in my mind: "What kind of person would do something like this?" What kind of person would trash such a beautiful place? With this heartfelt exclamation, my student gave voice to the cry of my own heart. And she unintentionally gave voice to the underlying insight of ecological virtue ethics—a focus on character. What character traits would allow someone to trash this or any place? What vices so blind us to the beauty and the integrity of the natural world that we can treat our nonhuman neighbors with such disrespect and carelessness?

A different day, some years later, was also picture perfect. A brilliant sun was shimmying up a clear blue sky, birds were singing to their hearts' content,

94. Leopold, *Sand County Almanac*, 130–32.

and the temperature was in the low fifties. My group of hikers—another band of Hope College students and my longtime fellow instructor on this May Term course called "Ecological Theology and Ethics"—broke camp and hit the trail toward our evening's destination. Late in the day, after many miles on the rocky trail, we rounded the bend and could not believe what met our eyes. The campsite by the trail was absolutely beautiful. There was no litter in sight. A stack of firewood was neatly placed next to a small fire ring. The old log lean-to was in tip-top condition. Tall white pines provided a protective canopy overhead. After a long silence, one of my students uttered the words percolating in my own mind: what a lovely spot to camp and what respectful, humble, loving people must have cared for this place over many years. With this heartfelt affirmation, this student also gave voice to the fundamental intuition of ecological virtue ethics: character is crucial in doing ethics. What character traits shaped the people who have treated this place with respect and care? What virtues enlighten us to see the beauty and integrity and God-given goodness of our home planet so that we are compelled by gratitude to care for the earth?

We humans are called to be earthkeepers. Each of us in our own humble and wonder-full way are to be keepers of what God has given us on the earth we inhabit with so many of our fellow creatures. May we be so inspired, from both our explorations of the natural world and our readings of Holy Scripture, that we become people of virtue—full of wonder and humility, wisdom and courage, faith and hope and love—who gratefully care for this precious and beautiful gift we call Earth.

Responses

From Richard Bauckham

The four essays in this volume seem to me to offer, to a large extent, complementary perspectives rather than exclusive alternatives. Steven Bouma-Prediger's study of ecological virtues is a distinctive and welcome contribution to ecological theology that can sit happily alongside any of the other three essays. I am particularly struck by the way that this emphasis on virtue ethics contrasts with Cynthia Moe-Lobeda's liberationist approach, with its emphasis on action against structural injustice. Different as they are, I think the two approaches can be helpfully complementary.

But before turning to the main focus of Bouma-Prediger's essay—ecological virtues—I feel obliged, as an exegete, to engage with his exegesis of Genesis 2 in his third section ("The Case for Earthkeeping"). (I did not have space in my own essay to discuss the Genesis 2 creation narrative.) While I agree broadly with Bouma-Prediger that, both in Genesis 1 and in Genesis 2, humans are portrayed as both unique among other animals and having much in common with them, there are two specific points at which I disagree with his exegesis of Genesis 2. In both cases he follows an exegetical trend among interpreters, but one that I think is demonstrably wrong.

Referring to the story of Adam naming the animals (Gen. 2:18–19), Bouma-Prediger says that naming "indicates a kind of authority." Commentators have often claimed that in the cultural world of the Old Testament, naming was an act of authority, but the evidence for this is quite inadequate, as George W. Ramsey has shown.[95] There are three cases in which kings bestow a new name on subjects (Gen. 41:45; 2 Kings 23:34; 24:17), but this is scarcely a basis for

95. George W. Ramsey, "Is Name-Giving an Act of Domination in Genesis 2:23 and Elsewhere?" *Catholic Biblical Quarterly* 50 (1988): 24–35.

supposing that naming was generally an act of authority. In the context of Genesis 3, if naming the animals were an indication of Adam's authority over them, then we should have to say that his naming of Eve is similarly an act of authority (Gen. 2:23; 3:20). It would be better to see naming as an act of recognition. Adam's naming the animals is comparable to the naming of children by parents (usually, in the Old Testament, the mother), which does not assert authority but recognizes the independent reality of a new person. Insofar as a name is appropriate, as in Old Testament cases it is often seen to be, naming could be considered an act of discernment. When modern scientists discover a previously unknown species and name it, they are not asserting authority over it but are giving it a recognized place in the world as humans perceive it. Adam, we might say, was the first taxonomist.

The second point at which I must take issue with Bouma-Prediger's exegesis concerns Genesis 2:15, which says that Adam was put in the garden God had planted "to till (*avad*) it and keep (*shamar*) it." Since this statement follows the description of the rivers of Eden (2:10–14), which associate it with Mesopotamia, where the rivers themselves were not sufficient to make most of the land fertile, Adam's task is probably to irrigate the land in order to sustain the trees God has planted there. Later he is sent to perform the same task outside Eden: "to till the ground from which he was taken" (3:23). The man from the soil must work the soil in order to live from the soil's produce. The task is probably much the same as that intended by the command to "subdue the land" in 1:28 (which, in my view, refers to agriculture), but here there is a stronger sense of humanity's close relationship with the soil. There is also, in the word "keep" or "preserve," the implication that Adam takes care of the soil. He avoids exhausting it.

Bouma-Prediger follows some recent interpreters in translating the two verbs as "serve" (*avad*) and "protect" (*shamar*).[96] This seems to be the textual basis for his use of the term "earthkeeping." Linking this verse to the "dominion" of Genesis 1:26–27, he deduces that "dominion must be defined in terms of service." It is true that the verb *avad*, when used with a personal object, means "to serve," but there is a consistent usage of the verb to mean "to work" or "to cultivate" when the object is inanimate (Gen. 3:23; 4:12; Deut. 28:39; Isa. 19:9; cf. Prov. 12:11; 28:19; Zech. 13:5). This is the obvious meaning in Genesis 2:15. The meanings of words depend on their contexts. I think it is a basic mistake

96. This interpretation is also adopted in Cynthia Moe-Lobeda's essay.

to understand Genesis 2:15 as a general definition of the human vocation in the world. It refers specifically to the practice of agriculture, which is primarily the way that humans make a living for themselves from the soil. Even the orchard of Eden did not yield its fruit to Adam without his having to work for it.

However, that section of his essay is merely preparatory to Bouma-Prediger's substantial study of ecological virtues, in which he outlines the nature of virtue ethics and focuses especially on wonder and humility as illustrative examples. I find his discussions persuasive and will limit my comments to a few ideas about how these lines of thought might be extended.

Given the importance of science and technology in our human relationship to the rest of God's creation, we could usefully think about wonder and humility as scientific virtues. Scientists often speak about feeling awe and humility in the face of what they discover—from the unimaginably distant galaxies to the equally unimaginable subatomic world. These feelings are not simply the "naïve" reactions of the vast majority of people who respond to the natural world as it presents itself to their senses. They are also the responses of those who study the natural world in the most rigorous way, with the most advanced techniques, and building on the work of many thousands of other researchers. But the need for the cultivation of these responses as scientific virtues is apparent because others value science and technology solely as means of increasing human power over nature so that we can remake it into a humanized world adapted to our needs and desires. The modern scientific-technological project has been characterized by hubris rather than humility and by a purely instrumental attitude to nature. In this tradition superstitious respect for nature (what we might otherwise call wonder) was an obstacle to making the best use of nature for human benefit.

How do we become "the kind of people" who treat the natural world with respect and care (to echo Boumer-Prediger's conclusion)? I think we should pay more attention to the fact that according to Scripture the virtues come from God. Paul calls the virtues "the fruit of the Spirit" (Gal. 5:22). James, in a different theological idiom, calls them "the wisdom from above" (James 3:17). They are the work of God in human life. In this connection, it is worth pointing out the biblical meaning of the word "holy," a word that features in the first section of Boumer-Prediger's essay, with its source in the work of Wendell Berry. Berry writes that "we are holy creatures living among other holy creatures in a world that is holy." "Holy" here does not mean "virtuous." Berry uses it in its biblical sense of "belonging to God" or "dedicated to God." We and other creatures and the world are holy because we and they belong to God. Holy people, "saints" (a term that in the New Testament applies to all believers), are holy because they are dedicated to God. Virtues are a necessary but secondary matter. They are the work of God in the person truly dedicated to God.

From Cynthia Moe-Lobeda

Steven Bouma-Prediger cogently and concisely articulates the case for replacing stewardship language and conceptual frames with "earthkeeping." With grace and detail he recounts the biblical grounding for earthkeeping as integral to the essence of human being as created by God. We are, he asserts, created as earthkeepers.

These moves are the background for his main point: that in order to be earthkeepers, we need to emphasize character as well as conduct. That is, earthkeeping requires attention to virtues and virtue ethics as well as to the duties and consequences addressed by deontological and teleological ethics. What we do depends upon who we are. Who we are, he goes on to argue, is shaped in significant part by the stories with which we identify, in which we see ourselves as players. Thus, what we do—including what we do in relationship to the earth and its elements and creatures—is shaped by "narratively formed character." Narratives shape character in part by bidding us engage certain practices of life, while these practices continue to shape our being and hence our doing. In sum, "We know what is truly good and how to live well by soaking in certain narratives of particular communities, with their corresponding practices." In making this argument, he draws on other ethicists' articulation of the character-forming power of narrative and practices, including Stanley Hauerwas, Alasdair MacIntyre, and James Smith.

What, then, Bouma-Prediger queries, are the narratively formed virtues that enable the human to be earthkeeper? In response, he credits the three decades of work ethicists, including himself, have done to develop ecological virtues and then focuses on two ecological virtues developed in his own volume on ecological virtues—wonder and humility. In elaborating these two virtues, he describes how practicing them enables earthkeeping and shapes us toward ever more earthkeeping.

I value tremendously the appeal to ecological virtues, and I agree that narrative plays a powerful role in shaping moral being—who we are and are becoming—and therefore in shaping what we do. (I agree also with his point that practices and the virtues we embody in them over time shape how we see the world. He could go further to note ways in which how we see the world shapes what we do.)

Here I build on this valuation of virtue ethics by pointing to two dangers in it. My intent is not to devalue ecological virtue ethics. Rather, my purpose is to implore that virtue ethics (including ecological virtue ethics) account for the social structural factors that limit virtues' power to shape moral doing.

First: Virtue Ethics as Necessary but Not Sufficient

Virtue ethics (including ecological virtue ethics), while necessary, is not sufficient to meet the call to earthkeeping because virtue ethics does not account for the social structural factors that (1) limit the impact of individual virtue, (2) limit the formation of individual virtue, and (3) act as moral players in other ways. Said differently, virtue ethics alone does not adequately address the power of societies (and other metasocial structures) as moral actors. Nor does virtue ethics account adequately for structural sin.[97]

To help illustrate this point consider the following story:

> I am reminded of a Cherokee tradition in which a wise elder narrates a story to the tribe's young people about a fierce battle between two wolves that live inside him. One wolf, clever and proud, is known for its greed, hate, envy, and violence. The other, strong and courageous, is known for its grace, love, peace, and humility. As the Cherokee elder describes the frequent and mounting tension between the two wolves, an excited boy implores him, "Please tell us which wolf will win!" "The one who will win," the elder replies, "is the one I feed."[98]

97. The following story and the two paragraphs succeeding it are drawn from my book *Resisting Structural Evil: Love as Ecological-Economic Vocation* (Minneapolis: Fortress, 2013).

98. Patrick Howell, "Lent Challenges Us to Make Positive Choices," *Seattle Times*, March 14, 2009.

This story holds rich truth. A principle of ethics is that we become what we do. What we "practice" shapes what we value, how we see the world, and our sense of what is right and good. The habits of everyday life—one's "lifestyle"—over time "feed" one wolf or the other. The wolf that is nourished better is the one that grows. In Bouma-Prediger's terms, character is "formed by practices over time that disposes us to act in certain ways."[99]

Yet, in the context of structural sin or structural violence, the story of the wolf also harbors a lie. Even people morally shaped by narrative and habit to practice the ecological virtues of wonder and humility are limited in capacity for earthkeeping if those virtues are not joined by a commitment to recognize and counter social structures that breed ecological destruction.

One might grow in ecological virtue in personal life (feed the good wolf) while continuing in paths of ecological destruction (sin) for a confluence of systemic reasons. I might practice wonder and humility and other ecological virtues while continuing to participate—knowingly or not—in systemic activity the collective impact of which is threatening Earth's climate, waters, air, and soil. For example, while practicing wonder and humility, I may continue to eat food produced by industrial agriculture. Granted, additional ecological virtues such as self-restraint and frugality might decrease the power of industrial agriculture by leading me to eat lower on the food chain, organically, and locally. Yet, in many contexts, social structures limit the practice of these virtues. I may live in a food desert, be too economically marginalized to afford local organic food, or work so many hours at low-paying jobs that I cannot afford the time to purchase it. Lack of public transit may make it nearly impossible to access organic local food distribution sites if I have no car or inadequate funds for its upkeep and gas. That is, an infrastructure of systemic factors may trap me into ways of eating, housing, clothing, and transporting my family that betray the ecological virtues. Or, to offer a second example, I may practice ecological virtues of wonder and humility and yet work for a company that—while greening its campus—is producing greenhouse gases at uncurtailed and untenable rates while trading carbon rights on the global market.

The point is this: while indeed practicing ecological virtues as individuals is crucial, it is not adequate. Many people do practice and cultivate these virtues, and countless more could do so *without applying them to the social systems of*

99. Bouma-Prediger applies to virtues what I here extend to character.

which they are integral players and through which they damage God's good creation. A pivotal question becomes: What would it mean to apply the ecological virtues to our lives as players in social systems, and how do we become the people capable of moving those systems toward the ecological virtues that we treasure in our private lives? How do we form ourselves and others into people who seek to shape the social systems that have life-or-death impact on millions of people and on Earth's health so that these systems align with the ecological virtues? To illustrate: this would include forming will and skill in the many arts of social change that will transform food systems from industrial agriculture heavy on meat consumption and chemical inputs to local and regionally based sustainable agriculture.

If practicing ecological virtues is crucial but not sufficient for earthkeeping, what is needed? Virtue ethics as a pathway to earthkeeping must be complemented by (1) steadfast commitment to ecological citizenship that aims at changing the economic, political, and cultural systems that shape society in earth-degrading ways, and (2) development of basic skills for ecological citizenship: skills in public policy formation, ecological and economic literacy, community organizing, economic advocacy, public protest, and more.

Second: Unacknowledged Morally Formative Narratives

I find compelling the argument that behavior is shaped by character and character is shaped by the stories in which we situate ourselves. The implication is that Christian communities may shape and reshape our people through reinterpretation of the faith stories. We will, for example, reread dominion, as does Richard Bauckham in his essay, from meaning dominance to implying caring for and serving the earth community. We will reread to see the earth as beloved and valued by God for its own sake, rather than as merely a stage on which the great God-human drama takes place.

Yet, for such rereading of faith stories to bear moral power requires acknowledging the other narratives—in addition to faith stories—that powerfully shape earth-human relations. For even if Christians change the story from humans as dominators to humans as earthkeepers, other narratives shape our actual practices as players in social systems. Many of those stories are unnamed and unacknowledged by the people living them. They include the narratives that feed our consumption orgy and especially our petroleum consumption orgy. They include narratives that equate human worth with buying power and equate economic growth with progress. Renarrating our faith stories to cultivate humans as earthkeepers and earth as beloved is a necessary ingredient of reshaping human life along lines that the earth can sustain. It must be joined by naming and refuting the other powerful narratives fiercely seducing us to live as players in those stories rather than as players in God's story.

In short, I value and endorse the two question with which Bouma-Prediger initiates his main point: If earthkeeping is integral to Christian faith, then what are the character traits of holy creatures living among other holy creatures in a world that is holy? How do we become people who embody ecological virtues? I believe that ecological virtues and retelling the faith narratives are truly essential. Yet I implore Christians also to recognize that personal ecological virtues are one of two hands in the earthkeeping life. The other hand is social structural change to reshape society toward earthkeeping. With this second hand we seek change in political and economic structures and seek freedom from cultural narratives that breed ecological destruction and lure us from God's story.

From John F. Haught

During the past two centuries science has discovered that the universe is still coming into being. Although the cosmos and the earth may seem quite old from a purely human perspective, when we view the natural world through the eyes of scientific cosmology, we cannot avoid the thought that our planet and the rest of nature are far from the end of their journey in time and space. What, then, is the appropriate motivation for Christian ecological ethics if the universe is still emerging and the natural world—including the story of life on our own planet—is far from being finalized? It is this question that my own chapter in this volume tries to address. It is still the main question I have after reading Steven's learned essay on the importance of virtue ethics in responding to our current ecological predicament.

With Steven I fully agree that the formation of a certain kind of "character" sculpted by the practice of specific virtues is indispensable to a genuinely Christian theological and moral response to our current ecological crisis. I very much appreciate his nuanced contributions to this volume. I agree also that the consistent practice of Christian ecological responsibility calls for a rich refinement of human character in accordance with the cultivation of all the virtues Steven lists. I do not disagree with his approach but simply want to add—and emphasize—that in my theological opinion the fundamental character-shaping virtue for Christian ecological ethics is *hope.*

By this I mean that the kind of moral character implicit in the Abrahamic vision is one in which the authentic life of discipleship, as represented, for example, by the figure of Mary in Luke's Gospel, consists of the habitual anticipation that God's promises *will* be fulfilled. I believe that prior to the formation of character on the basis of specific virtues—Aristotelian or otherwise—Christian thought requires that we first open our thoughts, hearts, and lives to the Abrahamic prospect that something really big is coming from up ahead—not just from "up above." In my own contribution to this volume, I have provided a sketch of how an anticipatory hope, combined with a scientifically informed awareness that our cosmos is not static but dramatic, allows us to appreciate the value of life in a new way, one that was unavailable until after Darwin and Einstein.

Theological justification for our caring for nature has usually consisted of two distinct approaches. The first is a text-based perspective that scans biblical and other authoritative writings of our Christian tradition in search of wisdom and imperatives that might recharge our ethical life with a fresh concern for the "integrity of creation." This approach takes for granted that Christian respect for nature has generally been lukewarm and sometimes altogether absent, ever since the beginning of Christian history. It assumes, nonetheless, that the Scriptures and classic Christian writings are resourceful enough to nourish the greening of our theological ethics. Ecological concern, in this text-based approach, is usually satisfied morally with *preserving* terrestrial life-systems that it assumes God's creativity has brought about in the beginning, and later on, by way of natural processes, including biological evolution. Steven has made use of the classic text-based approach in his thoughtful essay in search of a Christian foundation for ecological responsibility.

A second approach, quite distinct from the first, seeks to ground ecological responsibility in a *sacramental* vision of reality. It relies less on Scripture and classic theological writings and more on an intuition that the natural world is itself revelatory of the divine. Accordingly, human desecration of nature amounts to a blunting of our sense of the God who speaks to us not only through the "word" but also through the "world." The sacramental approach, traditionally more Catholic than Protestant, is epitomized in Thomas Berry's declaration that if we lose nature we lose God.[100] The sacramental way of grounding ecological responsibility attracts the attention also of some feminist ecological theologians and ethicists.[101] This approach corresponds to the analogical reading of nature that I discuss as one of three alternatives in my principal essay in this book. Protestant theologians, I should add, have often been wary of a purely sacramental perspective because of what they perceive to be its possibly idolatrous, pantheistic, and naturalistic tendencies.

I have proposed, for this volume, an alternative to the two approaches just sketched. It is based both on the biblical theme of hope and on our new scientific awareness that the universe is still coming into being. While not opposed to the two approaches just mentioned, my intention is to ground a Christian ecological vision primarily in an "anticipatory" reading of the universe, according to which the universe has in store presently unpredictable outcomes in the future. This futurist approach is consistent not only with recent scientific discoveries of an unfinished universe but also with an Abrahamic, promissory vision of reality.

In addition to Steven's axiological approach, my anticipatory way of reading the natural world corresponds closely to Teilhard's cosmic vision.[102] The latter's version of the anticipatory worldview is summed up in his implicitly metaphysical suggestion that our still-aborning universe "rests on the future" as its ultimate foundation.[103] The "metaphysics of the future" that I have endorsed in my writings on science, theology, and ecology has also been influenced at least indirectly by the writings of other thinkers, including Wolfhart Pannenberg, Karl Rahner, and Jürgen Moltmann. But it is mostly due to the influence of Teilhard that I have developed the anticipatory understanding of our unfinished universe that I am relying upon here. Consequently, I would ask Steven whether an anticipatory worldview and the biblical theme of promise

100. Thomas Berry, *The Dream of the Earth* (San Francisco: Sierra Club Books, 1988), 11.

101. For example, Sallie McFague, *The Body of God* (Minneapolis: Fortress, 1993).

102. See especially Pierre Teilhard de Chardin, *The Human Phenomenon*, trans. Sarah Appleton-Weber (Portland, OR: Sussex Academic Press, 1999) and *Writings in Time of War*, trans. René Hague (New York: Harper & Row, 1968).

103. Pierre Teilhard de Chardin, *Activation of Energy*, trans. René Hague (New York: Harcourt Brace Jovanovich, 1971), 239.

might not give a distinctively biblical accent to the shaping of both the virtue and the kind of character essential to an ecological morality.

As a scientific framework for this proposal, I have observed that once we accept the undeniable fact of an unfinished universe, everything in theology looks different from before, including, not least, our ideas of God. In addition, of course, the meaning of human life, the significance of Christ, the scope of redemption, the role of the Holy Spirit, the importance of church community—all these and many other theological themes take on a fresh meaning once we reflect deeply, and in a spirit of Christian hope, on the fact that the universe is still coming into being.[104] Taking this brief summary as background, then, I would adjoin my anticipatory approach to Steven's method of grounding Christian ethics.

In the Bible, to have "faith" means to become skilled in the habit of looking hopefully into the events in our personal and communal lives for the promise that lies within them—even when it seems that everything has come to a dead end. It is our indomitable hope for the future, it seems to me, that differentiates Christian moral motivation from that of Plato, Aristotle, Epicurus, Schopenhauer, Nietzsche, Camus, Sartre, Mill, Hume, Rawls, and most other philosophers. The new wave of hope that swept across much of the ancient world with the birth of Christianity, and that has flickered on and off for twenty centuries, should have some bearing now on how we deal with the destiny of nature. If Christian character could be shaped these days more by Abrahamic expectation than by such ideals as Platonic deliverance, Stoic resignation, Aristotelian moderation, or the various philosophical sources that underlie contemporary virtue ethics, would it not make a vital difference in how we understand and exercise our moral responsibility with regard to what the Bible takes to be God's creation?

The scientific discovery that the universe is an ongoing story allows theology to assimilate not just the history of humanity but also the whole of nature to a biblical vision of hope. Accordingly, I have proposed—in keeping with a Pauline vision of a universe coming to fulfillment in Christ—that an anticipatory outlook may help us cultivate an appropriate spiritual and ethical relationship to the natural world here and now. What obliges us to treasure

104. For a fuller treatment, see my book *Resting on the Future: Catholic Theology for an Unfinished Universe* (New York: Bloomsbury, 2015).

the beauties and riches of nature, in that case, is not simply their sacramental participation in an eternal present but their being installments of a future yet to come. Each person, each life, and each distinct being, when viewed from an anticipatory perspective, is also an advance disclosure of glories yet to come.

From the point of view of Christian faith, the promise residing in each present instance of cosmic becoming gives us a reason not only for treasuring and preserving the natural world but also for *preparing* God's creation to receive the promise of enhanced being and beauty in a new and open future culminating in new creation. Hope for the fulfillment of the promises of God is at the basis of all Christian theology and ethics, and hope for this fulfillment can rightly be called the fundamental ecological virtue as well.[105] Christian faith is epitomized in the eucharistic prayer: "We hope to enjoy forever the vision of Your Glory." And the vision of present natural beauty provides us with an irreplaceable introduction to the future promised us. The natural world, in its lavish and gratuitous profusion of diversity, is an installment of the extravagant future fulfillment toward which faith perceives all of life and the whole cosmic story to be summoned by God.

105. This point is made explicitly in a pastoral letter of the American Catholic bishops, *Renewing the Earth*: http://www.usccb.org/issues-and-action/human-life-and-dignity/environment/renewing-the-earth.cfm.

4 ~ The Unfinished Sacrament of Creation

Christian Faith and the Promise of Nature

John F. Haught

> At the end, we will find ourselves face-to-face with the infinite beauty of God (1 Cor 13:12), and be able to read with admiration and happiness the mystery of the universe, which with us will share an unending plenitude.
>
> —Pope Francis, Encyclical Letter *Laudato Si'*, #243

All over the earth, and especially in the most impoverished lands, sources of fresh water are drying up, forests are being cut down, topsoil is washing away, and deserts are spreading. Earth's atmosphere and oceans continue their decline into unprecedented impurity, the planet's climate is undergoing dramatic transformation, and species are disappearing at an alarming rate. Widespread warfare, patterns of excessive consumption, and increasing human numbers are adding to the stress we humans have already been placing on the life systems of our global home.

It is not hard to approach this ecological decline in a spirit of despair, or at least indifference. Countless people today are even expressing political hostility to those who make it their mission to awaken us to the fact that something has gone deeply wrong with our relationship to the natural world. Others, if they are religiously motivated, may take refuge in the assumption that the natural world was never made to last indefinitely anyway. They may consider religious faith primarily a matter of preparing our souls for a better home beyond our terrestrial quarters. Consequently, even today many Christian people and their pastors seem content to ignore ecological issues altogether.

Christian theologians are partly to blame for this indifference. Until recently, generally speaking, we have mostly ignored the natural world. In the

Christian West, theologians long ago handed nature over to scientists and poets, reserving for ourselves concern for the meaning of personal existence, human sexuality, preparing for death, intermingled at times perhaps with concern for social justice. At the beginning of the modern age, unfortunately, Christian theology lost contact with the natural world. Only during the past half century have theologians begun to revive interest in the relationship of faith to science and nature. By and large, however, even these efforts have yet to meet with much success in reshaping ecologically the spirituality of Christians in the world today.

Fortunately, the situation is slowly changing, and the recent encyclical of Pope Francis, *Laudato Si'*, is one among other encouraging signs. Christian theologians have begun reading the Scriptures and scanning their traditions in search of a doctrinally orthodox ecological theology. Some of these inquiries have led to the surprising discovery that spiritual and theological resources for Christian ecological responsibility have been lurking quietly all along in the Bible and traditional writings. Christian theologians are beginning to appreciate the ecological relevance of the biblical accounts of creation, of the theme of stewardship, of the inherent goodness of creation, and they are becoming increasingly alert to the ecological relevance of the religious virtues of humility, compassion, temperance, justice, gratitude, and hope. They are also finding new meaning in spiritualities grounded in the doctrine of God's incarnate presence in the physical world.

Ecologically sensitive theologians are discovering in classic theological writings a wealth of inspirational material previously unnoticed.[1] In this essay, however, I want to ask whether Christian ecological theology has looked earnestly enough into the theological motif that most explicitly differentiates biblical faith from other religious traditions as well as from secular ideologies that strongly influence contemporary Western cultural and intellectual life. I want to revisit here a question that has troubled me ever since I first became aware of the need for a theology of nature that can support a vigorous, intergenerational Christian ecological vision. To be specific, I want to

1. An early example of recent ecological awakening among Protestant theologians was the fine book by Paul Santmire, *The Travail of Nature* (Philadelphia: Fortress, 1985); among Catholics, an early example is the priest and pastor Charles M. Murphy, *At Home on Earth* (New York: Crossroad, 1989).

examine whether Christian attempts to ground ecological morality have not ignored—and even considered irrelevant—the most irreplaceable of all biblical themes, namely, that of hope for the world's future. Without playing down the ecological significance of the renewed interest in ecological theology by some of my fellow Christians, I want to ask whether Christianity's vision of creation as the embodiment of a divine promise is ecologically significant.[2] It strikes me as ironic that our ecological theologies have been dominantly apologetic, text-based, and at times sacramental in their theological style while suppressing the biblical theme that the whole universe, and not just human history, is the expression of a divine promise open to a future in which all of creation is to be renewed.

Technically speaking, to put it more directly, I am convinced that our theologies of nature have yet to draw out the implications of biblical eschatology for shaping an ecological vision and morality. A major reason for this neglect, of course, is that both secular environmentalists and even some Christian theologians have assumed that biblical eschatology's preoccupation with future fulfillment is for the most part ecologically menacing rather than salutary. Secular environmentalists have dismissed Christianity altogether because, to them, Christian hope seems too concerned with life after death than with the well-being of nature here and now.[3] Not only secular environmentalists, however, but also Christian environmentalists have generally avoided grounding their visions of nature in biblical eschatology. The Catholic priest and self-styled "geologian" Thomas Berry, to give a prominent example, has generally ignored the biblical preoccupation with future fulfillment. Berry, a prophetic figure in the ecological movement, has had considerable influence over the past few decades on some Catholic thinkers who fear that if we look too attentively toward the eschatological future, we will distract ourselves from facing up to the present situation of ecological devastation. Berry is not alone in finding it hard to integrate biblical hope into his own sacramental ecological vision and ethics.[4]

2. For more extended treatments of this question, see my books *The Promise of Nature* (New York: Paulist, 1993) and, more recently, *Resting on the Future: Catholic Theology for an Unfinished Universe* (New York: Bloomsbury, 2015), 149–58.

3. For example, John Passmore, *Man's Responsibility for Nature* (New York: Scribner's Sons, 1974), 184.

4. Thomas Berry, *The Dream of the Earth* (San Francisco: Sierra Club Books, 1988); another example is Charlene Spretnak's otherwise helpful book, *States of Grace* (San

Here, however, I want to ask whether a truly Christian ecological theology can profitably overlook the theme of promise that the majority of biblical scholars, especially since the late nineteenth and early twentieth century, have taken to be the most defining characteristic of biblical religion and Jesus's own faith as well as the main feature of early Christian expectation.[5] At first sight, "eschatology," a theological term derived from the Greek word *eschaton* (which literally means "last"), carries meanings that may not immediately motivate present concern for nature and that may even postpone conservation by looking gleefully toward the eventual apocalyptic destruction of the physical universe and the arrival in its place of something completely new. My argument here, however, is that such an impression is the result of a failure to look deeply enough into Christian concern for the world's future.

The term "eschatology" is also problematic, especially since in Christian tradition it has more often than not been defined as theological speculation about what happens to individual personal souls after death. In a wider and more biblical setting, however, eschatology has to do more fundamentally with the Kantian question of "what we may hope for." The prophetic traditions in the Bible, for example, are overwhelmingly concerned with the worldly fulfillment of hope in God's promises. They seek to expose the spiritual sensitivities of their contemporaries to the prospect of a new future not only for the people of God but also for all of human history and, at least in some cases, for the whole of creation.[6] The eschatological discourse of our greatest prophets,

Francisco: Harper & Row, 1991). Earlier, Lynn White Jr., in his essay "The Historical Roots of Our Ecological Crisis," *Science* 155, no. 3767 (March 10, 1967): 1203–7, had already indicted Christianity for interpreting the biblical theme of "dominion" as justification for economic progress and practices that have fouled the environment. As a response, he turns toward Benedictine theology and away from biblical eschatology. For other examples of the general ignoring of eschatology, see the articles by and about Thomas Berry collected in *Cross Currents* 27, nos. 2 and 3 (1988): 178–239.

5. To appreciate the story of this eschatological awakening, I recommend Jürgen Moltmann, *Theology of Hope*, trans. James Leitch (New York: Harper & Row, 1967), and Jürgen Moltmann, *The Experiment Hope*, ed. and trans. M. Douglas Meeks (Philadelphia: Fortress, 1975). Moltmann's theology of hope is deeply influenced by the Marxist philosopher Ernst Bloch's three-volume work *The Principle of Hope*, trans. Neville Plaice, Stephen Plaice, and Paul Knight (Oxford: Basil Blackwell, 1986).

6. See Jürgen Moltmann, *God in Creation*, trans. Margaret Kohl (San Francisco: Harper & Row, 1985).

underneath their sometimes threatening language about divine judgment, was intended to inspire and keep alive the general biblical theme of confidence in a God who makes and keeps promises, a God whose coming is expected to bring with it a new creation of this world and not an outcome having little if any connection with the present cosmic state of affairs.[7]

From the beginning, moreover, Christian faith in the resurrected Christ extends to the fulfillment of the whole of creation.[8] Since such hope lies at the very heart of Christian religion, I have often wondered why ecological theology usually leaves it out of its reflections on faith's implications for the well-being of nature. A genuinely eschatological faith encourages openness to the divine promise of a fulfillment yet to come, but our theologies of nature have failed to take into full account the fact that the universe may still have a future of new creation and "fuller-being" up ahead.[9] Eschatological faith passionately hopes that the coming of the "reign of God" and the sending out of the Holy Spirit will renew the face of the earth. It includes the conviction that God's initial creation (*creatio originalis*) continues even now (*creatio continua*) and that it will reach fulfillment only in the future (*creatio nova*), but Christian theology has yet to make eschatological faith the very heart of an ecological morality.

To realize that the world still has a future and that we have a moral obligation to make room for that future, we need first to become fully aware that over the past two centuries science itself has instructed us that we live in a universe that is still unfinished. The cosmos, as the evolutionary sciences have demon-

7. N. T. Wright, *Surprised by Hope* (San Francisco: HarperOne, 2008).

8. The notion of resurrection, prominent in apocalyptic sources of Christian faith, has unfortunately often been interpreted instead in a way that assumes a radical discontinuity between "this present age" and the "age to come."

9. That the universe has the capacity to bring forth "fuller-being" or "more-being" in the future is a fundamental theme in the works of Pierre Teilhard de Chardin: *Writings in Time of War*, trans. René Hague (New York: Harper & Row, 1968); *The Heart of Matter*, trans. René Hague (New York: Harcourt Brace Jovanovich, 1978); *The Divine Milieu* (New York: Harper & Row, 1962); *Human Energy*, trans. J. M. Cohen (New York: Harcourt Brace Jovanovich, 1962); *The Future of Man*, trans. Norman Denny (New York: Harper & Row, 1964); *How I Believe*, trans. René Hague (New York: Harper & Row, 1969); *Activation of Energy*, trans. René Hague (New York: Harcourt Brace Jovanovich, 1970); *The Human Phenomenon*, trans. Sarah Appleton-Weber (Portland, OR: Sussex Academic Press, 1999).

strated, is still coming into being. This fact changes everything as far as ecological understanding and morality are concerned. It means, at the very least, that our concern for nature must now include a special kind of care that the cosmic story and especially the story of life will have a future that extends far beyond what we can see at present. For all we know, this future will come to expression in modes of being, life, and consciousness whose shape we can barely imagine at present but for whose arrival we are ethically obliged to prepare.

Three Ways of Reading Nature

Making a case for this preparatory, as distinct from merely conservational, care for nature depends on how we read the universe here and now. There is more than one way to do so. It is useful to recall that not long after our religious traditions became literate, some of them began to compare the universe to a book, and since a book can be read at many levels of understanding, so also can the universe. Moreover, since grasping the deeper meaning and truth of any serious book requires a process of personal transformation and maturation in the reader's own life, would not a careful reading of the book of nature require a similar spiritual preparation? Most of our traditional religions have answered affirmatively. To see what's really going on in the universe, the great wisdom traditions have demanded that readers undergo a deeply personal spiritual conversion.[10] Contemporary scientific method, by contrast, requires no such transformation. The only condition for appropriately reading nature is that we learn to practice the objectifying methods of science that rely primarily on mathematical understanding.

Scientific method is a way of looking at things that always abstracts, in one way or another, from the complex ecological web of nature in which we and all other forms of life are entangled. From the perspective of Earth's spiritual traditions, therefore, scientific expertise is not enough to qualify one to read deeply beneath the surface of the natural world.[11] Perhaps, however, the image

10. On the need for personal transformation as a condition for competently "reading" the universe, see E. F. Schumacher, *A Guide for the Perplexed* (New York: Harper Colophon Books, 1978), and Jacob Needleman, *A Sense of the Cosmos* (New York: Dutton, 1976).

11. This is a point that Huston Smith makes in his books *Forgotten Truth: The Primordial Tradition* (New York: Harper & Row, 1976) and *Beyond the Post-Modern Mind* (New York: Crossroad, 1982). Smith's theology of nature, however, falls within the type

of a single book is no longer pictorially expansive enough to capture the enormous narrative breadth of the cosmos as it is now portrayed by contemporary science. At the beginning of the twenty-first century, geology, evolutionary biology, cosmology, and other sciences have now demonstrated that our universe is about 13.8 billion years old. To appreciate its temporal scale, I have found it helpful, both in teaching and writing, to picture the new cosmic story as taking up thirty big books, each 450 pages long, and each page standing for one million years in the overall narrative of the universe.

The story starts off with a "big bang" on page 1 of the first book. Our solar system arrives around the beginning of volume 21—somewhere between 4 and 5 billion years ago. Life on Earth has to wait until the twenty-second volume to begin stirring, and even then it remains very simple—unicellular for the most part—until around the end of volume 29. Then the Cambrian explosion takes place somewhere between 500 to 600 million years ago, bringing with it rapidly accelerating evolutionary developments. Dinosaurs, nevertheless, do not make their appearance until around the middle of volume 30, and a little after page 385 they vanish from Earth. Their disappearance, along with that of other large reptiles, permits mammalian life to begin flourishing at a relatively quickened pace. Human-like ancestors come on to the scene during the last four or five pages of the set, but anatomically modern humans do not arrive until the bottom fifth of the very last page of volume 30. In the last small paragraph of the very last page, reflective thought, ethical aspiration, and religious restlessness finally show up on our planet.

How we treat nature these days, I want to suggest, depends in great measure on how we read this multivolume story.[12] Presently—if I may be permitted to simplify things a bit—there are three main ways of reading the new cosmic story: archaeological, analogical, and anticipatory. Below I define and contrast each of these with the other two, and then I argue that the anticipatory reading can provide the conceptual backbone of a contemporary, eschatologically oriented Christian ecological vision. Although the three readings exist in hybrid versions in the real world, we may distinguish each from the others

---

that I will be referring to as analogical or sacramental, and thus it fails to consider the possibility of an eschatological interpretation of the natural world.

12. I have recently described these ways of reading in considerable detail in my book *Resting on the Future*, cited above.

with some degree of logical clarity. Briefly, the archaeological reading sees that the universe is a long story but finds no meaning in it. The analogical reading looks for meaning in nature but fails to appreciate the story and its length. The anticipatory reading sees the story but insists that an in-depth understanding of it requires our waiting for its meaning (and true value) to emerge. It is in terms of the anticipatory way of reading the cosmic story that I believe Christian theology may lead us now to develop a new approach to ecological spirituality and ethics. Let us look first, however, at the archaeological and analogical visions of nature.

The Archaeological Reading

This is the academically certified materialist way of looking at the natural world. It is a way of reading the universe that, in spite of opposition here and there, still dominates intellectual and academic culture. I call it archaeological because it seeks to account for present phenomena exclusively by burrowing back into the physical world's temporal past with the expectation of arriving at a "fundamental explanation" of all subsequent natural events and outcomes. After looking back as far as it can into the remotest states and physical conditions of the cosmic past, it then seeks to trace the physically causal steps that have led from primordial subatomic simplicity to the complexity of the present world of living and thinking organisms. "Archaeology," as we may call this reading, attempts to make complete sense of present realities by analytically breaking present things down into the cellular, molecular, atomic, and subatomic particulars from which they came. Confusing what is first or "archaic" in the order of time with what is primary or fundamental in the order of being, archaeological naturalism is led to believe that the present web of life on our planet is, in the words of the physical chemist Peter Atkins, really nothing more than past physical simplicity now "masquerading as complexity."[13]

Thus we may also refer to this academically popular worldview as a "metaphysics of the past." It is a worldview according to which living cells, organisms, and brains are at bottom nothing more than past lifeless elements now fleetingly gathered together into elaborate syntheses whose evanescence is

13. Peter W. Atkins, *The 2nd Law: Energy, Chaos, and Form* (New York: Scientific American Books, 1994), 200.

taken as proof of their ontological thinness. According to this metaphysics of the past, states of being that are temporally prior and physically elemental are taken to be equivalent to what is ontologically fundamental. In other words, a lifeless state of primordial subatomic and atomic diffusion is identified, in effect, as the ground state of being. All living and thinking beings, accordingly, are reducible to mere aggregates of subatomic elements that physics alone is equipped to understand.[14] The materialist philosopher David Papineau provides a good illustration of the archaeological reading of nature when he insists that everything that ever happens in the universe can be accounted for only by looking back into a temporally antecedent series of deterministic physical events: "Physics, unlike the other special sciences, is complete, in the sense that all physical events are determined, or have their chances determined, by prior physical events according to physical laws. In other words, we never need to look beyond the realm of the physical in order to identify a set of antecedents which fixes the chances of subsequent physical occurrence. A purely physical specification, plus physical laws, will always suffice to tell us what is physically going to happen, insofar as that can be foretold at all."[15]

Archaeology, by promoting a purely materialist, atomist, and analytical way of understanding nature, assumes uncritically that it is only by tracking chains of physical causes back to the temporal beginnings of the cosmic story that we can arrive at a reliable understanding of living and thinking organisms. In the archaeological reading of nature, life and mind can in principle add up to nothing more than the lifeless stuff from which they came. It is very difficult in this metaphysics, therefore, to understand why we should attribute special value to living and thinking beings, or even to the minds of the materialists like Papineau who attempt to convince us of the absolute truth of their atomistic worldview.

Allow me, nevertheless, to make an important clarification here. From the point of view of scientific method, archaeology is unobjectionable. Atomic analysis and excavation of the cosmic past are entirely appropriate, scientifically speaking. Digging back through many chapters of the cosmic story, and breaking present complexity down into its primordial physical units, is essen-

14. This is the firm belief, for example, of the Duke University philosopher Alex Rosenberg, *The Atheist's Guide to Reality* (New York: Norton, 2011).

15. David Papineau, *Philosophical Naturalism* (Cambridge, MA: Blackwell, 1993), 3.

tial to our understanding of nature. Apart from such exploratory excavations, we would never have discovered that the universe has a narrative makeup and that it is a story still going on. When I use the term "archaeology" in this essay, however, I am referring not to science's justifiable excursions into the cosmic past and its analytical reduction of complex things to their molecular, atomic, and subatomic components. Rather, I am referring to the scientifically unverifiable *belief* that the archaeological, analytical method is the *only* reliable way for the human mind to render present phenomena intelligible. Archaeology, as I use the term here, is a relentlessly materialist or "physicalist" way of reading the universe. It is a scientifically unverifiable and philosophically arbitrary expression of "faith" rather than empirically grounded knowledge. The pure archaeologist, then, is someone who *believes* that physical science's retrieval of the causal past is the only authentic access we have to a true understanding of the universe.

Underlying this archaeological/materialist belief system is an epistemological assumption that only the world that is in principle available to scientific analysis can be said to truly exist. It would seem to follow then that if life is reducible to lifeless elements, and if lifelessness is foundational to everything, there is little if any reason to attribute special value to living beings. And yet, ironically, some of the most blatantly archaeological contemporary scientific thinkers are unequaled in their highly moral promotion of ecological responsibility.[16] This is ironic because archaeology, as I am using the label, amounts to nothing less than what the great Jewish philosopher Hans Jonas has referred to as an "ontology of death." By this he means the intellectually appealing modern belief that nonlife alone has the status of true being and that lifeless matter is the "intelligible *par excellence.*"[17] Since, as the archaeologist reads the universe, only what is nonliving is subject to exact measurement, deadness alone can be thought of as preeminently real and comprehensible. Life, the mysterious quality we commonly attribute to certain complex cellular syntheses of atoms and molecules, is too empirically elusive to be intelligible, and so for the strict archaeologist life is in effect unreal.[18]

16. Here I am thinking especially of E. O. Wilson of Harvard University. See his book *Consilience: The Unity of Knowledge* (New York: Knopf, 1998).

17. Hans Jonas, *The Phenomenon of Life* (New York: Harper & Row, 1966), 9–10.

18. In its most extreme form, this belief goes by the label "eliminative materialism,"

Archaeology, therefore, rules out the possibility that the natural world can have anything more to it than an instrumental or practical value. An archaeological reading of the cosmic story is forced to reject religious claims that the natural world is the creation of God and hence that it has inherent meaning or value. According to archaeological naturalism, the universe amounts to nothing more than a series of physical states with no lasting importance. The universe is not a story of dramatic transformation but merely a series of physical transitions, each no more significant than its predecessors. By denying the existence of any overall meaning to the cosmic story, archaeology implies that the intellectually appropriate response to nature by human beings can only be one of "cosmic pessimism." Cosmic pessimism, by virtue of its logical structure, is compelled to deny that Christianity and other faith traditions that attribute meaning to the universe are anything more than imaginative human concoctions. Furthermore, the archaeological reading of the cosmic story maintains that all present and future states of cosmic history are strictly *determined* by what has happened in the cosmic past, and that what we take to be human freedom has no more basis in fact than our belief in the inherent value of life.[19]

Why is it, then, that so many materialist scientists are passionate environmentalists? There can be no doubt, after all, that many of them are. Think, for example, of Harvard entomologist E. O. Wilson. A strict materialist whose philosophy of nature reduces everything theoretically to lifelessness and mindlessness, Wilson nonetheless has written passionately and eloquently about the urgent need for all of us to love life and care for nature.[20] The Australian philosopher John Passmore, one of many ecologically sensitive archaeological naturalists, goes further than Wilson in expressing his suspicions about religion. He criticizes Christianity in particular for the ecological irresponsibility entailed by its hoping for everlasting life in the "next world." Christian expec-

as in the work of Paul M. Churchland, *The Engine of Reason, the Seat of the Soul: A Philosophical Journey into the Brain* (Cambridge, MA: MIT Press, 1995).

19. For a recent example of how determinism is taken for granted in scientific thinking today, see Stephen Cave, "There's No Such Thing as Free Will, but We're Better Off Believing in It Anyway," *Atlantic*, June 2016, http://www.theatlantic.com/magazine/archive/2016/06/theres-no-such-thing-as-free-will/480750/.

20. Edward O. Wilson, *Biophilia* (Cambridge, MA: Harvard University Press, 1984).

tation, he claims, diminishes our sense of obligation to care for *this* world.[21] By contrast, he argues that a consistent naturalism, the belief that nature is all there is, can alone move us to care for life on Earth. Life is precious, in his way of thinking, precisely because it is so perishable and precarious. By denying the existence of God and any afterlife, archaeological naturalists take for granted that humans are more likely to shoulder responsibility for preserving and nurturing life on Earth than if they allow themselves to be steeped in the hope for personal immortality.[22]

The archaeological dismissal of hope for the next life allegedly frees us to concentrate on the well-being of nature undistracted by concern for the supernatural. Since life was never intended by any deity to exist at all, and since the world is destined for nothingness in the end, at least in the meantime we can be all the more appreciative of living beings because of their fragility. Such an outlook allows us to approach living beings with a degree of delicacy and moral appreciation that biblical creation accounts and classical theology cannot arouse in us. According to this naturalistic reading of nature, we value life in direct proportion to its improbability and perishability. The otherworldly optimism of classical theism, on the other hand, only weakens our ties to nature and accordingly keeps us from caring deeply for the survival of life here and now.

Archaeological naturalists, in short, assume that nature is our only and final home. This belief should be enough, they insist, to make us want to care passionately for our natural habitat. Only by assuming that the natural world available to science is "all that it is, all there ever was, and all there ever will be,"[23] will we truly care for life on planet Earth or undertake serious ecological reform. A sense that the universe is utterly godless, along with an uncompromising conviction that life is accidental, rare, and destined to perish for good at some point in the cosmic future, will make us reverence and care for it rightly.

In their sharp indictment of otherworldly religion, materialist environmentalists are raising concerns that Christian ecological spirituality has yet to address head-on. Nevertheless, before attempting to do so below, I need

21. Passmore, *Man's Responsibility for Nature*, 184.

22. Passmore, *Man's Responsibility for Nature*, 184.

23. See Carl Sagan, *Cosmos* (New York: Ballantine Books, 1985), 1. Also see Charley Hardwick, *Events of Grace: Naturalism, Existentialism, and Theology* (Cambridge: Cambridge University Press, 1996).

to point out that scientific materialists generally fail to notice the extent to which their own understanding of nature theoretically prevents human *subjects* from ever feeling deeply at home in their purely *objectivist* understanding of the natural world. A sense of being at home in nature is a sentiment that most environmentalists take to be ecologically indispensable, but materialist environmentalists such as Wilson and Passmore tacitly subvert their own moral concern for nature and the need for us to feel fully at home in "this world" as soon as they insist that life and mind are ultimately reducible to lifeless and mindless elemental physical units. Their reductive physicalism, moreover, in principle undermines any claim that life has inherent value. By trying to convince us that, upon analysis, life turns out to be *really* nothing more than atomic or subatomic simplicity, they subvert any absolutist moral claims that we should resist nature's irreversible slide down the slopes of entropy toward final dissolution.

In short, archaeological naturalism, after leading our minds back down the corridors of cosmic history to an originally lifeless and valueless realm of physical being, offers no logically unassailable reason why we should resist here and now the chemical transformation our planet is at present undergoing from organic toward increasingly more inorganic states of matter. That is, they cannot tell us convincingly why we should resist the *actual* reduction of life and mind to a final state of absolute death. The early environmentalist Barry Commoner, it is instructive to note, warned us long ago that by reducing life to lifeless matter *in principle*, a purely materialist creed cannot expect to convince us that we should prevent this reduction from taking place *in fact*.[24] Logically speaking, therefore, the archaeological metaphysics of the past cannot provide solid intellectual or moral grounds for a serious ecological ethic for the present. And since it cannot provide a real home in its mindless material universe for human subjectivity and freedom, I must conclude that archaeological naturalism, in spite of the vocal protests of its most ardent defenders, is no less likely than Platonic dualism to promote the ancient Gnostic belief that we humans are "lost in the cosmos."

Recently a handful of scientific naturalists have acknowledged the intellectual weakness and moral heartlessness of materialist metaphysics, but their

24. Barry Commoner, "In Defense of Biology," in *Man and Nature*, ed. Ronald Munson (New York: Dell, 1971), 44.

objection, if we may call it that, has so far failed to penetrate deeply into Western academic and intellectual culture. I am thinking, for example, of Stuart Kaufmann and Terry Deacon, each of whom tries in his own way to liberate the scientific worldview from classical materialism by tackling the mystery of *emergence.*[25] These two scientists, along with a few others, are clearly unhappy about the currently dominant archaeological, materialist worldview that provides the main intellectual environment for the scientific research going on in the world today. Their qualified naturalism offers a less mechanistic and more holistic understanding of nature than is typical of most contemporary scientific thinking. Even these laudatory attempts to soften archaeological materialism, however, do not abandon what I'm calling the metaphysics of the *past.* They are not yet ready to give up altogether the modern archaeological assumption that the explanation of present phenomena can be provided only by going back into the past history of lifeless and mindless matter. Their softer naturalism is aware of the scientifically unpredictable emergent leaps that occur, at least occasionally, in the cosmic story, but they have not yet moved beyond the archaeological propensity to peer only into the cosmic past for adequate understanding of such interesting phenomena. Below I argue instead for an *anticipatory* reading of nature—one in which intelligibility and value can only be encountered by an epistemological stance of turning toward, and *waiting* for, the future. Anticipation, as I call it, is an ecologically favorable alternative to both the archaeological and analogical ways of reading the natural world.

25. By "emergence," I mean the remarkable arrival of new and unpredictable phenomena, such as living and thinking organisms, in natural history, phenomena that cannot arise apart from the introduction into natural history of novel "ordering principles" that are unspecifiable by physical or archaeological analysis alone. See, for example, Stuart A. Kaufmann, *At Home in the Universe* (New York: Oxford University Press, 1995), and Terry Deacon, *Incomplete Nature: How Mind Emerged from Matter* (New York: Norton, 2012). The logical incoherence of materialism has been forcefully, though too briefly, exposed in a recent work by the hitherto lifelong materialist philosopher Thomas Nagel, *Mind and Cosmos: Why the Materialist Neo-Darwinian Conception of Nature Is Almost Certainly False* (New York: Oxford University Press, 2012).

The Analogical Reading

To most Christian theologians even today, however, it seems that the only acceptable metaphysical alternative to materialist archaeology is the classical "metaphysics of the eternal present" that still underlies most theoretical renditions of Christian faith. I refer to this venerable way of reading the natural world as *analogical* and *sacramental.* It locates the "really real" world in a changeless, and presumably perfect and complete, realm of being that radically transcends the natural world. Finite beings, in this reading of nature, are imperfect representations or "analogies" of infinite being. They point to a transcendent sphere immune to all becoming and perishing. "Analogy," as I shall call our second way of reading nature, interprets the physical universe as a set of more or less transparent windows opening onto the eternal presence of God. Lurking in, beyond, behind, or in the depths of nature's constant shifting from one state to another, according to analogy, there exists the permanent, infinite, and absolute being of God.

In spite of new scientific understanding of nature as a gradual, horizontal story of emergence, analogy's "metaphysics of the eternal present" continues to read the natural world nontemporally as a vertical, ascending hierarchy of distinct levels of being in which the degree of value of each level is proportionate to the intensity of its *participation* in the timeless perfection of God. At the lowest level in the hierarchy lies the realm of lifeless "matter," and as the ladder of being ascends from one level to the next—through plants, animals, human beings, angelic spheres, all the way up to God—nature takes on increasing value in proportion to its transparency to the infinite in whose timeless being it shares imperfectly.

This analogical worldview provides the basis for a sacramental vision of nature, for the special hierarchical standing of living and thinking beings, and withal a good reason for reverencing and saving life on Earth. The term "sacrament" in traditional Christian, especially Catholic, theology stands for any thing, event, or person through which the sacred reveals itself. "Sacramentalism," as we may aptly label the analogical reading of nature, interprets the beauty, goodness, and vitality of natural beings as the manifestation or revelation of the timeless being of God in whom all created beings participate. Sunshine, oceans, rivers, waterfalls, winds, storms, breath, clean water, the hardness of rocks, the blooming of plants, the enormity of trees, the dark depth of forests, the expansiveness of deserts, the fertility of soil and sexuality, and (prior to the age of science) the luminosity of the seemingly changeless heavens above—all these natural phenomena, to the sacramental soul, are allurements that point beyond themselves to the infinite and everlasting being, creativity, and beauty of the Creator. To lose nature, then, would be to lose God.[26]

The sacramental quality of the analogical vision, as already noted, consists of the fact that everything finite shares in some way, and to some degree, in the perfection of God. Accordingly, the sacramental vision *should* have the effect of keeping us from looking upon the created order as reducible to past lifelessness or as nothing more than material stuff to be exploited by our narrowly human engineering projects. By looking upon the natural world as sacramental, the analogical reading shields it from being shrunken by our mundane, objectifying, scientific minds and industrial techniques into products corresponding to our insatiable acquisitiveness.[27]

According to the analogical vision, since the world of nature unceasingly participates in its maker's majesty, religious awareness of this connection should be sufficient to foster and justify ecological concern. Sacramentalists value nature precisely because created things are revelatory, to one degree or another, of God's infinite goodness and beauty. It follows then that the archaeological materialist criticism of Christian faith by secular environmentalists as ecologically noxious turns out to be groundless as long as we understand nature sacramentally. Furthermore, the sacramental vision, as compared to archaeological materialism, is much more prepared to face without flinching the prospect of our universe's eventual physical extinction while simultaneously valuing its perishable living treasures. How so? By intuiting the bond between natural phenomena and the eternal order they symbolize, sacramentalism is already prepared to let go of perishable things themselves since their passing makes possible a spiritual and climactic communion of the soul with God, a communion classically idealized, for example, in Saint Bonaventure's *Journey of the Soul into God*.

26. Berry, *The Dream of the Earth*, 11.

27. An excellent, brief example of the sacramental approach to ecological responsibility is the article by Michael J. Himes and Kenneth R. Himes, "The Sacrament of Creation," *Commonweal* 117 (January 1990): 42–49.

The materialist vision according to which "nature is all there is," on the other hand, is completely opaque to any eternal Source of all value. Consequently, archaeology offers nature no protection from the avaricious human instincts that so readily turn created beings into absolutes and thereby allow us to possess and even devastate our immediate environment, Mother Earth, as though she were herself infinitely resourceful. The analogical, sacramental reading of nature, on the other hand, allows us to embrace lovingly the finite beauties of nature not because of their precariousness but because of their participation in, and mediation of, the everlasting goodness and beauty of God. What makes life precious, in other words, is not its fragility or perishability—as archaeological naturalists often maintain—but the fact that life reflects fleetingly a timeless Majesty. By frankly acknowledging the sacramental character of nature, the analogical vision in effect teaches us to tread softly on planet Earth. By respecting nature without absolutizing it, analogy is assuming—as Saint Augustine so famously observed—that each human person is restless for the infinite and that only a final communion with an *inexhaustible* source of all being could ever possibly bring rest and peace to our souls. In principle, such a vision of reality allows us to withdraw our idolatrous demands on nature as we learn to worship only that which is in itself infinite.

To be sure, opening our hearts to the divine, according to analogy, requires of us a degree of detachment from the seductive allure of finite beings, including the evanescent beauties of nature. This detachment, however, is not a hostile, dualistic, world-escaping reactivity to the natural world but a necessary condition of our allowing nature to transport us toward a transcendent goodness and beauty. Only by being detached to a degree from nature can we receive it as a gift for which we can be grateful. Analogically speaking, therefore, the premier ecological virtue is gratitude, since it alone allows us to enjoy finite beings without draining them of their inner substance and thus destroying them. Analogy allows us to feast on the banquet of creation while also constraining our tendencies to possess and crush it. A sacramentally based ecological ethic, therefore, leans upon and learns from the religions of native peoples for whom ownership of land and its resources is foreign to their whole worldview.

To sum up, then, by reading the natural world as sacramentally transparent to the infinite, the analogical vision diverts our attempts to turn creation into material for our own projects. Nature's sacramentality, at least in principle, protects it from diminishment by our objectifying intellectual control and economic intemperance. Since the natural world is at heart a sacramental disclosure of God, it participates in its Maker's majesty and thus merits our continuing reverence. The sacramental vision is implicitly aware that no finite being or set of beings, including the entire physical universe, is immune to the threat of nonbeing. Unlike archaeological naturalism, however, it is justified in valuing things of nature, not for their perishability but for their always imperfect participation in the eternal resourcefulness of God. What gives life value is not its fragility but the intensity of its sharing, however flickeringly, in the eternal life of God. By gratefully acknowledging the finite goodness of nature, the analogical reading sets the world free from having to bear the stressful burden of being infinite itself. From the point of view of analogy, we may conclude that whatever damage humans have inflicted on the natural world is due not to religious faith but to a lack of it.

By reducing life to elemental lifelessness, on the other hand, archaeological naturalism has the inevitable effect of separating Earth's biosphere from any metaphysical horizon that might give us good cause for treasuring and saving it across many generations. When modern thought abandoned the idea of God and, along with it, any possibility of making plausible reference to a transcendent ground of goodness, it did not thereby quench the infinity of human longing. The insatiable thirst for "more" lives on in us as an anthropological constant—all the more achingly after each new acquisition. So the intellectual removal of the horizon of transcendence has left in its wake only an average-sized planet to sop up our endless passion for more. To analogy, then, it is the *loss* of our sacramental connection to the infinite, and not the idea of the infinite as such, that opens nature to our abuse. Reading nature analogically allows us to embrace the infinity of our longing as well as the finitude of the natural world by acknowledging creation's transparency to an infinite Generosity.

The Anticipatory Vision

Sacramentalism's analogical reading of nature is indispensable to any ecological theology that professes to be rooted in Christian tradition. Nevertheless, the analogical reading, while rightly looking for meaning and value in the natural world, fails to see clearly that the universe is still coming into being. Having originated long before the age of science, analogy still dominates religious thought and spirituality all over the world. After Darwin and Einstein, however, educated people now realize that the universe is still emerging and that its narrative unfolding is far from over. Theologically speaking, the universe is still groaning to reveal the divine in indeterminate ways that neither archaeology nor analogy can see or express. It would be a lost opportunity for Christian ecological theology, therefore, not to take into account the dramatic expansion of our sense of nature resulting from scientific discoveries in such fields as geology, biology, and now, especially, cosmology. Prescientific analogical spirituality may continue to inform Christian ecological theology, but it cannot bring out the ecological significance of either the biblical sense of the world's promise or the new scientific understanding of an unfinished universe.

It so happens, however, that during roughly the same recent historical period in which post-Darwinian and post-Einsteinian science has been expanding our sense of time, critical scholarship has been rediscovering the significance of the future in biblical understandings of redemption. Biblical studies have captured anew the early Christian concern for the "coming of God" and the primitive church's sense that the characteristic mode of divine action is that of *coming* (*adventus*) and making creation new again.[28] What I want to add now is that the biblical theme of divine advent and of history's promise may be interwoven tightly into the fabric of our new scientific picture of a universe that is still emerging. Such a synthesis can both enlarge our understanding of the universe and provide a fresh ecological appreciation of the natural world.

Christian expectation of the kingdom of heaven, in other words, may now be seen as confluent with a fresh concern for the future of the whole universe. The biblical promise of future fulfillment, having been central to Hebraic faith for centuries, did not have to be abandoned at the coming of Christ or in his resurrection from the dead. The theme of promise may now become the maternal womb of an ecological theology completely attuned to contemporary cosmology. Jesus's proclamation of the coming reign of God and the promises that accompany it now extend to encompass the horizon of a cosmic future previously unnoticed. Our longing for the coming of God need no longer be separated from hope for the ultimate fulfillment of an unfinished universe.

One of the main difficulties facing any ecological theology based primarily

28. As prominent examples, see the earlier citations of both Jürgen Moltmann and Pierre Teilhard de Chardin.

on an analogical, sacramental reading of nature is that it too easily assumes that the ancient biblical promise of salvation has now been fully realized except for the individual human soul's journey toward sharing in it. Understandably, because of its mostly prescientific reading of the natural world, analogy fails to take fully into account the fact that the universe itself is a continuing journey of ongoing transformation. Instead of facing toward the world's future and patiently awaiting new epochs of cosmic creativity, Christian sacramentalism seeks to transport our minds and hearts abruptly into what seems to be a fully finished sphere of being lying outside, inside, or above the natural world. Rather than anticipating the not-yet of the world's future, and instead of participating in bringing it about, sacramentalism interprets the life of faith as accomplishing little other than the purification of our souls and perhaps the redemption of our individualized bodies. By assuming that everything important has already been accomplished as far as God is concerned, the analogical reading of the world of time looks for no significantly new outcomes in the future story of nature. In that case, human existence too easily becomes a matter of spinning our moral wheels in a divinely designed "soul school" that allows us to develop moral character but one from which we can aspire at most to be released eventually.[29] In the analogical perspective, that is, the new scientific story of an unfinished universe may seem at best to be a mere curiosity. Nature may still be easily interpreted as an obstacle course for the believer's adventurous itinerary into God. The cosmic story now being told by science may even seem, to the strict sacramentalist, to be a distraction from our personal search for meaning.

An anticipatory reading of the universe story, on the other hand, seeks to preserve and expand upon the primitive Christian hope for the advent of God as the fulfillment of all of history, including what we now know to be the long story of nature. A theology of nature informed by the spirit of anticipation will not turn away from, but will instead jump astride, the narrative of a universe still coming into being. Longing for a new future *for,* rather than apart from, the world will then become a very good reason for taking care of Mother Earth here and now. According to anticipation, our expectation of "new creation" is not a reason to postpone, or consider secondary, the task of working right

29. A point that appears often in the writings of Pierre Teilhard de Chardin, for example, in his *Human Energy,* 29, and his *Activation of Energy,* 229–44.

now for the healing of nature. Anticipatory Christian faith will not attempt to leave the natural world behind in a final exodus to the hereafter. Rather, it will feel the promissory winds blowing not only throughout Scripture but also—as we may read the new scientific cosmic story—throughout our entire thirty volumes and any new ones that may be added up ahead in the ongoing adventure of nature's becoming. In this new setting, nature and Scripture may be read together as two layers of a single unfinished narrative.

Christian ecological theology will then celebrate evolutionary science and the new astrophysical and cosmological discoveries by linking the cosmic story tightly to the same divine "word" that hovered over creation in the beginning and that has faithfully breathed the spirit of promise into all things. A scientifically informed theological vision will think of God as creating the world not from out of the past but from out of the future. It may then think of the Holy Spirit as working to renew the entire universe no less today than ever. God's promise to Abraham, moreover, will apply not only to the future of the "people of God" but also, as Saint Paul eventually came to see, to the "whole creation" (Rom. 8:22). The anticipatory reading of nature compels us to move beyond a purely sacramental ecological spirituality and beyond narrowly apologetic reactions to secular critiques of Christianity. To be sure, from a biblical point of view, the human pilgrimage on Earth will still be an exodus journey and a desert wandering, but it will be a journey with, rather than away from, the universe.

An ecologically wholesome Christian faith will, in other words, remain a restless quest. If Jesus has "no place to lay his head," his followers too will keep marching toward Jerusalem without looking back. If so, however, a disturbing question may arise in the souls of some hopeful but nature-loving Christians: How can we hold together the biblical theme of exodus and Jesus's spirituality of homelessness, on the one hand, and the ecological axiom that we will not be motivated to take care of the natural world unless we think of it as our *home*, on the other? How can an anticipatory reading of the universe inspire an ethic that accords with the unanimous sense among seasoned environmentalists that we need to treat our natural environment as our *home* if we are to care for it enthusiastically—an assumption, incidentally, recently endorsed by Pope Francis in his remarkable encyclical *Laudato Si'*? In other words, how can we reconcile the liberating theme of religious homelessness with an ecological ethic built on a sense of our *belonging* fully to nature?

Embracing our religious rootlessness, after all, is a condition of spiritual liberation not only for Jesus but also for significant strands of other major faith traditions such as Judaism, Islam, Hinduism, and Buddhism. All of these, in one way or another, advocate the practice of detachment from worldly things. So the question of reconciling spiritual homelessness, or detachment, with cosmic at-home-ness is important interreligiously and not just within the wide world of Christian reflection on the meaning of salvation. How, then, may we reconcile a spirituality of pilgrimage, or of being on a long spiritual journey, with the ecological imperative to keep our feet firmly planted in Earth's soil? What, if anything, does the ideal of religious homelessness have to do with the ecologically necessary sense of feeling fully at home in nature?

Our new sense of the universe as an ongoing story may help us resolve the paradox. An anticipatory reading of the new cosmic story allows us to read the unfinished status of the physical universe as the foundation of both spiritual searching and ecological responsibility. Becoming fully aware that the universe is still coming into being may allow us, at least in principle, to embrace the venerable imperative of religious homelessness without having to translate it into an ecologically problematic cosmic homelessness. By reading the universe as an unfinished story rather than as an aimless series of physical states (as archaeology assumes), or as nothing more than a set of imperfect sacraments pointing to an eternal present (as analogy sees it), we may come to feel that we belong fully to the natural world without having to sacrifice the sense of being on a homeless and liberating religious pilgrimage.

To do so we must, first, gratefully embrace the scientific discoveries made over the past two hundred years telling us that the *cosmos* itself—billions of years ago—embarked upon a long pilgrimage that even today remains far from over. And, second, we may interpret our own brief life-journeys as an opportunity for grateful participation in the larger adventure of cosmic becoming, a narrative that will continue to go on long after each of us has settled into the dust from which he or she came. An anticipatory theology of nature will align our natural sense of being at home in nature with a simultaneous awareness that the whole universe to which we belong is restless until it rests in God. Our personal religious journeys, in an anticipatory reading of nature, will no longer mean escaping from the physical universe, even in death, but will mean entering ever more deeply into the universe's own journey into the compassionate heart of God. Since our cosmos is still unfinished—and therefore has not yet reached the goal of its own becoming—we can feel closely tied to it only if we link our own life stories *permanently* to the larger cosmic epic that still winds its way toward we know not where. By attaching our fleeting lives tightly to the universe's own fitful wayfaring, we may justifiably feel homeless religiously while remaining ecologically fully at home in the universe.

The cosmos, as we now realize, has been on a pilgrimage of its own for nearly 14 billion years. Even though we may feel at times like aliens who have been dropped into a dim world of lifeless matter from a separate, timeless world of life and light, scientific information now lets us realize that we feel a bit strange here not because we are solitary souls exiled from a distant heavenly shore but because we are fellow travelers with a universe that for now also remains estranged from its final repose in the mystery of God. As long as the journey of the universe is not over, therefore, we may embrace our religious restlessness as a fully natural manifestation of the deeper anticipation that *is* the universe. Ecological concern, at least from this narrative cosmic point of view, therefore, is completely consistent with our working to keep the universe open to a new and creative future. By linking our spiritual lives here and now to the universe's own homeless sojourning, our terrestrial religions, including Christianity, can remain tightly tied to the physical world simultaneously with our personally seeking liberation, salvation, and fulfillment.

The restless religious journey of human beings on Earth, starting perhaps as long as 200,000 years ago, is a new chapter in the story of a cosmos that has been tossing and turning in its sleep from the start. Our spiritual aspirations then are not departures from the cosmos but intense concentrations of the universe's own restlessness. Consequently, we need not feel religiously obliged to loosen our ties with nature but instead can link ourselves even more tightly to the cosmic restlessness. Not only our intellectual, moral, and aesthetic adventurousness but also our spiritual uneasiness may be interpreted as a sprouting of the universe's own ageless incubation. In that case, our sense of the sacred and of the divine mystery need not be interpreted as an invitation to leave the cosmos behind. Nor does our terrestrial habitat need to be thought of as a launching pad for the soul's journey into God. Nature, in an anticipatory reading, does not contradict but reinforces our native religious aspiring toward what is *more*. By embracing the universe's own homelessness, religious restlessness allows us to feel one with the rest of creation.

Conclusion

The ecological imperative, at least from the perspective of anticipation, requires our understanding and appreciating with increasing sophistication all the stages in the cosmic itinerary that led up to the present. Only by first learning about the narrative links that tie the terrestrial biosphere and the recent emergence of conscious life to an unfathomably long cosmic journey can we begin to value the natural world appropriately. The analogical vision, a reading of nature that still animates spiritual life all over our planet, is incapable by itself of arriving at this narrative appreciation of nature. An exclusively sacramental worldview remains innocent of the value of time and hence of the long cosmic story. Bound as it is to a predominantly spatialized understanding of the natural world, the analogical reading of nature cannot fully apprehend the temporal immensity and dramatic quality of a world that is still coming into being in the course of deep time. Only in the light of recent scientific discoveries is theology enabled now to move beyond the two-dimensional perspective of sacramentalism to a three-dimensional anticipatory reading of the universe.

New scientific awareness of the immensely long sequence of moments in natural history, as we now realize, has exposed the relative poverty of the vertical, static, and hierarchical pictures of the world that have been the infrastructure of sacramental piety for centuries. An anticipatory reading of the universe and its accompanying metaphysics of the future, I am arguing, can nowadays allow us to fathom fully the reality of nature and, in doing so, discover its cumulative *dramatic* value. Neither analogy nor archaeology can help us feel the spectacular significance of time and what can be accomplished only over long periods of natural history. Archaeology, I have noted, sees the cosmic story but reduces it immediately to a sequence of moments without any dramatic narrative thread that might allow it to carry a meaning or to build up value. Archaeology, no less than analogy, hides from the reality and significance of time by reducing everything that has occurred in cosmic history, including the making of lives and minds, to the pretemporal elemental simplicity from which it all arose. Analogy, for its part, reduces temporality to little more than an unfortunate deviation from the eternal present. Only an anticipatory reading of the cosmic story, it seems to me, holds time and nature together while also allowing followers of Christ to hope that the future of cosmic process may comprise endless epochs of indeterminate new creation.

It follows then that an anticipatory vision of nature requires new thoughts about the biblical God's commandment to humans to be faithful "stewards" of creation. If nature is not only sacrament but also promise, our stewardship can no longer consist solely of conservation. Conservation is necessary, of course, and we are obliged to show respect for the immense drama of creativity that has been occurring for billions of years. Now, however, stewardship must mean *preparation* along with preservation. An anticipatory reading of nature moves us to care for nature because, for all we know, the cosmos is pregnant with incalculable future outcomes that lie far beyond the range of what we can presently predict or plan for. If gratitude is the characteristic ecological virtue in the sacramental reading, therefore, in the anticipatory reading of nature the fundamental ecological virtue is hope.[30]

30. Identifying hope as an ecological virtue is a point implicit in Pope Francis's encyclical letter *Laudato Si'*: http://w2.vatican.va/content/francesco/en/encyclicals/documents/papa-francesco_20150524_enciclica-laudato-si.html (#61 and #71), but also—even more explicitly—in the American Catholic bishops' pastoral letter "Renewing the Earth" (1991): http://www.usccb.org/issues-and-action/human-life-and-dignity/environment/renewing-the-earth.cfm (section V.D).

Responses

From Richard Bauckham

It is significant that all four essays in this volume envisage a future for the whole creation in the purposes of God. They do not endorse the view that has been common in Christian history, especially in the modern period, that the nonhuman world is a temporary creation, radically different from human beings, for whom God's purpose is eternal life with God, perhaps in a different world—an eternal, heavenly one. In this traditional (though never universal) view, this present creation, which in its material and transitory nature is not fit for eternity, exists as a context for human beings on their way to a destiny beyond death and beyond this creation. Their bodies are material and transitory like the rest of this creation, but they are essentially spiritual beings who transcend this creation. The Christian hope has always (even if sometimes only tenuously) expected the bodily resurrection of the dead at the end of history, entailing the transformation of mortal bodies into an immortal form of embodiment. But nothing of this kind has been expected for the rest of the material creation.

In departing from this common view and affirming some kind of eternal future for the whole creation, the four essays in this volume belong to what seems to me an emerging consensus, especially among theologians with ecological concerns. There are a number of reasons for this trend. One is the recovery of the full scope of biblical eschatology, with the recognition that the New Testament's expectation of "a new heaven and a new earth" does not refer to a new world that replaces this one but to the radical renewal of the whole creation, analogous to the bodily resurrection of human persons. A second reason has to do with the understanding of the human person as an integral whole and as inseparably embedded in the material world. Both biblical interpretation and contemporary science have contributed to this holistic anthropology. It means recognizing that to be human is to be embodied (however one might think about the difference between mind and body), but also that human life is radically dependent on its complex relationships with other creatures, inanimate and animate. Human life is so ecologically constituted that a form of eternal destiny that extracts humans from this embeddedness in the rest of creation seems, to say the least, inappropriate. Thirdly, the common view was highly anthropocentric, attributing to the nonhuman creation the value only of serving humans on their way to eternal life. If God values other creatures for their own sake, then one may ask whether he intends to preserve that value in eternity.

John Haught's essay focuses on a different reason for envisaging a future for the whole universe in the purpose of God. He points out that we now know, on the basis of science, that the universe has had an immensely long history of change and development, and so we must recognize that "the universe is still coming into being" and "that its narrative unfolding is far from over." This is true, but I would add this proviso: the universe will continue to develop in ways that science can predict to a limited extent, *unless* God brings it, whenever God chooses, to its eschatological consummation through an act of new creation. We do not know how much temporal future is in God's intention for the universe—or, more specifically, for this planet. I shall develop this point below.

Haught proposes that, in view of the open future of the universe, ecological "stewardship must mean *preparation* along with preservation." This is because "for all we know, the cosmos is pregnant with incalculable future outcomes that lie far beyond the range of what we can presently predict or plan for." But I wonder, in that case, what "preparation" means. How can we prepare for a future of which we are entirely ignorant? I hazard a guess that Haught means we should conserve creation not only for its own sake but also because of the new possibilities with which it may be pregnant. In that case, preparation doesn't involve *doing* anything more than conservation. It just means having additional reason for preserving the natural world.

This is a very modest idea of "preparing" for the cosmic future. There are many people who think rather that we should project a plausible future and actively work in that direction. I am thinking, for example, of scientists working in artificial intelligence, some of whom have a vision of a "posthuman" future in which human nature will be artificially augmented and humans will effectively evolve into extremely intelligent machines. If human evolution is to continue beyond our present condition, it will be not by the natural processes that operated in our past but through deliberate design and intention on the part of humans (*some* humans, of course, not all). This is not a future to which we can adopt a simple "wait and see" approach. We must make choices. The same is the case with the many "geo-engineering" options for extending our technological power over the natural world. Enthusiasts for the "anthropocene" argue that nature unaffected by humans no longer exists. We now hold the rudder of planetary evolution and must steer it where we choose (in our own interests, of course). These are the kinds of challenges that surely must be engaged by Haught's proposal that our goal should be "to keep the universe open to a new and creative future." I think he means we should preserve biodiversity, stop polluting the oceans and felling forests. But who is to say that the new and creative future God intends is the one for which we "prepare" by conserving the natural world or the one for which we "prepare" by extending the technological project of human transformation of the planet?

Another aspect of Haught's eschatology I find puzzling concerns the eternal life of individual humans and its relation to the future of the cosmos. In biblical eschatology and traditional theology that stays close to it, the resurrection of the dead to eternal life is understood as a cosmic event in the future of the world. Resurrected humans will enter their eschatological future of participation in the eternal life of God along with all creation. Haught recommends that "we link our own life stories *permanently* to the larger cosmic epic that still winds its way toward we know not where." This clearly excludes eternal life for human individuals apart from the future of the whole universe. But can we still hope for a future for ourselves in that totally unknown outcome of the cosmic process? When writing briefly about biblical eschatology, Haught speaks, rightly, of "divine promise." I do not see how he combines the content of that promise, which surely includes both the resurrection of all the dead and the renewal of the whole creation, with the totally unforeseeable future that his anticipatory model of ecological theology projects.

I think there is a fundamental problem in the simple assimilation of biblical eschatology to scientific cosmology that Haught proposes. (He speaks of "an ecological theology completely attuned to contemporary cosmology.") The universe, as science understands it, cannot, from its own immanent possibilities, produce either the resurrection of the dead or its own new creation.

One might speculate about the possibility of overcoming death in the future (humans might evolve into hyperintelligent machines that can renew themselves as long as there is somewhere in the universe they can survive), but those who have died will not live again. Like all forms of utopianism, the human project to overcome death will only benefit those future people who are alive when it happens. Nor will anything the universe becomes bring back the ammonites, the dinosaurs, any of the billions of extinct species, or any of the lost landscapes of Earth. Christian hope is more radical than anything we can envisage the universe becoming: it is for *resurrection of the dead.* It does not privilege the future but holds out hope for the past. And, while resurrection itself is hope for humans, it can also be the analogy for thinking about the new creation of all things.

It is a pity that Haught makes no reference to Christology. Christian belief is that in Jesus Christ God has become, permanently, a member of the species *Homo sapiens* as well as, thereby, a participant in the whole community of creatures on Earth. Whereas Haught refers to the Christian hope as "the coming of God," the New Testament usually speaks of the coming of Christ. The difference is perhaps significant. Is Haught allowing for a future of the universe in which *Homo sapiens* may become as superseded as the dinosaurs? Would such a future relativize the incarnation and make the christologically focused eschatological hope of the Bible and the tradition anachronistic? These are serious theological questions for a view that leaves the future as completely open as Haught's proposal does.

It is also Christology that makes the resurrection of the dead the paradigm of new creation. God's promise for the future was given when he raised the dead Jesus to new and eternal life, making him the pioneer of eternal life for other humans and the whole creation. If resurrection from death is the paradigm, then the future thus promised cannot be one that develops out of the universe's inherent potentialities. It can only be given by a fresh creative act of the transcendent God. It will be an act in which all that has value in this creation, past and future, will be taken by God into a radically new mode of existence, participating in God's eternity. Just as the risen and exalted Jesus is still the Jesus who lived the life of a mortal human like us, transformed but not replaced, so the new creation will be this material cosmos, ourselves included, transformed but not replaced. This is the eschatological basis for valuing the whole created world: God has made and is making it for an eternal destiny.

So I think we should not fall for the temptation of assimilating the hope of new creation to the openness to the future that from a scientific perspective we can envisage for the universe. Whatever future the universe might ultimately have as a result of its own potential for development and disintegration, the new creation is not that future. Humans are mortal, and all created things are transient. Only from beyond this creation's own resources, only from the unlimited potentialities of the transcendent and creative God, can death and transience be transcended. Thus, although I find Haught's typology of the three ways of reading nature illuminating, I do not think his "anticipatory" reading measures up to the promise of eschatology. Yes, the universe has a history and invites a narrative reading. Its temporal future is incalculable, entirely within God's hands. But the Christian hope of new creation, the God-given destiny of all things, transcends that temporal future. It is an eternal future for all that God values in the whole diachronic, as well as synchronic, scope of the cosmic narrative. So I do not think that, in valuing and seeking to conserve all the creatures of Earth, we should be thinking primarily of their potential for leading to new developments in the future (of which we can usually know nothing). We value them for themselves, as creatures God loves, with a future he will give them as themselves. We do not value humans primarily for their potential for opening up new developments in the future. Even if we knew that the human race would be annihilated in some nuclear or ecological catastrophe of the future, so that human history turns out to be a dead end in the cosmic story, leading nowhere, we would value humans no less. We value each human being as a creature of God, precious in God's sight, and so we should value other creatures too.

From Cynthia Moe-Lobeda

~ I welcome John Haught's inquiry into Christian eschatology as a source of ecological vision, morality, and hope; his understanding of eschatology as divine promise "open to a future in which all of creation is to be renewed"; and his perception of creation as expression or embodiment of that promise. Inherent in these affirmations is the claim that Christian redemption includes the whole of creation. These perspectives are, as he suggests, firmly grounded in the biblical witness.

Welcome too is Haught's insistence that Christian theology should take seriously science's discovery that our universe is on a journey of becoming. In theological as well as scientific terms, creation is a movement of past, present, and future, not only a dynamic of the past. This is an appeal to theology to appreciate the spectacularly long, unfolding cosmic story, and to link life on this terrestrial biosphere to the vastly longer cosmic journey in which life on Earth is remarkably recent.

Furthermore, I appreciate Haught's recognition that a theology and eschatology of creation "becoming" have tremendous implications for morality. One implication—as he points out—is that we are called to care for the world that is becoming, and that it may include "modes of being, life, and consciousness whose shape we can barely imagine at present." Therefore, the moral dimension of human life on Earth must include not only conserving and preserving but also preparing for God's future of this creation, a future for Earth and the entire cosmos that lies "far beyond the range of what we can presently predict or plan for."

Before building on Haught's valuable claim about moral implications, I must note two aspects of his argument for a preparatory understanding (rather than a merely conservational understanding) of Christian obligation to care for creation that do not sit well with me. Haught argues that how we treat (what he calls) "nature" depends on how we read it. Said differently, our sense of moral obligation to care for creation is grounded in how we see or read the story of what is going on in it. With this I am in accord. He goes on to identify "three main ways of reading the new cosmic story." They are archaeological, analogical (sacramental), and anticipatory.

I do not fully concur with his portrayal of sacramental theology. According to Haught, sacramental theology (while deeply valuing the physical universe for revealing, mediating, and participating in God's infinite goodness and beauty) is problematic in at least five related senses. Sacramental theology (1) sees the universe in spatial (hierarchical) terms, not temporal terms, (2) "fails to see clearly that the universe is still coming into being,"[31] (3) reads the universe as "nothing more than a set of imperfect sacraments pointing to an eternal present," (4) interprets "the life of faith as accomplishing little

31. See also Haught's statement that "An exclusively sacramental worldview remains innocent of the value of time and hence of the long cosmic story. Bound as it is to a predominantly spatialized understanding of the natural world, the analogical reading of nature cannot fully apprehend the temporal immensity and dramatic quality of a world that is still coming into being in the course of deep time."

other than the purification of our souls and perhaps the redemption of our individualized bodies," and (5) "easily assumes that the ancient biblical promise of salvation has now been fully realized except for the individual human soul's journey toward sharing in it." As a result of these five held together, sacramental theology looks "for no significantly new outcomes in the future story of nature." Thus, sacramental theology works against a moral obligation or motivation to care for creation in a preparatory sense.

While these features may accurately describe some forms of sacramental theology, they do not describe most or the most influential sacramental theologies of recent decades. *Some sacramental theologies in fact bear the features that Haught attributes to the anticipatory reading of the universe story.* This way of reading the story recognizes and celebrates the unfolding cosmic journey of ongoing creation from the past and into the untold future, and directs human attention to participate with God in "working right now for the healing of nature" because of the promise that all of creation will be renewed. I would argue that some influential sacramental theologies also recognize and celebrate this cosmic journey and direct human attention toward working now for "nature's" healing. Because of his limited reading of sacramental theology, I question Haught's assertion that sacramental theology is not grounding for a preparatory sense of caring for creation.

Secondly, I question Haught's characterization of Christian ecological ethics and theology as thus far "consist[ing] solely of conservation" rather than also of preparation. Some Christian ecological ethics of the last decade have indeed assumed the need to prepare for God's unfolding future of life on this planet. Haught might more accurately critique ecological ethics as preparing primarily for a relatively *near* future (a few centuries) but not for the "future of cosmic process [that] may comprise endless epochs of indeterminate new creation" that Haught so insightfully evokes in his essay.

These two reservations expressed, I return to the valuable and provocative central claims of Haught's essay, articulated in his opening paragraphs and conclusion. One is that ecological theology and morality must be immersed in awareness that the cosmos and all aspects of life on the terrestrial globe are in fact in the midst of a vast cosmic journey that extends back 13.5 billion years and into the future infinitely. Another is the value of grounding ecological morality in eschatological hope because creation is an "expression of a divine promise open to a future in which all of creation is to be renewed." That is, the hope to which he calls Christians recognizes that God's promise is not just with the human community—late arriving as we are in this story—but also with the entire cosmic community on a splendid creative journey extending back over 13 billion years and into endless epochs of an equally vast and not-yet-known future. The third central claim—grounded in these two—is that caring for creation must be preparatory as well as conservatory.

These are invaluable claims for multiple reasons. To illustrate: The first is crucial for cultivating the ecological virtues of wonder and humility that Steven Bouma-Prediger so aptly describes. The second is necessary for reclaiming the biblical sensibility that the scope of God's redemption is cosmic. And the third propels us to a fuller sense of moral obligation.

I also invite further probing into the implications of these three claims for Christian ecological morality if we include Haught's additional emphasis that morality be preparatory for the cosmic future, not only the near human future. On the one hand, this is theologically sound. If God's promise is such a future, then we are indeed "ethically obliged" to prepare for that future. However, on the other, might this be a morally disempowering or discouraging claim, rather than a hope-producing claim? God's long-term past for this earth did not include the human species; why should God's long-term future include us? In hoping for a cosmic future that "may comprise endless epochs of indeterminate new creation" and a future that "will come to expression in modes of being, life, and consciousness whose shape we can barely imagine at present," we would be hoping for a future that well may not include human beings. My sense is that while abstractly we may recognize an obligation to prepare for that cosmic future, practically we are not likely to give it the importance of the nearer future, the next few centuries, or even the next span of millennia, in which we can practically image our human descendants to be alive and can seek to build a world in which they may thrive. Are humans capable of morality based on the hope of a cosmic future that might not contain human life? The response determines whether this vast cosmic future is a viable source of moral vision, hope, and action.

From Steven Bouma-Prediger

~ Many thanks to John for his insightful and informative chapter. I find myself in agreement with a great deal of what he says but also have some questions.

I agree that we Christian theologians, and the church more generally, "are partly to blame" for the indifference shown by many Christians to the various ecological degradations that beset us.[32] Far too many of us have ignored the natural world, even though our faith calls us to care for creation.[33] And I agree that the situation is slowly changing for the better, evident in the pioneering work of ecotheologian Joseph Sittler in the 1950s[34] up to the recent encyclical by Pope Francis,[35] and also manifest in denominational documents and interfaith creation care groups, church gardens, and summer camp programs.

So, as John acknowledges, there are many "spiritual and theological resources for Christian ecological responsibility," whether biblical interpretations of creation or theological accounts of stewardship or ethical treatises on virtues. It is simply not the case that Christians lack ways of thinking and acting and being in the world that do not support caring for this world.[36] It is the responsibility and privilege of those who have positions of leadership in the church to unearth these resources—something Richard and John and Cynthia, thankfully, have been doing for quite some time.

John is exactly right to identify eschatology as a crucial though often missing piece in the Christian case for care for creation. It is tragic (not just ironic) that the biblical view of God's good future, "in which all of creation is to be re-

32. For insightful historical analyses, see H. Paul Santmire, *The Travail of Nature: The Ambiguous Ecological Promise of Christian Theology* (Philadelphia: Fortress, 1985), and also Wesley Granberg-Michaelson, *Ecology and Life: Accepting Our Environmental Responsibility* (Waco, TX: Word, 1988), chap. 3. For prescriptions for what ails us, see Santmire's subsequent books: *Nature Reborn: The Ecological and Cosmic Promise of Christian Theology* (Philadelphia: Fortress, 2000); *Ritualizing Nature: Renewing Christian Liturgy in a Time of Crisis* (Minneapolis: Fortress, 2008); and *Before Nature: A Christian Spirituality* (Minneapolis: Fortress, 2014); and also Granberg-Michaelson's *A Worldly Spirituality: The Call to Take Care of the Earth* (San Francisco: Harper & Row, 1984).

33. I make this case in Steven Bouma-Prediger, *For the Beauty of the Earth*, 2nd ed. (Grand Rapids: Baker Academic, 2000).

34. For a collection of Sittler's influential work, see Steven Bouma-Prediger and Peter Bakken, eds., *Evocations of Grace: Writings on Ecology, Theology, and Ethics* (Grand Rapids: Eerdmans, 2000).

35. *Laudato Si'* can be found in Pope Francis, *Encyclical on Climate Change and Inequality: On Care for Our Common Home* (New York: Melville House, 2015).

36. That there are resources for caring for our home planet in virtually every religion is evident in the Harvard University Press book series World Religions and Ecology, under the general editorship of Mary Evelyn Tucker and John Grimm.

newed," has often been suppressed or ignored in our theology and ethics. And so John argues that we must "draw out the implications of biblical *eschatology* for shaping an ecological vision and morality" (emphasis added). I can only say: preach it, brother! Our eschatology shapes our ethics, whether for better or for worse. What we think about the future inevitably shapes what we do in the present. So we had better get our eschatology right.[37]

Alas, for decades, many Christians, especially evangelicals, have gotten their eschatology wrong. (As an evangelical, I speak from experience.) If you believe that at the second coming of Jesus the earth will be burned up to nothing, then you will likely have little reason to care for it.[38] If, by contrast, you believe that the earth will be renewed when Jesus comes to complete God's purposes for all creation, then you have another good reason to care for our home planet. The former view derives from a dispensationalist reading of Matthew 24–25, 2 Peter 3, and Revelation, to name some of the contested texts, while the latter is the testimony of the Bible as a whole rightly interpreted.[39] In short, John is spot on to identify biblical eschatology as crucial.

John is wise to point to Jürgen Moltmann as a theological resource, since he has emphasized the importance of eschatology and later in his career developed a sophisticated ecological theology and ethic.[40] Also, throughout his entire corpus Moltmann has emphasized the centrality of hope.[41] I confess that

37. For more on this argument, see Steven Bouma-Prediger, "Eschatology Shapes Ethics," in *Rooted and Grounded: Essays on Land and Christian Discipleship*, ed. Ryan Harker and Janeen Bertsche Johnson (Eugene, OR: Pickwick, 2016).

38. So claims environmental historian Roderick Nash in arguing that Christianity is to blame for much of our contemporary eco-mess. See Roderick Nash, *The Rights of Nature* (Madison: University of Wisconsin Press, 1989), 91–92. Evangelicals in the United States typically care the least about climate change. For data on religious beliefs and climate change, go to http://climatecommunication.yale.edu/publications/more-americans-perceive-harm-from-global-warming-survey-finds/.

39. Many authors and texts could be cited, but two of the best are N. T. Wright, *Surprised by Hope: Rethinking Heaven, the Resurrection, and the Mission of the Church* (New York: HarperCollins, 2008), and J. Richard Middleton, *A New Heaven and a New Earth: Reclaiming Biblical Eschatology* (Grand Rapids: Baker Academic, 2014).

40. Jürgen Moltmann, *God in Creation: A New Theology of Creation and the Spirit of God* (San Francisco: Harper & Row, 1985) and *Ethics of Hope* (Minneapolis: Fortress, 2012).

41. The book that initially made Moltmann famous was *Theology of Hope* (New

I was disappointed that Moltmann's theology was not employed when John described his preferred way of reading nature according to "the anticipatory vision." Moltmann could be useful to help unpack John's affirmation that "Christian faith in the resurrected Christ extends to the fulfillment of the whole of creation" and thus "hope lies at the very heart of Christian religion."

John offers an interesting typology of three ways of reading nature. His perceptive analysis of "the archaeological reading" highlights its main claims and various problems. As John convincingly shows, this materialist reading of reality is reductionistic in the extreme. The "*x* is nothing more than *y*" language employed by its adherents reminds me of Donald MacKay's critique of such explanations as "nothing-buttery."[42] The psychological phenomena of the mind are nothing but brain biology. The biology of the brain is nothing but organic chemistry. The chemistry is nothing but physics. The physics is nothing but mathematics. Nothing buttery.

John's critique is nothing short of devastating. He shows how this materialist reading is "a scientifically unverifiable and philosophically arbitrary expression of 'faith' rather than empirically grounded knowledge." The (typically atheist) purveyors of the archaeological reading are no less religious than the devout theists whose views they criticize.[43] Hence, this form of scientism—faith in science as the only method of finding truth, as distinguished from science (an important distinction John clearly makes)—is hoist on its own petard.

Furthermore, John perceptively demonstrates how a materialist worldview cannot logically support claims for why we humans ought to care for the natural world. If "the universe amounts to nothing more than a series of physical states with no lasting importance," then the natural world (including humans as merely physical organisms) has only instrumental value. But if the world is emptied of any moral value, then there is no legitimate reason for ecological

---

York: Harper & Row, 1967). For an in-depth analysis of Moltmann's theology, see Steven Bouma-Prediger, *The Greening of Theology: The Ecological Models of Rosemary Radford Ruether, Joseph Sittler, and Jürgen Moltmann* (Atlanta: Scholars Press, 1995).

42. Donald MacKay, *The Clockwork Image* (Downers Grove, IL: InterVarsity Press, 1974), chap. 4. See also MacKay, *Science and the Quest for Meaning* (Grand Rapids: Eerdmans, 1982).

43. This argument against the autonomy of reason has been made for over a century by Abraham Kuyper and his followers, e.g., Herman Dooyeweerd, *In the Twilight of Western Thought* (Nutley, NJ: Craig, 1980). See also Hendrik Hart, Johan VanderHoeven, and Nicholas Wolterstorff, *Rationality in the Calvinian Tradition* (Lanham, MD: University Press of America, 1983).

responsibility. At best, following the argument of John Passmore,[44] we care for the earth because life is precious, and it is precious (and thus of value) because it is perishable and precarious. This is meager gruel on which to build a robust ethic. The logical path of atheistic materialist worldviews is to follow Nietzsche to the conclusion that all moral claims are relative and thus the *Übermensch* rules.

John is perhaps most insightful when he points out that "scientific materialists generally fail to notice the extent to which their own understanding of nature theoretically prevents human *subjects* from ever feeling deeply at home in their purely *objectivist* understanding of the natural world." In other words, materialist environmentalists "tacitly subvert their own moral concern for nature and the need for us to feel fully at home in 'this world' as soon as they insist that life and mind are ultimately reducible to lifeless and mindless elemental physical units." How can we truly feel at home on this our home planet if we believe that we are merely bits of matter lost in a meaningless cosmos?[45] John notes that some formerly staunch defenders of the archaeological reading have "acknowledged the intellectual weakness and moral heartlessness of materialist metaphysics" but that "even these laudatory attempts to soften archaeological materialism, however, do not abandon what I'm calling the metaphysics of the *past*."

John's analysis of "the analogical reading" is no less insightful. This "metaphysics of the eternal present" implies that the natural world points beyond itself to its infinite and everlasting Creator and thus is valuable because it reveals God's goodness and beauty. The analogical or sacramental reading of nature "allows us to embrace lovingly the finite beauties of nature not because of their precariousness but because of their participation in, and mediation of, the everlasting goodness and beauty of God." The natural world reflects the majesty of God and thus is valuable not only because God made it but also because of its ability to point beyond itself.[46]

John asserts that the kind of detachment required by this reading of nature

44. John Passmore, *Man's Responsibility for Nature* (London: Duckworth, 1974).

45. For more on various forms of contemporary homelessness, including the postmodern nomad, and what resources exist in the Christian faith for responding to these kinds of homelessness, see Steven Bouma-Prediger and Brian Walsh, *Beyond Homelessness: Christian Faith in a Culture of Displacement* (Grand Rapids: Eerdmans, 2008).

46. For an excellent example of "reconstructing patristic and medieval concepts," to quote the subtitle, see Jame Schaefer, *Theological Foundations for Environmental Ethics* (Washington, DC: Georgetown University Press, 2009).

is not "a hostile, dualistic, world-escaping reactivity to the natural world but a necessary condition of our allowing nature to transport us toward a transcendent goodness and beauty." John argues, "Only by being detached to a degree from nature can we receive it as a gift for which we can be grateful." I agree, but it all depends on what one means by detachment. I worry that this world-affirming sacramental vision in practice too easily morphs into a world-negating spirituality that finds little lasting value in the natural world, since all that is really important is the spiritual world beyond this world.[47] In sum, while the analogical vision "*should* have the effect of keeping us from looking upon the created order as . . . nothing more than material stuff to be exploited," I worry that this way of reading nature can devolve into an ontological and anthropological dualism that devalues the earth and sanctions the exploitation of its creatures.

John has his own critique of the analogical vision. In his view, the analogical reading "fails to see clearly that the universe is still coming into being" and hence "cannot bring out the ecological significance of either the biblical sense of the world's promise or the new scientific understanding of an unfinished universe." I agree. The analogical vision does not capture either the biblical eschatology of a renewed world or the scientific understanding of an unfinished universe. But this is so not only because the analogical vision predates modern science but also because of some of the theological and metaphysical and anthological assumptions inherent within it.

In contrast to both the archaeological reading and the analogical reading, John advocates "the anticipatory reading." This view of nature seeks to expand our notion of Christian hope by "including what we now know to be the long story of nature"; hence, "longing for a new future *for*, rather than apart from, the world" provides "a very good reason for taking care of Mother Earth here and now." God's good future means the renewal of all things. It is not about only humans (or their souls), and it does not imply the destruction of the earth. John justifiably concludes that "the anticipatory reading of nature compels us to move beyond a purely sacramental ecological spirituality."

This anticipatory view of nature, furthermore, prompts the question of how to reconcile "spiritual homelessness, or detachment, with cosmic at-home-

47. It seems to me that this theology and spirituality is often tacitly shaped by the Neoplatonic theology of Pseudo-Dionysius.

ness." But this view of nature also hints at an answer: combine a proper sense of detachment with a rooted sense of being at home in the world.[48] John insightfully argues that "by reading the universe as an unfinished story . . . we may come to feel that we belong fully to the natural world without having to sacrifice the sense of being on a homeless and liberating religious pilgrimage." In other words, we are both homeless, sojourners longing for God's good future of shalom, and also at home, earth creatures aware that we are embedded in the world in which we live.[49] I would add, however, that it is not only a scientifically informed reading of the universe that prompts such a conclusion but also a biblically informed eschatology.

In his conclusion John briefly mentions the virtues of gratitude and hope. Gratitude is one of the central virtues of the Christian faith.[50] And hope lies at the very core of what it means to be a follower of Jesus.[51] I would love to see John further develop his ideas on these virtues. Only if we Christians embody such virtues will be able to truly live for the glory of God and the love of the world.

48. For an example, see Thomas Merton, *When the Trees Say Nothing*, ed. Kathleen Deignan (Notre Dame: Sorin Books, 2003).

49. For more see Bouma-Prediger and Walsh, *Beyond Homelessness*, chap. 8, entitled "The Indwelling God and the Sojourning Community."

50. For more on gratitude, see Diana Butler Bass, *Grateful: The Transformative Power of Giving Thanks* (New York: HarperOne, 2018).

51. For more on hope, see Jonathan Wilson, *Gospel Virtues: Practicing Faith, Hope, and Love in Uncertain Times* (Downers Grove, IL: InterVarsity Press, 1998).

Conclusion

In this present volume, we've held space for conversation in a form that itself reflects the dynamic nature of ecotheology as a burgeoning field. We hope such dialogue proves not only interesting and informative, but ultimately transformative for the ways it stimulates theological imagination, biblical engagement, and sustained responsible action.

A clear benefit to engaging theological discourse through conversation like the one in this volume is the occasion it provides for emergent resonance, or generative instances wherein variant perspectives prove complementary. These have happened already, to be sure, in this book. First, as a New Testament scholar, Richard Bauckham situates the larger conversation within a biblical theological context, and in so doing provides a critical exegetical framework indirectly utilized and referenced by the others. Bauckham's careful reading of biblical texts tethers the entire discussion to the Christian Scriptures that all contributors share and provides greater nuance to anthropological questions appearing throughout. More specifically, Bauckham's careful analysis of *creatio imago Dei* qualifies the limits of the public spheres of life when read alongside Cynthia Moe-Lobeda's clarion call for deeper human moral reflection and social action and adds texture to John Haught's understanding of human creativity toward the enhancement of unfolding life. In the realm of ecotheology, it's not passé or overstated to note the ongoing importance of linking biblical theology to Christian theology. Adherence to Scripture is always generative of new theological insights, but this discipline is especially important in communicating the call to ecojustice in our churches through the world. Biblical study will remain a critical ingredient in ecotheological reflection.

Far from narrowly connecting to the doctrine of creation, various theological foci also complement one another throughout the dialogue, painting together a more expansive view of Christian ecotheology. A clear example of this is the juxtaposition of Steven Bouma-Prediger's emphasis on personal character and action with Moe-Lobeda's focus on public witness and advocacy, and both of these working archetypes, as Haught types them, in contrast to anticipatory views of the unfolding future. In his response to Haught, Bouma-Prediger humbly notes that at times evangelical communities like his own have too readily focused on matters of Christology and related immaterial conceptions of salvation and would therefore do well to follow Haught's lead by centralizing a hopeful, embodied eschatology. Likewise, Moe-Lobeda's and Bouma-Prediger's implicit theological conceptions of discipleship hold one another in tension and speak to what Moe-Lobeda refers to as "the two hands" of Christian vocation. Moe-Lobeda sees personal virtue as necessary but not sufficient, and pushes to apply the ecological virtues to social systems. Bouma-Prediger, on the other hand, questions the solvency of said systems and argues for a more personalized approach. In this debate and elsewhere, Bauckham's theocentric perspective provides categories for ultimate and penultimate theological concerns by uplifting God's sovereignty in the eschatological consummation of creation and qualifying both advocacy and virtue as "the work of God in the person truly dedicated to God." Because ecological questions are, as the etymology of their name suggests, interrelated, integral questions, they speak to an array of theological concerns—the doctrine of God, creation, anthropology, Christology, eschatology, and the like. Reading scholars from varied theological traditions in concert with one another makes plain the ways one supplements another, and to some extent all complement each other.

For the many ways our contributors' perspectives complement one another, they also chart and map a great deal of common ground, which results in key similarities within the many differences. First, all attend to the radical interconnectedness of all creation and articulate suspicion and concern over modern and postmodern anthropologies that envisage humans as extricable from and sovereign over the material world. The very title of Bauckham's essay, "Being Human in the Community of Creation," speaks to this concern. With great care, he addresses common ways of interpreting the creation of human beings *imago Dei* and ultimately suggests that humans are wholly interrelated to the realm of all creation while yet given a distinct responsibility to recognize the mutuality we share with "other" creatures. Calling upon many scientific conclusions, Bauckham articulates the difficulty of drawing clear lines between human life and other-than-human life and therefore suggests Christian interpreters of the Scriptures focus more on the ways humans *do* resemble God and less on differences between creatures, as they too carry the indelible mark of the Divine.

While Bouma-Prediger also adopts, in his words, "earthy and earthly" depictions of human identity, he favors a more functional approach. For Bouma-Prediger, humans occupy a privileged place of authority, but one oriented toward service, even to the point of suffering on behalf of creation. So, while at once interconnected with creation, humans are yet called to serve and protect planetary life, and this is why for Bouma-Prediger cultivation of personal virtue is critical. In the end, the action of serving is born out of being.

So, what negotiates the being? For Bouma-Prediger and to a greater extent Moe-Lobeda, narratives play a major role. Anthropologies are shaped by story. The stories we inherit, engage, and create shape our desires and moral imagination. The theologically constructed self is also a socially constructed self; as people, we participate in social systems, which necessarily means we inhabit the realm of story. And so, if any among us assumes either the Baconian, modern story of personhood wherein humans as subjects are utterly distinct from the material world as object, or the hyperindividualized, experiential conception of personhood characteristic of postmodern thought, we risk detachment from reality. In Moe-Lobeda's words, theologically and biologically we are a we, and therefore enact the radical incarnate love of God by collaboratively acting out our parts in the collective and communal.

Like his colleagues, Haught is taken with narrative and convinced of human interdependence with creation. However, for him we humans are markedly unique in the ways we look for promise despite desperate circumstances; the *imago Dei* disposes us to move past what is for us the surprising. It isn't that we're actors in a story or play that's been written, but more that we as authors are in the process of writing the final act! To this end, Haught seeks to push Bauckham and Bouma-Prediger especially by emphasizing the extent of human creativity in the context of an unfinished universe.

The importance of recovering an ecocentric eschatology is yet another point of shared perspective among the contributors. All four lift up an embodied view of what is to come that has great implications for human and other-than-human life alike, albeit in different ways and through different means. Eschatology is central to Haught's argument in the manner that the future, including our planetary future, comes from up ahead. This is decidedly different from many modern, Kantian conceptions of the end, wherein the important question is, "What might we hope for?" No, for Haught and his companions in this compendium, the promises of God are sure, if even yet unclear, and absolutely corporeal. All agree, the ecological aspects of biblical eschatology are not salutary but paramount. In understanding neighbor to mean more than the human next door, Moe-Lobeda makes this clear when she argues that the second Great Commandment, "Love thy neighbor as thyself," isn't really a commandment at all but rather a declarative statement of what will be. Justice-making-love is under way, and when we participate in its becoming, we play a role in God's great, eschatological redemptive work. So, it isn't that we Christians merely await some final, climactic revelation of God. Instead, we extend gratitude for the ways God is already at play within our earthy kin to change and renew the world through "the healing, liberating, and transforming Word of God in the creatures and elements of this earth."

Bauckham agrees that Christian eschatology speaks to the redemption of creation as a whole. The solidarity humans find with other creatures will not be sundered but perfected in the new creation. And yet, this doesn't mean Christian eschatology should privilege the future, as is the case in Haught and Moe-Lobeda's perspectives. Biblical eschatology, Bauckham argues, holds out hope for the past—for God's restored creation. So rather than preparing for something completely unknown or anticipating a radically new way of life, Bauckham suggests eschatological emphases should lead us in humility to simply find our place within the community of creation as was once, is, and will be.

In keeping with eschatology, our four contributors share a vital, essential focus on hope. In Haught's words, all seek to "see promise even in the most unpromising of circumstances" and to allow such Spirit-filled hope the germinal space it needs to change our individual and communal outlooks. Bouma-Prediger and Haught see hope as foremost among the ecological virtues and remind us that all virtues are practiced in and through habit. In fact, Haught goes so far as to say that "putting on the habit of hope" is part and parcel with Moe-Lobeda's call to moral responsiveness. Despair, while affectively real in our day and age, can easily lead to moral inertia rather than moral agency. And so, as with all things under the rubric of Christ's victorious resurrection, the death and destruction, grief and anger of the cross is welcome, but it does not, nor will not, have the last word.

And of course, neither will this book have the final word. Even as it goes to press, our global ecological realities fluctuate. As a result, our attention and energy shift and our solutions can fail and are refashioned. Indeed, many of the challenges of our day noted in this volume—from socioeconomic matters like climigration, water scarcity, and public health scares to biological concerns such as bleaching reefs, lost and endangered creatures, and vanishing glaciers—call for nimble, sophisticated responses, and among them decidedly theological offerings. As demonstrated throughout our shared work, ecotheology speaks to the relevance of belief as well as practice. It provides context for the lived internal experience of individuals and communities, who have a direct impact on organisms, creatures, and entire ecosystems. For this reason, theological reflection plays an ever-integral role in the larger work of the environmental humanities. What's more, this particular collection of voices speaks to the radical promise of Christian thought and practice in highly consumptive contexts like the United States. When taken alongside our contributors' constructive essays, far gone are yesteryear's critiques of Christianity's longstanding anthropocentricism and absent are concerns about otherworldly obsessions. In concert with each other, all four offer a rich, fecund, incarnate theology for "nature," the likes of which Joseph Sittler and others called for half a century ago. But the volume is more than a fine apology. Beyond the clear and persuasive conclusion made by each and the nuanced challenge found within one another's response lies a greater gift for today's church—that of example. Now more than ever in our participation within natural history, we need thoughtful, creative collaboration toward shared aims of life on planet Earth. We require varied perspective. We require conversation and accountability. We require theory coupled with praxis and lament yoked with hope. As longtime participants in the formation of Christian ecotheology, Richard Bauckham, Cynthia Moe-Lobeda, Steven Bouma-Prediger, and John Haught have modeled such innovative discourse for us and the Christian communities we comprise. As individuals, their work has shaped the field of Christian ecotheology in significant ways, but here as conversation partners their work extends beyond the realm of church, demonstrating the promise of Christian theology for any who share a love of the world.

Contributors

Katharine Hayhoe (PhD, University of Illinois, 2010) is an atmospheric scientist and the Political Science Endowed Professor in Public Policy and Public Law at Texas Tech University in Lubbock, Texas. Her research focuses on quantifying how climate change affects human and natural systems. Dr. Hayhoe has served as a lead author for the Second, Third, and Fourth US National Climate Assessments and has published more than one hundred peer-reviewed articles, chapters, and reports. She has been recognized as a United Nations Champion of the Earth and an Oxfam Sister of the Planet and has received, among others, the National Center for Science Education's Friend of the Planet award and the Sierra Club's Distinguished Service award. Dr. Hayhoe currently chairs the Earth Science Women's Network Advisory Council and also serves on advisory boards for organizations including the Faraday Institute for Science and Religion and the Smithsonian Natural History Museum.

Richard Bauckham (PhD, Cambridge University, 1972) is Professor Emeritus at St. Andrews University, Scotland, formerly Bishop Wardlaw Professor of New Testament Studies. His work as a biblical scholar addresses a wide range of topics, including the theology of Jürgen Moltmann, Christology, Jewish and Christian apocalyptic literature, the Old Testament Pseudepigrapha, Jesus and the Gospels, and theological approaches to environmental issues. He is the author of many books, including *The Bible and Ecology: Rediscovering the Community of Creation* (2010) and *Living with Other Creatures: Green Exegesis and Theology* (2011). From 1996 to 2002 he was General Editor of the Society for New Testament Studies Monograph Series. Dr. Bauckham is an Anglican and served as a member of the Doctrine Commission of the Church of England for many years. He now resides in Cambridge to continue ongoing research.

Cynthia Moe-Lobeda (PhD, Union Theological Seminary, 2001) is Professor of Theological and Social Ethics at Pacific Lutheran Theological Seminary, Church Divinity School of the Pacific, and the Graduate Theological Union in Berkeley. She has lectured or consulted in Africa, Asia, Europe, Latin America, Australia, and North America in theology; ethics; and matters of climate justice and climate racism, moral agency, globalization, economic justice, ecofeminist theology, and faith-based resistance to systemic oppression. Her most recent book, *Resisting Structural Evil: Love as Ecological-Economic Vocation* (2013), won the Nautilus Award for social justice. Dr. Moe-Lobeda presently serves as a theological consultant to the Presiding Bishop of the Evangelical Lutheran Church in America.

Steven Bouma-Prediger (PhD, University of Chicago, 1992) is the Leonard and Marjorie Mass Professor of Reformed Theology and Chair of the Campus Sustainability Advisory Committee at Hope College in Holland, Michigan. An ethicist by training, his research interests intersect Christian virtue ethics with environmental concerns. Dr. Bouma-Prediger is the author of many books and articles on Christian environmental ethics, including *Earthkeeping and Character: Exploring a Christian Ecological Virtue Ethic* (2020) and *For the Beauty of the Earth: A Christian Vision for Creation Care* (2001). Dr. Bouma-Prediger serves on the board of the Au Sable Institute for Environmental Studies, a nonprofit supporting environmental research and work of evangelical Christians.

John F. Haught (PhD, Catholic University, 1970) is Distinguished Research Professor Emeritus, Georgetown University, Washington, DC. His area of specialization is systematic theology, with a particular interest in issues pertaining to science, cosmology, evolution, ecology, and religion. Dr. Haught has published twenty books and numerous articles and reviews, including the recent *The New Cosmic Story: Inside Our Awakening Universe* (2017) and *Resting on the Future: Catholic Theology for an Unfinished Universe* (2015). A Catholic layman, Dr. Haught regularly consults on ecclesial matters. Now in retirement, Dr. Haught frequently leaves his Florida home to lecture internationally on many issues related to science and religion.

Alan G. Padgett (DPhil, University of Oxford, 1990) is Professor of Systematic Theology at Luther Seminary, St. Paul, Minnesota. His research and publishing cover a number of related topics, including New Testament studies, philosophy, Christian theology, and the theology and science dialogue. Dr. Padgett has published thirteen books and numerous essays, articles, and reviews, including *God, Eternity, and the Nature of Time* (1992), *Science and the Study of God* (2003), and the *Blackwell Companion to Science and Christianity* (coeditor, 2012). A United Methodist minister, Dr. Padgett is a Senior Fellow in the John Wesley Fellowship and a Fellow of the International Society for Science and Religion.

Kiara A. Jorgenson (PhD, Luther Seminary, 2016) is Assistant Professor of Religion and Environmental Studies and Director of the Environmental Conversations Program at St. Olaf College, Northfield, Minnesota. Dr. Jorgenson writes and teaches on matters related to Protestant ecotheologies, ecofeminism, climate justice, the theology of motherwork, and childhood studies. Her recent book, *The Ecology of Vocation* (2020), explores the ecological promise of Protestant renderings of vocation, past and present.

Index of Names and Subjects

Index of Scripture References